T0305037

Malaysian Economics and Politics in the New Century

Malaysian Economics and Politics in the New Century

Edited by

Colin Barlow

Visiting Fellow, Department of Political and Social Change, Research School of Pacific and Asian Studies, Australian National University, Australia

Francis Loh Kok Wah

Professor of Political Science, School of Social Sciences, Universiti Sains Malaysia, Penang, Malaysia

Edward Elgar
Cheltenham, UK • Northampton, MA, USA

Published by
Edward Elgar Publishing Limited
Glensanda House
Montpellier Parade
Cheltenham
Glos GL50 1UA
UK

Edward Elgar Publishing, Inc.
136 West Street
Suite 202
Northampton
Massachusetts 01060
USA

A catalogue record for this book
is available from the British Library

Library of Congress Cataloguing in Publication Data
Malaysian economics and politics in the new century / edited by Colin Barlow and Francis Loh Kok Wah.
    p.cm
  Based largely on papers from the second biennial Australia-Malaysia Conference, held in Canberra in May, 2000.
  Includes bibliographical references and index.
  1. Malaysia—Economic conditions—Congresses. 2. Malaysia—Politics and government—Congresses. I. Barlow, Colin. II. Loh, Francis Kok-Wah, 1951–
III. Australia-Malaysia Conference (2nd : 2000 : Canberra, A.C.T.)

HC445.5 .M342 2003
320.9595—dc21
                                                                          2002037940
ISBN 1 84064 599 7 (cased)
Printed and bound in Great Britain by MPG Books Ltd, Bodmin, Cornwall

Contents

Dedication

This book is dedicated to the distinguished Malaysian scholar and economist, Professor Dr Ishak Shari, who passed away on 30 June 2001, at the age of 53 years. Ishak's chapter for the volume was completed just before he became sick, and reflects his abiding concern with social issues and the less well-off in Malaysia.

Ishak was a modest, humorous, brilliant and compassionate man, whose sympathy for the poor was a driving force for most of his life. He was also a person encouraging and illuminating others, and the words of the great scholar Iqbal, which he used in his Inaugural Lecture as Professor of Development Economics at the Universiti Kebangsaan Malaysia in 1991, especially reflect his character.

Iqbal wrote:

> The journey of love is very long, but sometimes with a sign you can cross that vast desert. Search and search again without losing hope. You may sometimes find a treasure on your way.

Ishak often helped provide signs to his students and other friends, including some contributors to this book. He will be sadly missed by all who had the good fortune to associate with him.

May Allah shower His Blessings upon his soul, and may he rest in peace.

Tables

Contributors

Colin Barlow is a Visiting Fellow in the Department of Political and Social Change at the Australian National University, Canberra. He has worked on rural economic and social development throughout Southeast Asia, focusing on the production and marketing of cash crops and ways in which public and other interventions are best organized to secure adoption of new techniques raising living standards. He and his wife, Ria Gondowarsito, are currently leading a international study of socio-economic aspects of the global oil palm industry, concentrating mainly on Malaysia, Indonesia, Africa and palm oil markets. He is also interested in the political and economic scene in Malaysia, and has convened three Australia-Malaysia Conferences on this topic. His recent edited books include *Institutions and Economic Change in Southeast Asia* (1999) and *Modern Malaysia in the Global Economy. Political and Social Change into the 21st Century* (2001). He is President of the NTA - East Indonesia Aid, an Australian non-government organization promoting village development in West Timor and Flores.

William Case is a Senior Lecturer in the School of International Business, Griffith University, Brisbane. He has taught at the University of Texas at Austin, the MARA Institute of Technology in Shah Alam, Malaysia, the Australian National University in Canberra, and the Australian Defence Force Academy in Canberra. He was also a Research Associate at the University of Malaya while conducting PhD research in Malaysia from 1989 - 1990. William Case is the author of *Elites and Regimes in Malaysia: Revisiting a Consociational Democracy* (1996) and many book chapters and journal articles on Southeast Asian politics.

Ishak Shari was until 2001 Professor of Development Economics and Director of the Institute of Malaysian and International Studies (IKMAS) at the Universiti Kebangsaan Malaysia at Bangi, Selangor. His primary research emphasis was on poverty and income distribution in Malaysia, taking into account the impact of globalization on these problems. He was a consultant to the United Nations Development Programme, the Economic and Social Commission for Asia and the Pacific and the World Bank. His published works included: *Development Policies and Income Inequality in Peninsular Malaysia* (1986, with Jomo K.S.); *Development and Underdevelopment in Rural Kelantan* (1989): *The Fishermen Economy: Capital Accumulation, Technological Change and Economic Differentiation* (1990); *The Earth for All Mankind: Coping with Economic Inequalities during the Globalization Era* (1999). All but the first of these books are in the Malay language. Ishak also served as the President of the Malaysian Social Science Association.

Francis Loh Kok Wah teaches Politics in Universiti Sains Malaysia (USM). He received his BA from Dartmouth College and his PhD from Cornell University in Politics and Southeast Asian Studies. His latest publications include *Fragmented Vision: Culture and Politics in Contemporary Malaysia*, co-editor (1992); *Sabah and Sarawak: The Politics of Development and Federalism*, editor (1997); and *Democracy in Malaysia: Discourses and Practices*, co-editor (2002). He coordinates a team of USM researchers involved in the multi-country project *Globalisation, National Governance and Local Responses*, funded by SIDA, Sweden. He is Secretary of Aliran, a Malaysian non-government organization devoted to social and political reform, and is one of the editors of *Aliran Monthly* where he regularly publishes on current affairs in Malaysia.

Lim Kit Siang was born in Batu Pahat, Johore, Malaysia, and holds an LLB (Honours) awarded by London University in 1977. He is a Barrister-at-Law (Lincoln's Inn), and was called to the Malaysian Bar in 1978. He began his career as a teacher in 1961 - 1965, and also worked as a journalist. He was Secretary-General of the Singapore National Union of Journalists in 1962, and in 1966 - 1969 was the National Organizing Secretary of the Democratic Action Party in Malaysia. He was Secretary-General of the Party from 1969 - 1999, and has subsequently been National Chairman. He has been elected as a representative of his Party on many successive occasions, beginning as a Member of Parliament for Bandar Melaka in 1969 and continuing to elections as a State Assemblyman for Penang and the MP for Tanjong (Penang) in 1995. He was the Malaysian Parliamentary Opposition Leader from 1975 - 1999. Mr Lim has been detained without trial on several occasions, and has engaged in numerous other activities and campaigns.

Anthony Milner is Professor of Asian History and Dean of the Faculty of Asian Studies at the Australian National University, Canberra. From 1991 - 1994 he was Director of the Australian - Asian Perceptions Project of the Academy of the Social Sciences in Australia, and this Project produced a series of research papers, a radio series for the Australian Broadcasting Commission and the books *Australia in Asia: Communities of Thought* (1996); *Australia in Asia: Comparing Cultures* (1996 and 1998); and *Australia in Asia: Episodes* (1998) (Oxford University Press). Professor Milner is a member of the Foreign Affairs Council of the Australian government and has been editor of the *Asian Studies' Review* of the Asian Studies' Association of Australia, He also holds several other prominent positions with public and academic bodies. He was educated at Dookie Agricultural College and Monash University in Australia, the University of Malaya, and Cornell University in the United States. He has taught at Monash, Cornell and the University of Kent in England, and was made a Fellow of the Academy of Social Sciences in Australia in 1995. Professor Milner's writings on Malaysia include *Kerajaan: Malay Political Culture on the Eve of Colonial Rule* (1982), *The Invention of Politics in*

Colonial Malaya (1995), and (jointly authored) *Perceptions of the Haj* (1984), and he has written numerous other books.

Michael Ong is a Research Specialist in the Library of the Australian Federal Parliament. He taught politics at the University of Malaya from 1970 - 1987, and was Associate Professor and Chairman of the Division of Public Administration, Faculty of Economics and Administration. He was a Council Member of the Asia-Pacific Political Science Association from 1984 - 1986, and Vice-President from 1986 - 1988. He was a Research Associate at the Centre for Southeast Asian Studies at Monash University from 1981 - 1982, and a Visiting Fellow in the Department of Political and Social Change at the Australian National University from 1987 - 1988. He has since 1997 been a Member of the Steering Committee of the Centre for the Study of the Southern Chinese Diaspora, Australian National University, and a Committee Member of the non-government organization, Racial Respect.

Rais Yatim has served in various capacities in the governments of Tun Abdul Razak, Tun Hussein Onn and Datuk Seri Dr Mahathir Mohamad. He has held a several major political posts, including those of Deputy Minister for Law and Deputy Minister of Home Affairs in the late 1970s, and of Chief Minister of Negeri Sembilan from 1978 - 1982. Dr Rais was Malaysian Information Minister from 1984 - 1986, and then became Foreign Minister. He resigned from the latter post in 1987 following the 'Team A-Team B' political tussle in the United Malays National Organization, resuming practice in his former law firm. He won the Jelebu Parliamentary seat in the 1999 general election, and was appointed by Dr Mahathir to his present post as Minister of Justice in the Prime Minister's Department. Rais obtained his LLB (Hons) degree from the University of Singapore in 1973, and was called to the Malaysian Bar. He graduated with a PhD in law from the University of London in 1994. His book *Freedom under Executive Supremacy in Malaysia* (1995) focuses on public law issues relating to executive power in Malaysia, and his latest work, *Zaman Beredar Pesaka Bergilir* was published in 1999.

Shamsulbahriah Ku Ahmad is Director of the Asia-Europe Centre at the University of Malaya in Kuala Lumpur, and a Lecturer in the Department of Development Studies, Faculty of Economics and Administration of that University. She specializes in the political ec onomy of development. She holds a BEc (Hons) from the Universiti Kebangsaan Malaysia, an MPhil from the University of Sussex in England, and a PhD from the University of Cambridge in England. Her academic interests include labour markets and their interactions with politics, society, gender and economics, and she has published numerous papers in these areas.

Russ Swinnerton retired from the Royal Australian Navy in 1997, after a thirty-year career. He has had extensive sea experience in the region, and was

Australian Defence Adviser to Malaysia from 1994 until 1996. He remained in Kuala Lumpur until 1998, working as a freelance writer and analyst. He has contributed to a range of publications on defence, maritime security and strategic issues. He is now a strategic analyst with the Australian Department of Defence.

Tan Tat Wai qualified in 1969 with a Bachelor of Science in Electrical Engineering and Economics from the Massachusetts Institute of Technology, United States of America. He secured a Masters degree in Economics from the University of Wisconsin in 1970, and a PhD in Economics from Harvard University in 1977. He started his career in 1978 as a Senior Economist in the Economics Department of the Bank Negara Malaysia in 1978. From 1984 to 1987 he worked as a consultant to the Bank Negara and subsequently to the United Nations University. He also from 1981 to 1992 worked as the Secretary and then a Member of the Council on Malaysian Invisible Trade. He is the Group Managing Director of Southern Steel at Prai, and sits on the Board of Nanyang Press Holdings, Shangri-la Hotels (Malaysia), and Titan, all of which are companies listed on the Kuala Lumpur Stock Exchange. He also holds directorships in other public and private companies.

R. Thillainathan holds a Bachelor's degree from the University of Malaya, and a Masters degree and PhD from the London School of Economics. He is currently the Director of Finance of Genting, Berhad, and prior to this was a university don and a banker. He was the President of the Malaysian Economic Association from 1996 until 2002. He is a Member of the National Economic Action Council II, the Employees Provident Fund (EPF) Investment Panel and the Malaysian Accounting Standards Board.

Preface and Acknowledgements

This is the second volume in the new 'Australian' series on Malaysia, and is derived mainly from the second biennial Australia-Malaysia Conference, held in Canberra in May 2000. The theme of that exciting and stimulating Conference was 'Malaysia after the Financial Crisis and General Elections: Economic, Social and Political Implications', and the present book deals with aspects related to this theme. The emphasis of this book contrasts with that of the first volume in the series, 'Modern Malaysia in the Global Economy: Political and Social Change into the 21st Century' (Edward Elgar, 2001). Thus this book chiefly looks towards Malaysia's future, whilst the earlier volume was partly concerned with historical changes leading to the situation in the 2000s.

Subject to two caveats below, all authors are entirely responsible for their opinions. This includes the editors' introductory Chapter 1 and concluding Chapter 13, which were not written in consultation with other contributors.

We edited this book in two locations. One was at the Department of Political and Social Change at the Australian National University in Canberra, where Colin Barlow is a Visiting Fellow. The other was at the School of Social Sciences at the Universiti Sains Malaysia in Penang, where Francis Loh Kok Wah is a Professor of Political Science. We especially wish to thank Professor Ben Kerkvliet at the Australian National University, and Associate Professor Abdul Rahim bin Ibrahim at the Universiti Sains Malaysia, for facilities and continuing support to our editing project.

We also want to express our gratitude for financial contributions towards the May 2000 Conference costs, including those of producing camera-ready copy. Our thanks go to the following institutions and companies: the Australian National University, Canberra; the Malaysian High Commission, Canberra; the Australian Agency for International Aid, Canberra; Cutler and Co., Melbourne; IDP Education Australia; the Malaysian Mining Corporation, Sydney; Lang Australia, Sydney; Federal Hotels, Sydney; Tenix Defence Systems, Canberra; P.J. Dawson and Associates, Canberra; Energy Services International, Canberra; and Proton Cars, Sydney. We wish as well to acknowledge a contribution from the Australian National University towards publication costs. We are indebted to the staff of Edward Elgar Publishing at Cheltenham and Aldershot, England, for their highly professional assistance in production of the book.

We should like to thank all participant authors for their extended work in writing chapters for this volume, and for their patience with us during the editing process.

We should finally express our great appreciation to Colin Barlow's wife, Ria Gondowarsito, for her continued support and advice during editing, and for

xiv   *Malaysian Economics and Politics in the New Century*

very capably undertaking on her own account the onerous production of camera-ready copy according to the requirements of the Elgar house style.

Two contributing authors wish to make special comments regarding their chapters. R. Thillainathan notes that his contribution is a revised version of a paper presented at the Bank Negara Malaysia's 18th Central Bank Course on 30 September 1999 in Petaling Jaya, and submitted to MAPEN II. The views expressed in his chapter are entirely his own, however. Russ Swinnerton wants to record that the views in his chapter are predominantly his, and do not necessarily reflect the attitudes of the Australian government or its Department of Defence. He prepared sections of his contribution with the assistance of a colleague, Mr J.N. Mak.

We should note that the third biennial Australia-Malaysia Conference was convened by Colin Barlow at the Australian National University in Canberra in March 2002, and had as its theme 'Industrialization in Malaysia'. A book based on this third Conference will be the next in the 'Australian' Malaysia series, and is already being prepared. It will concentrate on the economic, political and social aspects of the industrialization process which has helped change Malaysia so much over the last four decades.

Most values in this book are quoted in Malaysian ringgit (abbreviated as 'RM'), whose mean rate of exchange against the United States dollar stood at 3.80 from the time of its pegging to the latter currency in September 1998, up to at least mid-2002. Some other values in the book are quoted in United States dollars (abbreviated as '$').

Where the sign '-' appears in the cells of tables, it means that relevant data are not available.

For the convenience of some readers, a map of Malaysia is presented as Figure 1.1.

PART I

Introduction

1. Introduction

Colin Barlow and Francis Loh Kok Wah

Malaysia at the start of the new century seemed poised to continue the economic development which had seen such heady advances in the years before the 1997 financial crisis. But the grave setbacks of that crisis had raised vital questions for Malaysians, including those about how the economy and society were organized, about how the benefits from economic development were distributed, about the relations of government to major national institutions, and about the nature of the political process. Manifestly the country was again progressing well in broad economic terms, but the underlying questions remained prominent and answers were being actively sought by people at large.

The first book in this series[1] set out the remarkable transition in Malaysia from the early 1960s to the late 1990s, as it moved from a predominantly rural to a largely industrial society. That book outlined and analysed the economic, social and political background to the huge changes over those three decades, examining the economic and political initiatives and underlying policies, the trends in income and income distribution, the special problems of East Malaysia, and the role in the changing society of different ethnic groups and of women. The book looked too at the impact of the major structural alterations to society effected from the early 1970s under the New Economic Policy (NEP), the implications of the significant emergence of non-government organizations, and the development of Malaysian foreign policy in an era of rapid national and international change.

The present book builds to some extent on the earlier work, and readers unfamiliar with the Malaysian story are advised to check that work as one source of their insights. This book essentially hinges on a watershed in the late 1990s attributed to the interrelated effects of the financial crisis, the arrest of Anwar Ibrahim, and the subsequent 1999 general election. Thus the financial crisis exposed serious weaknesses in the banking system, financial markets, and the behaviour of many corporate entities, while Anwar's arrest and its outcomes brought to public view deficiencies in the administration of justice and public order. The 1999 election results reflected public dissatisfaction with the ruling *Barisan Nasional* (BN), illustrated especially by the partial swing of Malay votes from the United Malays National Organization (UMNO) to the opposition *Parti Islam SeMalaysia* (PAS). But while the strength of UMNO was reduced at the election, it and the associated parties of the BN remained in power and appear indeed to have subsequently regained some popular support.

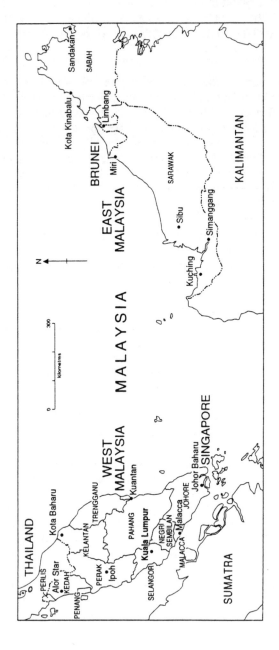

Figure 1.1 Malaysia in 2002

The questions of the first paragraph as well as the events and issues surrounding them, are scrutinized in succeeding chapters, with economic and strategic aspects being mainly examined in Part II, and political and other aspects in Part III. Sometimes in these discussions the earlier historical roots of current situations are explored, so as to secure a better understanding of what took place.

First, in Chapter 2 of Part II, R. Thillainathan examines the Malaysian banking system and financial markets, looking too at attendant developments in the wider Malaysian economy. He reviews and documents economic conditions and policies before and after the economic difficulties caused by the 1997 financial crisis, turning then to reasons for the crisis both in the wider Asian and more restricted Malaysian contexts. He highlights speculation, inadequate risk management, the 'Asian' feature of concentrated shareholdings, and deficient legal infrastructures as main reasons requiring attention. Dr Thillainathan argues strongly for a switch from the present bank-centred to a market-centred financial system, suggesting banking reforms to eliminate moral hazard, financial reforms to promote capital market development, and other market-based changes to encourage corporate restructuring. While he feels the Malaysian economy has adjusted well since 1997, he also believes the country must further reduce 'its chronic over-dependence on banking with its recurrent boom-bust cycles' (p. 26).

Next, in Chapter 3, Tan Tat Wai, with the insightful perspective of one practically involved, looks at the impact of the financial crisis on the corporate sector, examining differences between the 1985 and 1997 recessions and seeing the economy in the latter year as better positioned to withstand crisis. He analyses the effects of the abrupt credit withdrawals after 1997, examining the differential impacts of non-performing loans on key economic sub-sectors. He addresses the substantial restructuring subsequently undertaken by Malaysian corporations, looking at how this took place with different kinds of companies. He criticizes the facile under-valuation of Malaysian restructuring by the international press, which has focused on big *Bumiputera* businesses propped up by government funds. He uses published records of the Kuala Lumpur Stock Exchange (KLSE) to examine the subsequent fundamental restructuring by most large companies which were losing money, scrutinizing the take-overs and other moves which have 'laid the groundwork for a more efficient economy' and better future performance (p. 41).

In Chapter 4, Shamsulbahriah Ku Ahmad addresses the Malaysian workforce, concentrating on the working and salaried middle classes and quantifying the substantial size to which the latter has grown. She pinpoints the varying possession of skill amongst the working class, with its relatively low level reflecting a shortage of better trained workers. She discusses the types of 'knowledge workers' in the middle class, ranging from the less skilled 'routine non-manual' component to the smaller 'professional-managerial' component which itself has internal competence differentials (p. 47). She highlights the export-oriented industrialization strategy of Malaysia and other regional countries, affirming its goal of attracting foreign investment as an engine of growth, and suggesting this disadvantages the unskilled working class. She emphasizes the importance of foreign workers in Malaysia's tight labour market, proposing that continued vacancies in the unskilled sector show these people do not compete with Malaysians for jobs. She argues as well for more training of unskilled as well as skilled workers to service the growing economy.

In Chapter 5, Ishak Shari addresses social implications of the crisis, noting it was mainly foreign labourers who lost their jobs. But the impacts on local Malaysian workers included reduced wages, lower overtime, less demand for informal services, and rising prices, with women, rubber labourers, the urban poor and aboriginal people being most adversely affected. People could not access social services and buy medicines, or had to move from private to inferior public facilities. Professor Ishak cites the political implications of social reverses, which taken with the Anwar affair led to public dissatisfaction and a questioning by young urban Malays especially of whether 'government under the existing leadership was desirable' (p. 70). Yet he points too to the continuing peacefulness of Malaysian society, attributing this to past government successes in eradicating economic disparities and facilitating participation by Malays and others in the multi-ethnic middle class. He nonetheless believes the 'undercurrent of social discontent' may only be satisfied by 'reconstructing institutions characteristic of a modern democratic society' (p. 73).

In Chapter 6, Russ Swinnerton looks at the evolving security environment of Malaysia, tracing the development of the armed forces and their change, in response to successive challenges, from an internal security force in the 1960s and 1970s to units capable of maritime and forward defence in the late 1990s and the new century. He highlights the 'multipolar security structure' of the early 2000s. This reflects uncertainty exacerbated by the regional economic slowdown and the 'war on terror' following September 11th, where possible economic disputes hinging on the Spratly Islands, sea lanes in archipelagic waters, nautical limits and illegal immigrants all require appropriate military preparedness. The Malaysian government now emphasizes military self-reliance, along with regional and ASEAN cooperation, defence dialogue and external assistance. This is under circumstances where, despite aversion to extra-regional and Western-led security treaties, Malaysia still participates with Singapore and Commonwealth countries in the Five Power Defence Arrangement. The country's basic attitude in defence is one of non-aligned self-sufficiency, however.

Then in Chapter 7 of Part III, Francis Loh addresses the emergence in Malaysian politics from the late 1990s of a new element of 'participatory democracy' embodied in the *reformasi* movement. This element has to some extent supplanted the earlier dominance of 'ethnicism', and takes effect in a political environment also characterized by 'developmentalism' which is the cultural by-product of the developmental state. There is now an era of contestation between the three elements, and this is characterized by 'ferment and fragmentation' (p. 94). Professor Loh explores recent events, highlighting the increasing prominence of non-government organizations and rise of opposition to the *Barisan Nasional* (BN) by the Malay middle class. He covers the recent switch of government towards 'utilitarian' goals, de-emphasizing Malay symbols and encouraging non-Malay parties as well as Malay to promote public services. He analyses the results of the 1999 election, showing how Malay and Chinese voters responded to the new situation. He concludes there was a 'permanent shift' in voting patterns, with less certainty of a BN victory in this time of contestation.

In Chapter 8, Michael Ong reviews the changing power configurations in Malaysia, suggesting that the possible 'sea change' in the events of the late 1990s was no such thing (p.106). He maintains that the progressive undermining of constitutional provisions and other institutions since 1957 have secured the position of the BN, limiting the possibility of real threat to it for the time being. He reviews constitutional developments, successive modifications to the electoral system, changes in the rules and procedures of parliament, and the introduction of an array of discretionary laws including a modified Internal Security Act and Sedition Act. All of these taken together and combined with restrictions on the press effectively inhibit the operations of a normal democratic society. Mr Ong mentions the *coup de grace* to what he terms the 'rule by law', embodied in the 1988 sacking of Tan Sri Salleh Abas, lord president of the judiciary, and of two other senior judges. He concludes that despite the high expectations of the *Barisan Alternatif*, this nascent and fragile plant needs committed and disciplined leadership to survive.

In Chapter 9, William Case documents the astonishing fall from grace of the deputy prime minister, Anwar Ibrahim. He explores the role of the judiciary in Anwar's downfall, reviewing the legitimacy at various levels of what occurred. Following an account of the increasing confrontation between Anwar and the prime minister, he examines the legal charging process, the proceedings of the first trial with its successive amendments in the prosecution's case and severe ultimate sentence, and the unsavoury second trial putting Anwar on the sidelines for the next fourteen years. Against the background of these trials, Dr Case pinpoints Malaysia's unique position in the region as a country where government has neither upgraded its judiciary to enhance its power, nor extended the judiciary in the interests of democracy. The government has rather reined the judiciary in, as 'a diminished tool of an increasingly paramount prime minister' (p. 129). He concludes that Anwar's experience heightened Malaysians' concerns over the erosion of their judiciary. While such erosion may have assisted central control and speeded industrial progress, it was a contradiction which may later obstruct the process of modernization.

In Chapter 10, Anthony Milner scrutinizes Dr Mahathir's role in 'the rescue of the Malays'. He reviews Dr Mahathir's writings on the topic from the late 1940s, looking at their initial emphasis on 'backwardness' and 'hereditary rights' and then at the stress in his 1970 book *The Malay Dilemma* on both these aspects and Malays' need for special economic opportunities as they broke away from custom towards new thinking. He describes how much later, in his Vision 2020, Dr Mahathir anticipated a resilient indigenous community fully competitive with other ethnic groups. He explains how Dr Mahathir vigorously promoted these ideas through practical policies, which dramatically enhanced the role of Malays in the modern sector. Professor Milner notes the tenacity of Mahathir's pursuit of his visionary Malay policy, with its roots in the views of Munshi Abdullah in the early nineteenth century as well as those of other commentators. He sees this policy as contradicting the 'egalitarian aspirations' of Australian society, and as accordingly likely to generate continuing tension between Malaysia and Australia, whatever personalities are involved (p. 141).

In Chapter 11, Rais Yatim addresses Malaysian civil liberties from the stance of both an academic lawyer and a minister entrusted with administering justice. He asserts that democratic rights and freedoms should be determined with regard to a country's circumstances, and not according to the views of outsiders. He lays out basic components of human rights, suggesting as well that local culture is significant and that Asian in comparison with Western societies place more importance on society as a whole rather than the individual. Hence broad internal security and public order may be emphasized more than the rights of the single person. Dr Rais reviews the influence on the Malaysian legal system of English common law, and considers 'executive priorities' of the colonial past springing from needs to quell militant communism and other social unrest. He checks more recent security legislation pertaining to such problems, addressing the treatment of fundamental rights in the Malaysian constitution. He concludes that Malaysia's 'own brand of civil liberty' requires continuous review according to circumstances, but that it always needs to match the larger interests of Malaysian society (p. 157).

In Chapter 12, Lim Kit Siang considers the challenges of opposition politics, addressing the 1999 general election and formation by four parties of the *Barisan Alternatif* (BA) under the shock of the Anwar affair. He analyses the BA's joint manifesto, and examines some adverse factors and abuses in the conduct of the election. He scrutinizes the development subsequent to the election of more 'arbitrary and authoritarian rule', reporting some adverse comments on the Malaysian political situation by foreign legal and other groups. He argues for a strengthened opposition front 'to break down the divide and rule politics dominated by race and religion', but sees a recent resort by UMNO to the latter approach. He urges that the controversial issue of an Islamic state must be squarely addressed by PAS and other BA parties, so as to avoid 'baseless fears of a primordial nature' regarding the restrictions imposed by such a state. Mr Lim concludes by arguing for 'inter-civilizational dialogue', leading to a superior political architecture free of 'ethnic and religious baiting' and more acceptable to all Malaysians (p. 169).

Finally, in Chapter 13 of Part IV, Colin Barlow and Francis Loh Kok Wah bring together the major issues of each chapter, scrutinizing them under the heads of 'the organization of economy and society' (p. 175) and 'political and legal processes and outcomes' (p. 181). They consider the issues in relation to the ideas of individual authors and each other, drawing from them broad indications over the directions of Malaysian economics and politics in the new century.

The discussions of the book reflect wider debates in Malaysia about future directions of the national economy, polity and society, and should convey to its readers a better appreciation of current conditions in this dynamic and fascinating country. But to counter tendencies towards pessimism which problems recited in various chapters might create, it is noted that Malaysia is still one of the faster growing economies of the world, with the highest average standard of living in Southeast Asia after Singapore. The nation has an admirable comparative record of race relations and public order which further stimulate economic enterprise and social well-being, while affirmative action under the NEP has created a better balance between different ethnic groups. The country's large and growing middle classes are increasingly well educated, seeming poised for added dynamic change in the tradition of bold and frequently successful initiatives which have featured in the country's development since it gained independence in 1957.

This second book in the 'Australian' series on Malaysia is a joint product of Malaysian and Australian enterprise. Its underlying purpose is to present to a wider audience the views on Malaysia of scholars, businesspersons, politicians and others actively engaged with economic and social change in that important nation. Its thrust is consciously non-partisan, endeavouring to present a range of attitudes on each problem whilst leaving readers to make their own assessments of events and implications. The emergence as a modern society of this middle-sized state of Southeast Asia is a signal occurrence in world development, with lessons for numerous countries as yet unable to progress so far. It is hoped that this book and those following it will effectively continue this pedagogical role.

NOTES

1. *Modern Malaysia in the Global Economy: Political and Social Change into the 21st Century (Cheltenham, UK and Northampton, MA:* Edward Elgar, 2001).

PART II

Economics and Strategy

2. Malaysia and the Asian Crisis: Lessons and Challenges

R. Thillainathan

The Malaysian economy made a 'V-shaped' recovery from the economic crisis that devastated the region and country from mid-1997 to mid-1999. This chapter first reviews the economy before and after the crisis. It then attempts to analyse whether and to what extent the crisis was caused by speculation, excessive risk-taking, weak risk management, a weak financial system and a weak legal infrastructure. The chapter finally considers what financial market reforms are necessary to avoid such a crisis in the future, where this includes an evaluation of Malaysia's approach to bank and corporate restructuring and its implications for future growth. The chapter does not attempt to analyse whether the recovery that has taken place can be attributed to the new regime of exchange controls, however, and whether this regime should be continued. That task is undertaken in a separate volume by Athukorala (2001).

THE ECONOMY BEFORE AND AFTER THE ASIAN CRISIS

At the outbreak of the Asian crisis, the Malaysian economy was registering high growth, over-full employment, and low inflation. There was also a big over-supply in properties and in infrastructure facilities, exposing the economy to the risk of the boom-bust cycle of asset markets (Table 2.1). The external current account deficit had also been persistently high, while the service sector was over-protected and the exchange rate had appreciated in US dollar terms.

The government was running a fiscal surplus, but the stance of monetary and exchange rate policy in the mid-1990s was not sound, with a near-pegged exchange rate regime and excessive growth in money supply and credit. Even in respect of its fiscal position, government finance was satisfactory only if one ignores the liabilities it had assumed in implicitly guaranteeing the safety of bank deposits, in guaranteeing a minimum return on its collective saving and investment schemes,[1] and in taking on the obligation to step in if certain privatized projects went bust. Growth was generally prioritized over distribution, but over-reliance on privatization to achieve a distributional goal undermined efficiency and increased macroeconomic vulnerabilities.

The government's initial response to the crisis was unsatisfactory. The stance of macro-policies was tightened to restore market confidence, and imposition of a regime of stringent credit control led to an over-kill. These policies together with the contagion plunged the economy into a deep recession. Anti-market pronouncements, an unwillingness to consider a market solution and conflicting statements on mega-projects aggravated the crisis. The policies were replaced by a new regime of capital controls in September 1998, with a limited easing in macro-policies.

The original collapse of the economy was followed by a strong rebound in the V-shaped recovery. Threats of deflation and inflation were averted, and the currency, stock and property markets recovered from their lows. Unemployment once again approached its historic low. Yet there was still in 2001 a big over-hang in the property market and the infrastructure sector. The restructuring of banks, and to a lesser extent of the corporate sector, had been decisive but not market-based. While *Danaharta*, the official asset management company, had set a time frame for completing its asset disposal programme, this was still proving to take a long while.

The recovery was led by a strong growth in export-oriented manufacturing in particular, as well as in government spending. Monetary policy was more accommodative but credit growth was still lacklustre. While the government's response to the mid-1980s crisis was to liberalize the goods sector - which led to a phenomenal recovery of the economy - the country in 2001 was more inward-looking and less market-oriented. Following a mid-1980s stance would call for liberalizing the service sector, but this had not been done to the extent one might have expected. Thus the service sector was not being exploited as an engine of growth, and was instead a drag on the rest of the economy. That was especially so as this sector accounted for more than 50 per cent of the nation's output.

When Malaysia instituted its new regime of exchange controls, some assumed the worst. A few, including the author of this chapter, were aware that capital controls would reduce an economy's long-term growth potential, but that the country would be bankrupted only if the controls were accompanied by resort to irresponsible macro-policies. Those with this view recognized that without checks provided by the market, capital controls had increased the risk profile of the Malaysian economy. But they argued that the authorities were unlikely to pursue imprudent macro-policies or to let that happen for any length of time.

The fact that the economy made a strong recovery is not baffling, given the initial slack capacity, increased government spending, a very weak ringgit and strong export demand. However, if capital controls became more permanent, as appeared to be the case, then in the long run the economy would only grow at or below 75 per cent of its potential. Apart from capital controls, the long-term economic growth potential was also constrained by a distribution-bias of policy (albeit lower than before), an increasing tendency towards industrial targeting, and the unwillingness or inability of the government to open up its service sector. If the United States economy succumbed to a recession, this would even cloud the short and medium-term prospects of the Malaysian economy[2], given that capital controls would make the country less attractive for foreign investors than other competitor countries in its region.[3]

Table 2.1 Key Economic Indicators before and after the Crisis*

		Before the Crisis				After the Crisis		
	1986	Mid 87 - mid 97	1995 - 1997	1996	1997	1998	1999	2000
State of the Economy								
Real GDP Growth Rate (%)		8.5			7.5	-7.4	5.8	8.5
Unemployment Rate (%)	8.8				2.4	3.2	3.4	3.1
Inflation Rate (%) CPI		<4.0			2.7	5.3	2.8	1.6
PPI					2.7	10.7	-3.3	3.1
External Current Account								
Surplus/Deficit as % of GNP		>-6.0			-5.9	13.9	17.1	10.0
Stance of Policy								
Government Surplus								
(+)/Deficit (-) as % of *GDP*					2.5	-1.8	-3.2	-5.8
Broad Money (M3) Growth Rate %			>20		18.5	2.7	8.3	5.0
Credit Growth Rate (%)			>25		26.5	1.3	0.3	5.4
Exchange rate (RM per US$)		2.60	2.54 - 2.52		3.89	3.80	3.80	3.8
Financial and Debt Structure								
Debt as % of GDP								
Domestic Debt	234				267			
- Banking System	102				149			
- Debt Market	62				57			
External Debt	71				61			

Table 2.1 (Continued)

Financial and Debt Structure					
Debt Composition	100	100			
Domestic Debt					
- Banking System	43	56			
- Debt Market	26	21			
External Debt	31	23			
Share of Net Funds Raised					
Banking System	50	58			
Domestic Debt Market	33	11			
External Debt	3	16			
Equity Market	13	14			
State of Asset Markets					
Property Market Occupancy Rate (%)					
Office Space		94.9	79.9	76.2	75.4
Retail Space		90.5	61.7	76.6	78.8
% Change in Average Monthly Rentals					
Office Space		-5.0	-19.3	-8.7	14.3
Retail Space		0.0	-39.3	8.0	10.9
Stock Market					
KLCI Index Level	1,238	594	586	812	68.0
KLCI Index Change (%)		-52.1	-1.3	38.6	-16.3

Table 2.1 (continued)

	1986	Before the Crisis Mid 87-mid 97	1995-1997	1996	1997	After the Crisis 1998	1999	2000
Indicators of Banking and Corporate Distress								
NPL (Non-Performing Loan) Trend (%)**								
Net					4.1	13.6	11.0	9.6
Gross					6.0	21.3	24.1	
Corporate Distress Trend of PLCs (%)								
Net Profit Margin				12.0	6.9	2.8	1.3	
Firms not Covering Interest Expenses from Operational cash-flow***				5.6	17.1	34.3	26.3	

Sources: Claessens et al. (1999); International Monetary Fund (1999); Malaysia. Bank Negara Malaysia (1986 - 2000 and 1986 - 2001).

Notes: * The abbreviated terms used are defined as follows:

  CPI - Consumer Price Index

  PPI - Producer Price Index

  KLCI - Kuala Lumpur Stock Exchange Composite Index

  PLC - Public Listed Company

** The NPL ratio has been computed either on a net basis after deducting specific provisions and interest-in-suspense, or on a gross basis before deducting specific provisions and interest-in suspense and before sales to *Danaharta*. The latter set of numbers is taken from the International Monetary Fund (1999). The 1999 number is as at March 1999.

***The numbers on interest cover margin in this panel have been taken from the International Monetary Fund source listed above, and the data is in respect of the first half of 1999.

CAUSES OF THE ASIAN FINANCIAL CRISIS

1. Speculation

Speculative attacks triggered the Asian financial crisis. But at the outbreak of the crisis, the Asian economies had been made vulnerable by the unsustainable pace of economic growth and by certain structural weaknesses including massive over-building and over-valued exchange rates. The crisis was aggravated by the wrong policy response, anti-market rhetoric, panic, and excessive risk-taking which damaged the balance sheets of banks and corporates. Even if there had been no regional crisis, the Malaysian economy would have crashed by the beginning of the new century if the stance of official policy had not been changed.

The relationship between firms, government and banks in Malaysia in the pre-crisis period cannot be described as being so 'cosy' as that in certain other Asian countries. There was no overt policy of 'directed lending' to big firms, and to that extent one cannot say that the financial constraints on big firms were weak. Nonetheless, there were certain visible defects. The government's commitment to a high growth policy based on a high ratio of investments to gross domestic product led eventually to the promotion and support of certain 'mega' projects, to the implicit assumption by lenders that the government would not let those projects fail, and to lending decisions by bankers based not just on project cash flows but also on collaterals and implied government support. Such over-investment led aggregate demand to outstrip aggregate supply, with a consequently persistent external deficit. It also led to poorer cash flows and more problem loans.

2. Deficiencies in Risk Management

These deficiencies caused the Asian crisis to be prolonged and severe, with huge mismatches between the assets and liabilities of enterprises leading them to assume excessive liquidity, interest rate and currency risks. While Asians love to take risks, the problem was not dealt with by requiring mandatory disclosures warning investors and depositors on what risks were taken. Equally, adequate opportunities to hedge risks by letting markets develop had not been provided.

Currency mismatches were modest in Malaysia, however, as the exchange control regime required approvals for foreign currency borrowings. Yet several prominent corporations were allowed to raise foreign currency loans, although they only had ringgit cash flows. With the sharp ringgit depreciation these corporations faced massive foreign exchange losses or insolvencies, because of their currency mismatches and inabilities to hedge exposures.

The chronic over-dependence of the Malaysian economy on short-term, floating-rate bank debt had increased from about 100 per cent to 150 per cent of gross domestic product between 1986 and 1997. In 1995, for instance, 40 per cent of the loans of commercial banks, the dominant component of the banking system, were callable on demand. Another 40 per cent comprised term loans of four years and above, but these were funded with short-term deposits with the weighted average maturity of deposits being only 15.2 months. Given this high leverage together with over-reliance on short-term floating-rate financing and the maturity mismatch, the credit squeeze and jump in interest rates accompanying the outbreak of financial crisis in mid-1997 greatly damaged the balance sheets of the Malaysian banking and corporate sectors.

Macroeconomics is extremely relevant for risk management, given Asia's chronic over-dependence on banking. If inherently risky banking is taken with bad macroeconomics, this can be an explosive mix for any corporate entity which has over-borrowed and assumed too much maturity or currency mismatches. The high-risk nature of banking (in distinction to funds management, for instance) arises from its high gearing and massive asset liability mismatches, and in particular from its tendency to borrow short and lend long. Malaysia's chronic over-dependence on banking is readily evident from Table 2.1, and from the fact that the share of the domestic banking system in total debt increased from 43 to 56 per cent between 1986 and 1997.

Over-dependence on banking increases Asia's macroeconomic vulnerabilities and systemic risk. A confidence crisis causing a run on banks can convert a liquidity crisis into a panic, and thereafter turn it into a solvency crisis. This is so for three reasons. Firstly, banks influence money supply, and a run on banks can cause a multiple contraction in credit. Secondly, banking is a high-risk business, both for the reasons already given and because its under-capitalisation and over-gearing leads to risky lending. Thirdly, banks, unlike other financial institutions, are engaged in providing payment services and are therefore susceptible to or cause systemic risk.

The over-dependence on banks in Asia has been caused by their over-protection, as well as by the over-regulation of capital markets. This has in turn led to the under-development of non-bank financial institutions, capital markets, risk management products, risk intermediaries, trading and market-making. The over-dependence of the high-risk banking industry becomes catastrophic when it operates under a regime of pegged exchange rate and open capital flows, or has to function under inconsistent macroeconomic policies. The recent experience of Asia, and to an extent of Malaysia, provides ample testimony to this eventuality.

3. Form of Corporate Governance and Equity Markets

Unlike the dispersed shareholdings of the Anglo-Saxon world, Asia is characterized by concentrated shareholdings. Non-competitive product markets and weak legal protection encourage this, as do governance by large shareholders rather than managers, reduced opportunities for managements to specialize, poor diversification of investments, and increased risks of expropriation of outside shareholders by insiders. Concentrated shareholdings accordingly make for a less-developed equity market.

In Malaysia the equity market is very sizeable, in spite of concentrated shareholdings, the reasons for this being set out by Thillainathan (1999). The news at the outbreak of the regional crisis of corporate governance breakdowns, and the weak responses to this of regulators, led to a big stock market sell-down. The problem was compounded by new rules on scrip delivery[4] which were imposed to check the sell-down, and these rules were scrapped soon thereafter. But initiatives to facilitate the development of suitable mechanisms for improved corporate governance were taken only later, and doubts still persist on issues related to enforcement.

4. The Legal Infrastructure

An alternative explanation of the crisis attributes it to Asia's under-reliance on markets, and to over-reliance on a relationship-based system to make decisions on such matters as borrowing and lending as well as investment. According to this view, Asia's inadequate reliance on markets is due to its weak infrastructure for private contracting, which is in turn attributed to its poor laws or weak enforcement of those laws. Investment decisions based on the relationship model rather than on market prices and contracts need not turn sour so long as the supply of capital relative to investment opportunities is limited. They are likely to go wrong, however, where there is a plentiful supply of capital relative to investment opportunities, as was the case in Asia with the massive capital inflows of the 1990s.

To protect their interest, foreign lenders to Asian corporations and banks invariably made short-term loans, relying on the threat of not rolling over the loans to ensure borrowers serviced the latter. When the Asian crisis struck, the decision of some lenders to call back loans made others do the same and caused a stampede of capital outflows. This was a rational response and not a panic, for it did not make sense for lenders to take their time and go to the courts to enforce their rights, given the poor laws and weak enforcement.

On this analysis of the crisis, some form of capital control can be justified as a temporary or medium-term measure, providing a breathing space to build the legal infrastructure and develop domestic markets. There is merit in such an analysis for Indonesia and Thailand with their weak laws and unrestricted capital flows, but rather less merit for Korea which had weak laws but a tightly regulated capital account. There is even less merit in the argument for Malaysia, which had a more satisfactory legal infrastructure as well as exchange controls to combat speculation. It thus seems that the other three factors just listed account more for Malaysia's misfortune.

FINANCIAL SECTOR REFORM AND CAPITAL MARKET DEVELOPMENT

In contrast to a bank-centred system, a market-centred financial system reduces macro-economic vulnerabilities and systemic risk. This is illustrated by the funds management industry, which is a key component of a market-centred system. In this case risks are borne by investors, and any differences in liquidity needs of individual investors and the maturity profile of the investment portfolio is met by a liquidation of underlying assets. Such liquidations lead to price volatility, the risk of which has to be borne by the investor. But as any funds outflow has to be exactly matched by an inflow, liquidity and systemic risks are minimized.[5]

To bring about the development of a market-centred financial system, the banking industry needs to be opened up to competition, while financial markets need to be deregulated. The required reforms in Malaysia are now outlined.

1. Reforms for Averting a Future Banking Crisis

The current push in Malaysia for a prudential and disclosure-based regulatory regime is not adequate, and more needs to be done. There is a requirement for the phased opening up of the banking industry to global competition, for strong management which may be achieved by hiring the best from around the world, for enlightened supervision based on adequate risk controls, and for a realignment of the incentives of owners, managers, depositors and regulators in line with prudent banking practices with respect to the matching of risks with returns.

The Malaysian banking industry has been exposed to the problem of moral hazard, as bankers have had an incentive to engage in more risky lending. This incentive is greater, the lower the capitalization of a bank or the higher its gearing. High gearing characterizes the banking industry in Malaysia and elsewhere in Asia because of the explicit or implicit government guarantees of deposits. High gearing under such circumstances increases the incentive for owners to engage in risky lending, as the profits generated from such lending are for the account of owners whereas losses are borne largely by taxpayers.

In this environment, and unless this moral hazard problem is rooted out by eliminating the explicit or implicit guarantees of deposits, even a private enterprise economy can be made very vulnerable to over-investment and to the boom-bust cycles of the property and share markets. But to do away with these guarantees in an efficient and equitable manner, retail depositors require the support of a deposit insurance scheme, and wholesale depositors require the freedom to deposit without restriction between banks and across countries. The opening up of the banking industry is not likely to happen soon, given the favoured position of bankers in Asia.

2. Reforms for Promoting Capital Market Development

(a) **The Funds Management Industry**. The balanced development of this industry *vis-à-vis* the banking industry requires a reform of the financial sector in general, and of the Employees' Provident Fund (EPF) in particular. Increasing reliance has to be placed on the financial and capital markets to price, mobilize and allocate savings between competing debt and equity market instruments, as well as to price and allocate risks between different market players based on their willingness and capacity to bear the risks. This is in the new environment of enhanced market volatility, and will in turn necessitate the liberalization and deregulation of financial markets. The latter is so that traders and investors have the incentive to take positions, and to hedge or make markets without unnecessary restrictions and incurring high transactions costs.

One key reason for the under-development of the funds management industry in Malaysia is the capture by the Employees Provident Fund of a sizeable portion of national savings through its forced-savings scheme for employees, and through the centralized investment of these savings. The EPF is under-invested in marketable securities, and has not invested in global equities or bonds. Given the benefits of diversification and investment on a portfolio basis, the problem of increasing the supply of marketable securities and reducing restrictions on investment in them must be addressed as a matter of priority. The problem of over-centralized investment can be addressed not by breaking up the EPF, but by parcelling its funds for external management.

The role of the EPF after such parcelling would then be twofold: to manage funds which are earmarked for passive management, and to ensure that adequate investment choices are offered to contributors on a competitive basis. The choices at such a juncture would be between different asset classes (including domestic and international), different management styles (including passive and active management), and different providers of annuity products. The goal would be to allow contributors to exercise their individual choices based on considerations including expected returns and risks, costs, risk preferences, and risk-bearing capacity. This new situation contrasts with the current practice of adopting a common investment plan, irrespective of the age profile or risk-bearing capacity of contributors.

(b) **The Bond Market**. Unlike the equity market, the bond market in Malaysia is inactive and illiquid, and therefore under-developed. This is not because of a weak market infrastructure in respect of trading, clearing and settlement, but owing to over-regulation and the pursuit of incorrect policies. A similar situation holds in most other Asian economies.

The secondary market for Malaysian government securities is *inactive and illiquid* because of a captive demand for them, a shortage of these instruments, an illiquid cash market and the lack of a futures market. It is not therefore possible to separate the problem of determining the risk-free rate from the problem of pricing credit risk, and this can also curb activity in the issuing and trading of private debt securities. To create a more active and liquid market as a benchmark for pricing fixed rate debt issues, the government has to issue Malaysian government securities periodically (even if it does not have to borrow) and to consolidate its existing issues of these securities into fewer, larger issues. Without the consolidation and large periodic issues, the market for Malaysian government securities can be easily cornered. Then it cannot play a meaningful role in yield discovery.

To develop an active and liquid secondary bond market, it is necessary to free yields, to reduce or eliminate reserve and liquidity costs, to reduce interest rate risk premiums, and to create an institutional framework for borrowing and lending securities as well as to remove existing restrictions on 'repo' and 'reverse repo' transactions.[6] The incidence from time to time of high reserve and liquidity costs[7] combined with the phenomena of depressed Malaysian government security yields[8] has often made it unprofitable for dealers and traders to make a market or trade in bonds. Restrictions on the borrowing and shorting of securities as well as the lack of a futures market have rendered these activities highly risky, and made for a big risk premium.

Yields can be freed and liquidity costs reduced by liberalizing the liquid asset requirements, and this is presently being implemented under the Bank Negara Malaysia's new liquidity framework. Reserve costs can be reduced by lessening reliance on statutory reserves as a tool of monetary policy, or by exempting financial institutions from holding reserves against their bond inventories. The interest rate risk premiums can be brought down by improving opportunities for hedging. A well-developed cash and futures market will increase the supply of fixed income products, whose short supply has been a contributory factor in the Employees' Provident Fund's under-investment in marketable securities and in constraining the development of a market in annuity products.

(c) **Securitization.**[9] The securitization of debt can reduce asset-liability mismatches and the capital requirement of banks. It can also increase the supply of private debt securities for investors. Securitization in Malaysia will be boosted by several reforms implemented in the post-crisis period, provided the cash and futures market in bonds becomes more active and the legal infrastructure is more conducive.

(d) **The Cross-Currency Swap Market**. In the absence of a well-developed and liquid bond market, the yield curve generated by the cross-currency swap market can also be used as the proxy for issuing and trading private debt securities and for boosting their supply. Thus the yield curve generated by the cross currency swap market was used as the proxy during the mid-1990s for issuing and trading private debt securities in their onshore market. The international and domestic rating of certain Malaysian corporates as well as the arbitrage activities between the onshore private debt security market and offshore cross-currency swap market were adequate to ensure a narrowing of the onshore and offshore yield curve. This enabled a more widespread use of the latter as a proxy in the onshore private debt security market.

So long as the Malaysian bond market remains under-developed, reliance can be placed on the cross-currency swap market to generate a proxy yield curve. This makes it essential for the government to remove restrictions which have led to the shut-down of the ringgit cross-currency swap market from September 1998. Otherwise the lack of a proxy yield curve can curb the level of issuing and trading activity in the private debt security market. The re-establishment of the ringgit cross-currency swap market is also necessary to enable investors and borrowers to hedge their interest and exchange rate risks more easily and at lower cost.[10] That will increase overseas interest for investing in Malaysia, and reduce the risk of Malaysians who have overseas exposures. The move is more necessary where the value of ringgit is market-determined.

(e) Legal and Regulatory Infrastructure. A good legal infrastructure is essential to making the transition from a relationship-based investing model to a market-based one. Markets have to be opened up and the infrastructure for contracting has to be strengthened. This must be done if a financial system is to be developed with increasing reliance on financial markets where transactions are based on market prices and contracts.

Thanks to its history, Malaysia has been endowed with a superior legal infrastructure compared to that prevailing in the other crisis-stricken countries[11], which are now undertaking far-reaching legal reforms in response to what happened. Malaysia too is undertaking some reforms, however. Thus a recent high-level report of the Ministry of Finance on corporate governance (Malaysia. Securities Commission 1999) called for more codification, as well as for the introduction of statutory derivative action to strengthen civil enforcement action. Aside from codification of a director's fiduciary duties, the report also recommends codification of the minimum functions of boards of public limited companies. This move towards codification has been motivated by a desire to clarify the law or (as some speculate) to make judgements more consistent, reliable and predictable.

Yet it is impossible for the law to be written up to cover all contingencies, and some element of discretion should always be preserved. Any reform in the law should also not be at the cost of the time-honoured 'business judgement rule' that keeps the courts out of corporate decisions. It is pertinent too that the rule of law requires an efficient, independent and impartial judiciary as well as an independent bar, and there has been a growing perception of a decline in the standards to which laws have been upheld in commerce in recent years. As the rule of law is a critical determinant of economic growth and as justice must be seen to be done, there is a need for the government to address what has led to this adverse view. Otherwise, the perception of a weak legal infrastructure may dictate Malaysia's continued reliance on an investing model that is relationship-based, with its attendant vulnerability to recurrent economic crises.

(f) Bank and Corporate Restructuring. The recent banking crisis and corporate distress in Malaysia were triggered by a collapse in demand and asset prices. But in contrast to Indonesia or Thailand, corporate distress in Malaysia was not systemic, being concentrated primarily in construction, property development, the building materials industry and the infrastructure sector.

Market-based and government-facilitated and financed restructuring options became available in Malaysia with the setting up by government in 1998 of *Danaharta* (an Asset Management Company), *Danamodal* (a Bank Restructuring Agency), the Corporate Debt Restructuring Committee, and the amendment of Section 176 of the Companies Act.[12] While corporate restructuring or bankruptcy proceedings often take years to complete where cases are complicated by multiple, diverse creditors with conflicting interests, restructuring or rehabilitation in Malaysia has been quite fast. This is because in some cases restructuring has been government-facilitated, government-directed and even government-financed. In these cases it is taxpayers and not creditors who are at risk.

Creditors in this situation often emerge as the beneficiaries, subjecting the process once again to the moral hazard problem. The process also leads to opportunistic behaviour by encouraging those with inside information about such government-financed restructuring programmes to buy up debt or equity-linked debt papers at a bargain. In fact in a private restructuring exercise, the shareholders are invariably required to absorb the losses on the 'first-loss' principle.

Incentives for market-based restructuring have increased with the recent amendment to Section 176 of the Companies Act, however. Yet the government is still actively intervening and guiding the restructuring of banks and large companies, as well as owning the only asset management company and bank restructuring agency with large financial resources. A time-bound exit strategy for *Danaharta* and *Danamodal* has been announced only recently, but the allowed time is still too long and may diminish pressures for the full restructuring of distressed companies. A strong case can therefore be made for greater reliance on the market-based approach to restructuring, with banks or other private parties establishing asset management companies. This approach can be extended by using the remedies available under the Companies Act for resolving less complicated cases of corporate distress. In these cases, restructuring or liquidation could be left to the banks, since there is a well-functioning secondary market in properties.

Danaharta has indicated that it will not function as a warehousing agency, and began its asset disposal programme from the second half of 1999. It announced in 2001 that it would complete this programme by 2005. This time is still too long, however, and the organization's exit strategy is a key issue for the government. The slower the pace of asset disposal, the greater the overhang in the market. So long as this overhang exists and asset prices are above their market clearing levels, new development activities and the pace of economic growth are severely hampered. It is important as well that *Danaharta* should be cautious in the use of its funds to support partially completed projects, either directly or through joint ventures. It should rely on the auction or tender process, letting the market decide the fate of these projects.

A comprehensive restructuring exercise requires the judicious use of debt-equity conversions, with the resulting change in ownership structure and management creating the right incentives for efficient behaviour by all stakeholders. There have to date been several financial restructurings, but not as many management changes at the corporate level. If *Danaharta* ends up as a warehousing agency, or if it or the Corporate Debt Restructuring Committee does not impose proper burden-sharing on stakeholders of enterprises restructured through their interventions, the right incentives will not be created to rid the corporate and banking sectors of the moral hazard problem.

CONCLUSIONS

This chapter examines what Asia, and Malaysia in particular, should do to reduce their chronic over-dependence on banking with its recurrent boom-bust cycles. It is possible to reduce this over-dependence by developing domestic financial markets, but not by insulating them from global markets. Both Asia's and Malaysia's regulatory and legal infrastructures are inadequate to facilitate an optimal shift from bank financing to financing accessed directly from the financial markets. The required reforms to make this shift have been discussed, and it appears that increased reliance on the private sector will not be adequate unless there is a corresponding increase in dependence on market prices and contracts and less dependence on relationships. The stance of macroeconomic policies should also be prudent.

The massive over-building and asset-liability mismatches of the mid-1990s, arising from inappropriate policies and a distorted incentive structure, have now been contained or even reversed by the outbreak of the regional crisis, and by subsequent price adjustments and extensive but limited financial restructuring. The Malaysian economy is leaner, and, subject to the global economic environment, possesses good medium-term growth prospects. But there has been little change in the risk profile of the economy, since business continues to be conducted in essentially the same way. In fact, the country's new exchange control and pegged exchange rate regime may have increased its risk profile. This risk profile undermines Malaysia's growth potential, and can lead to a renewed build-up of pressures within the economy. These pressures could cause another shake-up within three to five years unless changes are made in the way the economy is managed.

NOTES

1. This was the case in 2001 with the Employees Provident Fund, which guarantees a minimum return of 2.5 per cent per annum. It was also the case with several unit trust schemes operated and managed by the National Investment Corporation (PNB), which explicitly or implicitly guaranteed not only the principal but also a high return (well above the market returns).
2. The strong recovery of the Malaysian economy from mid-1999 after its sharp collapse in 1998 was followed by a substantial slowdown in 2001. This reversal of fortune can be attributed partly to the weakening in external demand and partly to lacklustre private investment. The weakening in external demand was caused by the slowdown in the US economy. The lacklustre private investment was due to the continued overhang in excess capacity and the persistence of asset prices above the market-clearing level, as well as to the pursuit of less market-friendly policies.
3. The capital controls imposed on foreign portfolio investments had all been removed by 2000. However, the capital controls imposed on Malaysians remained in place. Before the crisis only Malaysians with domestic borrowings had to have the prior approval of the central bank to invest abroad, whereas after the crisis even Malaysians without any domestic borrowings required the prior approval of the central bank to invest abroad.
4. The word share 'scrip' is an abbreviation of share subscription certificate. The optimal arrangement is for scrips to be delivered by the seller and payments to be made by the buyer simultaneously, usually about three days after a trading deal is executed. The new rule on scrip delivery imposed in the aftermath of the crisis requires scrips to be delivered before a sale order and before the receipt of payment.
5. If the maturity preferences of suppliers and end-users of funds are not fully matched, then the services of a financial institution will still be necessary to provide the required maturity transformation and to assume the resulting maturity mismatch risk. A well-developed financial sector is likely to minimize such mismatches between providers and end-users of funds, and to transfer the remaining risk to those entities willing or able to bear them (which may not necessarily be banks). The under-development of capital markets causes an over-concentration of risks in banks, while the lack of risk management products means that the banks are not able to transfer risks to those who are best able to bear them.
6. Under a repurchase agreement or 'repo', an institution enters into an agreement with a buyer to sell a security for cash and to buy it back at a pre-agreed price after a specified period of time. The seller is in fact using the 'repo' transaction to finance its investment in the security on a collateralized basis. In a reverse repurchase agreement or a reverse 'repo' transaction, an institution is in fact lending against the collateral of a security. A reverse repo transaction can in fact be used by an institution to borrow a security against the collateral of cash for the purpose of short selling the security.
7. The high reserve cost is owed to over-reliance by the central bank on the use of statutory reserves as a tool for the conduct of monetary policy. The high liquidity cost is due to the imposition by the central bank on the banking system of high liquid asset requirements as a measure of prudence.
8. Malaysian government security yields will be depressed when shortage of supply causes an intersection of the supply curve on the captive segment of the demand curve.
9. Securitization is the process of bundling or combining loan assets or accounts receivable that are not securities, registering the bundle as securities and selling them directly to the investing public. Securitization enables an institution to specialize in the origination of loans as well as to unbundle and sell participation in the risk and financing burden of these loans to those who are willing and able to assume them. Thus securitization enables an institution to liquefy its balance sheet and/or conserve its capital.
10. The cross-currency swap market must be an onshore as well as an offshore market, and there should be little or no restriction placed on hedging or speculation. After the abolition of the

offshore ringgit market in September 1998, the authorities attempted to develop an onshore market in cross-currency swaps. But given the existing restrictions on hedging and speculation in 2001, it seemed that this market would never take off.

11. This is presumably the reason why the government decided from 1985 to terminate appeals to the Privy Council of the United Kingdom (a court of final appeal). The potential for appeals was a relic from the colonial period.

12. *Danaharta* was set up to buy and manage the non-performing loans of banks, while *Danamodal* was set up to recapitalize banks. The Corporate Debt Restructuring Committee was set up to facilitate voluntary restructuring. The amendment to Section 176 of the Companies Act in late 1998 requires that a company obtain the consent of creditors representing at least 50 per cent of its debts before it can apply for court protection from creditors.

3. The Impact of the 1997 Financial Crisis on Malaysia's Corporate Sector and its Response

Tan Tat Wai

Malaysia also experienced a severe recession in 1985 - 1986. However, there were major differences between the nature of the latter and the recession triggered by the East Asian financial crisis of 1997 - 1998. It is important to understand the key differences between these two recessions in analysing their impact on, and the response by, the Malaysian corporate sector.

This chapter first scrutinizes differences between the recessions, so as to form a macro-framework with which to analyse their micro-impact on the corporate sector. It next highlights the magnitude of the crisis at the level of major firms, proceeding to sum up the extent of restructuring up to early 2000 and to reach conclusions in light of that analysis.

DIFFERENCES BETWEEN RECESSIONS

In 1984, the Malaysian economy was clearly heading for a very severe financial crisis. To begin with, the world economy had slowed down in 1982, leading to a general decline in commodity prices in that year. In the meantime, the Malaysian government and the private sector had both been spending at a fast pace between 1977 and 1982.[1] Some key characteristics of the economy at the start of the 1985 crisis are presented in Table 3.1.

When the decline in commodity prices commenced, the government attempted to spend its way out of the difficulties. When commodity prices failed to rebound and foreign direct investments remained sluggish, the counter-cyclical spending served to worsen both the fiscal and current account deficits to an unbearable degree. The government thus had no choice but to immediately restructure the economy. A contraction in fiscal spending was announced in the budget for the year 1985, and a number of policy measures were implemented.[2]

The result was of course predictable. The economy went into a broad-based and prolonged recession. Gross domestic product (GDP)[3] at constant prices contracted by 1.0 per cent in 1985 and grew by a mere 1.2 per cent in 1986. Gross national product[4] at constant prices declined by 3.2 per cent in 1985 and a further 8.3 per cent in 1986. The latter would not recover until 1988, even as GDP started to rise strongly from 1987. Both consumption and investment fell over this period. Exports also fell in both 1985 and 1986, and unemployment rose sharply as there were many retrenchments and some bankruptcies. No one was spared from the crisis, and both foreign and local firms were affected. The construction sector and those supplying it were hit particularly hard, with the sector contracting for four consecutive years and not recovering until 1989.

Table 3.1   Key Characteristics at the Start of the 1985 and 1998 Crises, Malaysia

	1985	1998
Recurring Fiscal Deficit (% of GDP)	16.6	5 years of surplus
Current Account Deficit (% of GDP)	-2.2	+13.0
(5 years cumulative total) (% of GDP)	-42.0	-14.0
Exports to GNP (%)	49	103
Commodity Exports (% of total exports)	65	17
Gearing of the Economy	-	-
Domestic Loan: GDP (%)	85	148
External Debt: GDP (%)	75.6	60.9
External Debt Service: Export (%)	18.9	6.7
Unemployment rate (% of workforce)	7.6	3.9

Source: Malaysia. Bank Negara Malaysia (1986-2000)

However, in such an environment of a broad-based but slow slide downwards, firms generally had time to react to and deal with the contraction. The exceptions were firms actively trading on the Kuala Lumpur Stock Exchange (KLSE). These firms were first hit by the Pan El crisis in late 1986,[5] which was followed by the New York city stock market crash in October 1987. Those events set off runs first at the Malaysian cooperative societies which had taken deposits and invested heavily in KLSE counters and properties. The banking system was also threatened in the aftermath, and the Bank Negara Malaysia had to organize a massive operation to take control of cooperatives, banks and finance companies in trouble.

As the Bank Negara tried to sort out the mess in the financial system, it also proceeded to tighten rules and regulations to improve the long-term prudence of the system. Some key policies adopted at that time and likely to have made a big difference in the subsequent 1998 crisis were:

1. Increases in capital and the capital adequacy ratio.
2. Imposition of a six months' interest non-payment as the standard for classifying non-performing loans.
3. Tighter requirements on Bank Negara approvals for companies raising foreign loans, with ability to repay in foreign exchange being a key consideration.

It is necessary to stress the key point that many troubled firms had been able to drag their feet on restructuring until the advent of the Pan El crisis, because of the slow nature of the downwards slide. There had basically been no quick recall of bank loans, and non-performing loans were on the basis of 12 months' non-payment of interest while there was also no capital adequacy ratio. In the slow slide situation, cash flow got squeezed gradually, allowing firms and banks to assume a mutually advantageous deliberate work out of their difficulties.

Some firms in not such deep trouble were able to progressively increase their capital. They could alternatively or at the same time add new business so as to enhance cash flow. In contrast, had financial institutions been forced by a more generally unfavourable environment to quickly pull back on and even withdraw loans in a panicky response, firms in a tight but otherwise manageable situation might have been forced to undertake hasty adjustments. The crisis would then have been worsened, and could indeed have been much broader.

The 1998 Financial Crisis

In similar fashion to the 1985 - 1986 recession, Malaysia went into 1997 with a prolonged current account deficit (Table 3.1). This time the spending spree was private sector driven, even if it was encouraged by government policies. Much of this private spending was funded by debt, with part of this being in foreign currency borrowings.

There was as in 1984 a substantial bubble building up in the domestic economy, again in the property and stock markets. Some parts of the government recognized this aspect, and attempted to correct it. Hence the then economic adviser to the prime minister, Tun Daim, warned investors several times that the KLSE Composite Index was rising fast and was already too high. The Bank Negara also recognized this trend, and tried to control it by setting a credit ceiling on lending to the broad property sector. Unfortunately, that effort was aborted under intense business lobbying and political pressure.

On the other hand, and contrasting with the 1985 - 1986 recession, the economy was characterized by full employment and a sound government fiscal position. Not only was unemployment merely 2.9 per cent, but more importantly there were 1.5 million foreign labourers in the country. Unofficial estimates even put the total legal and illegal foreign labour force as high as two million persons. In 1984, in contrast, unemployment was more than 6 per cent although the economy had been growing since 1977. There was thus no likelihood in 1997 of a massive retrenchment of Malaysian labour, even if GDP declined sharply for a couple of years. Domestic consumer confidence should hence not have been depressed by fear of retrenchment. It was almost certain that in any retrenchment exercise foreign labourers, who had been repatriating most of their incomes rather than spending them locally, would be hit first.

Regarding the fiscal position there were five years of continuous surplus up to 1997. This compared with the significant deficit equivalent to 16.6 per cent of GDP in 1984. In 1997, the fiscal deficit had been largely financed by external debt since the 1980s, and the level of external debt servicing was already pushing towards the internationally acceptable norm of 20 per cent of exports. Again in contrast to 1985 when the government had to quickly cut back on its borrowings and spending, it could in 1998 afford to spend large sums of money to cushion any significant fall in domestic demand. In particular, since the foreign debt service level was less than 7 per cent of exports and exports had increased from 49 to 103 per cent of GDP, the ability of the economy to borrow externally was considerable. If the government could persuade foreign funding sources that it could repay, foreign financing of any fiscal deficit would be feasible.

It thus seems that if there had been a well-managed publicity campaign backed up by specific actions to build domestic and international confidence, there should have been no massive erosion of confidence. Unfortunately, severe disagreements within the government on how to handle the crisis led to inadequate, if not wrong, policy responses. In particular, the initial drive to emulate International Monetary Fund policies, and especially the two-pronged attack to cut expenditure and force an immediate contraction of loans, greatly worsened the crisis.

THE MAGNITUDE OF THE CRISIS AT THE FIRM LEVEL

Given that the 1997 crisis was much more one of confidence than one across the board, as occurred in the 1980s, it is obvious that impacts at the firm level were very uneven. Not unexpectedly, the hardest hit firms were those who had invested very substantially during the run up to 1997. It is possible to identify these firms, first by distinguishing sectors that had run up big loans.

The Malaysian banking system went overboard in funding the 'bubble' that took place prior to the crisis. Table 3.2 shows that the manufacturing sector, which had been the fastest growing sector in the economy for many years, doubled in outstanding loans between 1993 and 1997. This was in itself a very fast pace of growth. Yet lending to the property and stock and shares sectors grew even more. The latter are the two sectors that would be hardest hit in times of contraction, especially if there were attempts at forcing the pace of adjustments.

Indeed, the government allowed and encouraged the banking system to tighten credit sharply from the fourth quarter of 1997. As financial institutions clamped down on credit and circumstances worsened, they themselves became the first sector to go into crisis. The banking system lost RM2.3 billion in 1998, as against a profit of RM7.7 billion in 1997, while the stockbroking industry lost RM3.5 billion against a previous year's profit of RM2.5 billion.

Table 3.3 denotes that finance companies led the contraction in credit. Over the twelve months of 1998, they withdrew RM17 billion from customers, or 16.5 per cent of their total outstanding credit at the end of 1997. This withdrawal was equivalent to 4.2 per cent of the outstanding credit provided by the whole banking system at the end of 1997. In the next twelve months of 1999, finance companies' credit contracted by another RM7 billion, or 8 per cent of their total outstanding credit at the end of 1998.

Table 3.2 Loans of Banking System by Sector, Malaysia (RM billion)

	1993 (RM Billion)	1997 (RM Billion)	Increase (RM Billion)	(%)
Property	54	130	86	159
Stocks and Shares	6	39	33	550
Manufacturing	32	64	32	100
Total	175	421	246	141

Source: Malaysia. Bank Negara Malaysia (1986 - 2001).

Table 3.3 Total Amounts Lent by the Banking System, Malaysia, 1996 - 1999 (RM Billion)

	Dec. '96	Sept. '97	Dec. '97	Jun. '98	Dec. '98	Jun. '99
Commercial Banks	218	260	276	277	286	285
Finance Companies	83	102	103	99	86	77
Merchant Banks	19	23	23	23	22	21
Total	320	385	402	399	394	383
Stocks and Shares	-	-	39	-	33	-
Purchase of Vehicles (Finance Companies)	-	-	42	-	34	-

Source: Malaysia. Bank Negara Malaysia (1986 - 2001).

In fact, the true impact of the credit squeeze was far more than indicated by the reduction in credit from the finance companies. In the nine months from

January to September, 1997, total credit provided by the banking system grew by RM65 billion or 20.3 per cent. However, the system was instructed in October, 1997, to ensure that total credit growth would not exceed 15 per cent by the end of December in that year, and this implied that credit would have to contract by RM20 billion in the last two months of the year! Given that many projects were already committed, with promises of new credit facilities or a drawing down of available facilities, the only way the banking system could ensure near compliance would be to withdraw significant existing credit or approved credit already in the pipeline.

It seems in retrospect that if the government had followed through its earlier directive to control credit to the broad property sector in March 1997, it would have done much to reverse the rapid build up of the property and share market bubbles. Such a move would have preceded by one year the impact of the financial crisis on Malaysia. Many new projects would not have taken off and some consolidation would have occurred before the crisis hit, helping to control the speed and magnitude of the adjustments.

Given the actual state of affairs, non-performing loans ballooned in 1998, and the reclassification at that juncture of such loans as those with three months' non-payment (from the previous six months) served to worsen the panic. By the end of 1998, RM20.9 billion of the total of RM140 billion property loans had become non-performing loans, as against RM 9 billion for manufacturing and RM7.5 billion each for consumer credit and stocks and shares (Table 3.4).

Table 3.4 Breakdown of Non-Performing Loans, end-1998 (RM Billion)

	Property	Stocks & Shares	Consumer Credit	Manufacturing
Commercial Banks	13.2	4.1	2.6	7.2
	[12.2]*	[17]	[15]	[12]
Finance Companies	6.2	2.4	4.9	1.2
	[20]	[26]	[15]	[24]
Merchant Banks	1.5	1.0	-	0.6
	[19]	[24]	-	[22]
Total	20.9	7.5	7.5	9.0
	[14]	[20]	[-]	[-]

Notes: * Figures in brackets are percentages of total non-performing loans in the category.

Non-performing loans in consumer credit have a direct impact on private consumption. As credit lines are withdrawn and consumer goods reprocessed, consumers' wealth and confidence, especially amongst lower and middle income groups, are hit hard. This in turn has a second round impact on demand for goods and services.

Non-performing loans in stocks and shares impact the economy in different ways. A smaller part of these loans is likely to be for individuals with high net worth. The greater part is probably for companies and businesspersons using the stock market for reverse takeovers and acquisitions. As the stock market falls and finance institutions force the selling of shares used as collateral, the companies, businesspersons and finance institutions concerned suffer a permanent destruction of wealth. However, the impact in this case is not widespread but limited to these latter three parties.

The effect of non-performing loans to property companies is far more severe than that of those extended to stock and shares. It is bigger on the financial institutions, partly because of the size factor but also because the security value cannot be realized quickly. This gives rise to severe cash flow problems for both the institutions and the property companies. The accumulation of a glut in unsold and uncompleted properties also means contractors and suppliers of construction raw materials suffer from both bad debt and the plunge in demand. The impact of non-performing loans on the manufacturing sector is uneven.

As may be expected from the foregoing analysis and as is clear from Table 3.5, the biggest drops in production after the 1997 crisis were in consumer durables and construction raw materials, especially transport equipment (i.e., cars), room air-conditioners and steel bars. However, the case of the transport equipment was somewhat unique. Yet although the fall in 1998 was very great, the rebound in 1999 was equally sharp.

Table 3.5   Changes in Industrial Production, Malaysia, 1998 and 1999 (Per Cent of Total Value of Production, Year on Year)

	1998	1999
Manufacturing Total	-10.2	12.9
*Consumer Durables**		
Transport Equipment	-52.2	53.5
Room Air-Conditioning	-38.9	-11.3
Household Refrigerator	-17.3	-5.8
*Construction**		
Steel Bar & Rod	-43.6	19.3
Cement	-17.9	-2.8
Plywood	-18.6	0.8
*Others**		
Fuel Oil	-24.2	-24.8

Note: * These are industries generally dominated by big firms, mostly on the KLSE main board.

The corollaries to these varied responses to non-performing loans after the 1997 crisis were huge losses and a need for adjustment. But the differences

between sectors and sub-sectors naturally produced different types of response
to the difficulties.

Table 3.6 Concentrations of Losses amongst Malaysian Companies*, 1997 -
1998

	Percentages of Companies in Each Category by Size of Loss per Company (RM million)		
Sub-Sector	<50	>50	Total
Industrial Products	21	17	38
Consumer	35	5	40
Construction	6	30	36
Trading & Services	13	32	45
Property	19	25	44

Company Size Group	<50	>50	50-500	>500
10 Major Conglomerates	3	41	38	58
Others	97	59	62	42
Total	100	100	100	100

Source: Kuala Lumpur Stock Exchange (2000).
Note: * Those on the Main Board of the KLSE only.

Table 3.7 More on Losses amongst Malaysian Companies*, 1997 - 1998

	Total Companies	Number of Companies in each Category by Size of Loss per Company (RM million)				
Sub-sector		<50	50-100	100-200	200-500	500-1000 >1000
Industrial	102	21	5	7	4	20
Consumer	57	20	1	2	0	0
Construction	33	2	2	4	1	21
Infrastructure	5	0	0	0	0	0
Trading Services	80	10	5	8	7	42
Property	70	13	7	5	5	10
Total	347	66	20	26	17	83
Company Size Group 10 Major						
Conglomerates	33	2	6	13	5	52
Others	108	64	14	13	12	41

Source: Kuala Lumpur Stock Exchange (2000).
Note: * Those on the Main Board of the KLSE only.

Using companies listed on the KLSE as a guide, 44 per cent of companies in property development and 38 per cent of companies in industrial products suffered losses, while 40 per cent of consumer goods companies were in this category (Table 3.6). Fifty eight per cent of ten major conglomerates each had massive losses of over RM500 million, while 42 per cent of other companies listed on the Exchange were also affected in this way. More details of the apportionment of losses are given in Table 3.7.

THE RESTRUCTURING OF MAJOR CORPORATIONS

The Malaysian government moved decisively to tackle the problems of the financial institutions. It coerced the absorption through mergers and acquisitions by a mandated ten Malaysian 'anchor' banks of 22 finance companies, non-bank owned merchant banks and smaller banks. Foreign owned banks were not included in this exercise. The government also set up an asset management company called *Danaharta* to take over RM45.5 billion of the bigger non-performing loans from all financial institutions. In parallel, *Danamodal* was established as an investment company to provide RM6.15 billion of loans to recapitalize banks and finance companies with weak balance sheets (Malaysia. Bank Negara Malaysia 1986 - 2001). Further background on this process is given in Chapter 2.

As a follow-up in 2000, the government proceeded to foster through mergers and acquisitions the restructuring of local stockbroking companies into up to a dozen 'universal' brokers. These brokers have to satisfy a minimum capital condition of RM250 million, possess good management, and have acquired or merged with at least three other stockbroking companies. These proposed mergers and an increase in the capital of insurance companies were underway in the early 2000s.

Last but not least, another new official restructuring institution, the Corporate Debt Restructuring Committee, was set up to facilitate debt restructuring between firms and their financiers. Up to the end of 2000 it had dealt with 68 cases totalling RM36.5 billion, of which 19 cases totalling RM14.1 billion had been finally settled (Malaysia. Bank Negara Malaysia 1986 - 2000).

The purpose of these official exercises was to ensure the fundamental restructuring of the financial sector, so as to better handle non-performing loans and other excesses of the kind occurring during the financial crisis. However, even more fundamentally, there was the purpose of ensuring that the smaller number of merged banks and other financial institutions possessed the capital base and professionalism to cope with globalization. By and large, weaker institutions were taken over by stronger ones, despite some degree of tampering to ensure that the New Economic Policy objective of creating a pool of *Bumiputera* entrepreneurs was also observed.

Resulting from these exercises, only three of the ten anchor banks in the early 2000s were Chinese-controlled, while the other seven were either government or *Bumiputera*-controlled. Some degree of compromise had been necessary in trying to balance the need for strong institutions able to withstand the opening up of the financial market with the requirement to ensure strong *Bumiputera* ownership under the philosophy of the NEP. Nonetheless, at least five of the ten anchor banks were led by banks with proven track records through the crisis and in the hands of sound management.[6]

Types of Restructuring

Many types of restructuring are possible, depending on the nature of the crisis and the perception of its severity and length of the crisis by businesspersons concerned.

In general, every company in stress suffers from heavy losses, a high level of debt, or both. The heavy losses could be the result of inefficiency, a severe drop in business volume due to the recession or high financial charges. A high level of debt can be the result of an original steep level of borrowing, or of substantial borrowing in foreign currency. In the latter case, the depreciation of the ringgit has the effect of reducing shareholders' funds through an inflation of the debt measured in ringgit and a consequent need to provide for foreign exchange losses. Manifestly, a heavy concentration on short-term debt worsens the situation and triggers an immediate crisis. The severity of the 1997 financial crisis suggests that most heavy loss-making companies were affected by industry-wide structural issues as well as their own financial profiles.

Looking to specific sub-sectors and to the case of construction raw materials, years of double-digit growth had propelled players to aggressively expand capacities. In both steel and cement for example, capacities were being doubled as the crisis set in. Demand then collapsed by nearly 50 per cent for cement and by 60 per cent for steel bars.[7] In such circumstances, industry-wide consolidation is necessary and mere financial restructuring is unlikely to solve the fundamental problem.

In the case of the property development companies, the problem is usually a need to write off or sell some assets, inject new capital and focus on more viable projects in good locations. From the time of the 1997-1998 crisis until the early 2000s, it was the low and medium-cost housing valued at below RM150,000 that maintained brisk sales. Even so, property companies in bad locations and with wrong concepts would not have survived regardless. This is because projects that cannot sell have zero cash flow - unlike manufacturing companies. It is unusual for the latter to end up with zero flow, and as long as the flow is positive it is possible to buy time for another day. In each company in crisis, it is necessary to check the following:

1.   Whether the crisis is one-time or more fundamental and structural.

2. The urgency of the situation as seen by the degree of gearing, tenure of loans, and strength of cash flows after the drop in demand and prices.
3. The relative strength and weakness of the organization in relation to competitors.
4   The ability and willingness of major shareholders to fund capital call.

In cases where the crisis is perceived as temporary and the cash flow can sustain the servicing of a bank loan, the firm's reaction is likely to be one of procrastination. Financial restructuring is undertaken by rescheduling loans, reducing existing capital, agreeing to debt to equity conversions and selling non-core assets. New minority partner(s) may be roped in for the new equity injection. There is no merger and acquisition, which lead to a change in ownership and management structure.

On the one hand, a sharper than 'natural' decline in circumstances due to violent fund movements including the pulling of bank loans tends to reinforce the feeling of both private sector and government decision makers that the crisis may be transient in nature. Both parties in this scenario want to buy time for an orderly restructuring, hopefully without the businespeople involved losing control and without the government confronting an upset in social order including adverse effects on the *Bumiputera* business community.

On the other hand, in cases where a structural crisis with strong cash flow issues is perceived by those involved, there is a feeling that radical restructuring should be urgently undertaken. This entails inviting foreign (or if available, local) partners, to the extent of losing control. Here the preservation of shareholder value and the firm itself takes precedence over the interests of continuing ownership and control, while awaiting an upturn.

The world financial community, including the International Monetary Fund and World Bank, concluded after the recent crisis that East Asian countries had inefficient firms which were not necessarily profit-maximizing. Hence it called for quick and drastic action, with fire sales to foreign firms as the only logical solution. Inevitably, expectations were generated of sales of core assets and the giving up of controlling stakes to major multinational rivals. The failure by crisis firms to quickly sell out at deep discounts attracted widespread criticism and a withdrawal of foreign investments. Malaysia, in particular, was regarded as the worst culprit.[8]

In reality, substantial restructuring occurred in Malaysia. But unfortunately there has been no comprehensive documentation of its extent and depth, while world opinion has been swayed by the Malaysian government's use of state funds in attempting to salvage leading *Bumiputera* businesses under the wealth restructuring prong of the New Economic Policy. The repeated bailouts of the Renong group, the purchase of Malaysia Airlines shares from its major shareholder at double the then prevailing market price, the reluctance to let the Perwaja steel mill fail, and the request to fellow ASEAN countries to postpone

by two years implementation of the ASEAN Free Trade Agreement for the
automobile sector, have been held as clear illustrations of Malaysia's will to
protect its failing businesses at any cost.[9]

Table 3.8 Details of Company Sales (All Values in RM Billion)*

	Debt	Asset Sold	Cash Raised	Buyer
DRB-HICOM Gp.	5	Proton	1	Petronas
	2	Eon	pending	Proton?
		Kedah Cement	0.4	APMC Blue Circle
Sungai Way Gp.	2.7			
Sungei Way	1.4	SW. Quarry	180	Pioneer Australia
Sun City	1.1	SW. City	180	GIC Singapore
Sun Tech	0.1	SW. Pyramid	182	GIC Singapore
Konsortium Perkapalan	>2	Lion Corp.		
Konsortium Perkapalan		Pac. Carrier	0.6+$200m debt	MISC**
PNSL		ALTPNSL***	0.4+$100m debt	MISC**
		ALT2PNSL***		
		11 ships PNSL		
MRCB	>5	23% Malakoff	0.7	MMC
		15% Malakoff	0.5	National Power
		30% PD Power		of UK
Binariang	-	33% Binariang	1.8	British Telecom
MUI	-	50% APMC	2.1	Malayan Cement Blue Circle of UK
Sapura	-	100% Adam		Time Engineering
Berjaya	-	21% Prudential Assurance	0.24	Prudential Assurance
		30% Mutiara Swisscom		Swiss Telecoms
		48% Intan Utilities	0.3	Vivendi
Pernas	-	30% Malayawata	0.2	Ann Joo Resource
Taiping Consolidated	-	Hotel Malls		YTL Corp.
Arab Malaysia	>2	22% Powertek 20% AMMB	0.23	Tanjong

Source: Kuala Lumpur Stock Exchange (2000).
Note: * Up to mid- 2000. ** Malaysian International Shipping Corporation. ***Subsidiaries.

Actually, much restructuring has occurred outside these prime examples of bailouts. An analysis based on Kuala Lumpur Stock Exchange data of the highly publicized restructuring of the financial sector and the quieter restructuring of the manufacturing sector shows that Malaysia's business sector has started to lay the ground work for a more efficient economy. It may be expected *a priori* that the bigger companies recorded by the Exchange would have suffered more in the financial crisis. Malaysian financial institutions have generally been quite tight in lending to small companies, but tended to shower big publicly-listed companies with huge loans not always adequately evaluated or collateralized.

Table 3.9 Companies in Reverse Takeover by New Owners, Malaysia, 2000

New Name*	New Core	Old Name	Old Core
Already Restructured			
MK Land Holdings	Property	Perfect Food Ind.	Food
Tong Hup Group	Plantations	Union Paper	Paper products
Formis	Computer services	Orlando	Garments
Chonggai	Garments	Eksons	Wood products
Jerasia Capital	Ladies' garments	MCL Corporation	Garments
CHG Industries	Veneer plywood	CHG Ind.	Veneer plywood
Restructuring in Process			
Focal Aims Holdings	Property	Great Wall Plastic Industries	Plastic packaging
	Property	Sanda Plastic	Plastic packaging
	Wood products	EMC Logistic	Transportaton
	Conglomerate	Eden Enterprises (M)	Restaurants
		DataPrep Holdings	Computer services
Safuan Holdings	Property	Promet	Construction
Khoo Soon Lee Group	Property	Kelanamas ind.	Property
Forum Master	Property Construction	Esprit Group	Construction
	Property	Abrar Corporation	Construction
Asia Pacific Latex Ind.	Latex glove	Red Box (M)	Photo albums

Source: Kuala Lumpur Stock Exchange (2000).
Note: * In restructured form.

The Record of Fundamental Restructuring

Of the 141 KLSE main board companies losing money in 1998 and 1999 (Table 3.7), only 55 had failed to announce restructuring plans by the end of March 2000.[10] A further 26 of these companies had either turned around, possessed big shareholders' funds relative to their losses, or were supported by major shareholders with this characteristic. Such companies did not require restructuring. Another 18 of the 141 companies had effected financial restructuring, 18 more had undergone fundamental restructuring with changes in ownership and control, and the balance of 24 companies had restructured by selling significant assets and inviting in foreign partners.

Table 3.8 provides details of fundamental restructuring, showing that many companies involved sold control of parts of their core businesses, sometimes to foreigners. Hence Blue Circle Ltd. of the United Kingdom ended up buying control of 50 per cent of the Malaysian cement industry by purchasing a half share of its subsidiary, APMC. It should be noted that the KLSE Main Board listed company, Malayan Cement, did not own and control Kedah Cement (Cement and Concrete Manufacturers' Association 2000).

Again, the Pioneer Group of Australia ended up by owning 50 per cent of one of the largest quarry and readymix cement operations in the country, with an option to buy control from the Sungai Way group. Ann Joo bought control of Malayawata, which represented the first consolidation of the Malaysian steel industry. Ann Joo already owned a medium-sized rolling mill, and had wanted to build its own steelmaking and rolling complex prior to the crisis.[11]

In the case of telecommunication companies, the sale by Sapura to Time Engineering of the Adams asset represented industry consolidation, while the sale by Berjaya and Binariang of key minority stakes in their mobile telephone subsidiaries, Digi and Maxis, to Swiss Telecoms and British Telecom respectively, represented major efforts at getting foreign managerial and technological capabilities. The same is true of the sale of a minority stake in the independent power plant operator, Malakoff, to the National Power Company of the UK. New owners with viable businesses also took over other companies exercising basic financial restructuring. For all intents and purposes, the original major shareholder(s) who got into crisis had to admit defeat, accept their losses, and give up control. This was obviously not a matter of bailing out, and a summary of what occurred in these other instances is given in Table 3.9.

The Impact of Foreign Loans and Role for Foreign Takeovers of Crisis Firms

Unlike Indonesia, Thailand, and perhaps even South Korea, the foreign debt level in Malaysia at the time of the financial crisis was relatively small (Malaysia. Bank Negara Malaysia 1986 - 2001). Right through the crisis, the level of liquidity remained robust, with the savings rate going up to 42 per cent in 1998 from an already high level of 38 per cent in previous years (Malaysia. Bank Negara Malaysia 1986 - 2000). Hence the need for funding was not severe, contrary to the speculations of many analysts at the time. The corollary was that the pressures of foreign loans at the firm level were also tolerable, especially as the tenure of such loans was generally longer term.

A survey of KLSE main board companies shows that not more than 30 of these had significant foreign loans. In most cases such loans were not the deciding factor in their problems, although they severely impacted bottom lines. However, they sometimes triggered a need for immediate restructuring. The biggest impact of foreign loans was for very large companies like Tenaga Nasional, the National Electric Power Company, Telekoms, and Malaysia Airlines. Yet while both Tenaga and Telekoms had the cash flow and balance sheet to handle their foreign loans, Malaysia Airlines could not achieve this owing to its under-capitalization, massive ongoing expansion and weak management not familiar with the aviation industry.

CONCLUSIONS

The speed of advance and adverse effects of the East Asian financial crisis of the late 1990s were initially enhanced by inappropriate official policy responses, especially those involving cuts in expenditure and the contraction of loans. There were also some corporate manoeuvres prior to the crisis which backfired when the latter took effect, with companies suffering because of much reduced demand coupled with a major expansion. Gearing shot up under the twin blades of a plunge in sales and cash flows, coupled with expansion on borrowed funds. Comparisons of the 1985 and 1998 crises indicate that the slower downward slide in the former enabled companies to respond more easily to their problems. They also denote that measures taken by the Bank Negara in the late 1980s in reaction to 1985 are likely to have made a big difference in the subsequent crisis. It is evident too that at the advent of the 1998 crisis the economy was sound, in the sense of being characterized by full employment and a good government fiscal position.

In so far as Malaysia's fundamental economic problems were less severe than those of other crisis-hit economies and its recovery relatively fast, the problems for firms in trouble were more manageable. Malaysia also did not persevere too long with its International Monetary Fund style austerity programme, and was proactive in setting up a special institutional framework to deal with restructuring financial institutions. Again, since Malaysia was more heavily dependent on multinationals and electronic industries, crisis-hit firms tended to be in domestic demand-oriented construction and consumer durable-related industries.

While Malaysia in general as well as individual companies both had foreign borrowings, foreign currency loans are not seen as the key factor in the corporate crisis. Such loans just worsened a bad situation, while liquidity as seen by the high level of savings shows that the need for foreign capital was not acute. This too was different to the situation of other crisis-hit countries.

Restructuring was almost inevitably needed to sort out the problems of companies with difficulties. But while Malaysia has been cited as an example of a lack of corporate restructuring, that is only true if attention is focused on a few well-linked corporations with massive loans. Thus in the early 2000s there were at least two major groups which had a total debt exceeding RM20billion and were still muddled in a hopeless financial restructuring process.

Yet apart from the latter there were many cases of real corporate restructuring, where owners realized the need and took action, even if the preferred approach appeared to focus on financial restructuring. Hence the majority of the 141 KLSE Main Board companies losing money in 1998 and 1999 moved positively in this way. Some companies undertook fundamental restructuring, including inviting the participation of foreign partners.

It should finally be noted that lack of published data means the analysis of this chapter is confined to firms listed on the Kuala Lumpur Stock Exchange, and does not cover the Malaysian corporate sector comprehensively. KLSE-listed companies are generally among Malaysia's elite, with better long-term performance track records. Small and medium-scale enterprises are unfortunately missed out, although they are in fact likely to have been less exposed in terms of over-borrowing because of a tighter availability of credit. Other large unlisted companies are also omitted. It is felt, however, that the use of available data in this way enables a timely analysis, which at least throws light on a vital part of the Malaysian business sector.

NOTES
1.   Hence both private and public sector demand grew substantially between 1977 and 1982.
2.   Public sector spending was greatly trimmed from 1984 to 1985.
3.   Gross domestic product is gross value added, at purchasers' prices, by all resident producers in the economy, *plus* any taxes and *minus* any subsidies not included in the value of the products.
4.   Gross national product is GDP *plus* net factor income from abroad, which is the income residents receive from abroad for factor services (labour and capital) *less* similar payments made to non-residents who contribute to the economy.
5.   Pan Electric Ltd. was a large company under the influence of the Malaysian Chinese Association's Multipurpose Group. It had severe financial difficulties following intensive speculation, triggering the collapse in 1986 of both the Kuala Lumpur and Singapore Stock Exchanges as well as several other major financial institutions.
6.   Amongst the anchor banks, the country's largest bank, Maybank, and the country's largest Chinese-owned bank, Public Bank, went through the 1985 - 1987 recession and the recent financial crisis unscathed. In addition, the Bank of Commerce, Southern Bank and Hong Leong Bank also weathered the crisis without needing capital injections from *Danamodal*. The RHB Bank entered the crisis absorbing the acquisitions of the Kwong Yik Bank and the United Malayan Banking Corporation (UMBC) in quick succession. The UMBC was in deep financial trouble when it was acquired by RHB, and this somewhat affected the financial position of the latter despite a good management team. The ability of the Multipurpose Bank, Eon Bank and Perwira Affin Bank to compete as major banks remains to be seen, since they

are basically smaller entities taking over other financial institutions generally hit hard by the crisis.

7.   Cement capacity increased from 12.5 million tonnes in 1996 to 24.3 million tonnes in 2000, while demand dropped from 17.8 million tonnes in 1997 to 9.3 million tonnes in 1999. Steel bar capacity increased from 2.7 million tonnes in 1997 to 4 million tonnes in 2000, while demand fell from 2.7 million tonnes in 1997 to 1.1 million tonnes in 1999.

8.   This can be surmised by reading the *Asia Wall Street Journal, Business Week, The Far Eastern Economic Review, Asia Week* and other such magazines at the time of the crisis. Indeed, *Business Week* ranked Malaysia below Indonesia in managing the East Asian Economic Crisis!

9.   In these Malaysian cases, no distinction was made between bailing out a key enterprise and bailing out the owner. Bailing out an enterprise would have been more justifiable and acceptable. Bailing out the owner, sometimes without solving the problem of the enterprise, is never acceptable. This is best illustrated by the government's buying Malaysia Airlines shares at cost from its privatized owner, but not in the end addressing the huge debt problem of that company. The rationale of the government was of course the need to preserve the *Bumiputera* millionaires created over the years of the New Economic Policy, thus balancing the wealth structure of the country for the purpose of political stability.

10.   More companies have undergone fundamental and financial restructuring since March 2000, but are not analysed here.

11.   This was followed in March 2001 by the proposed acquisition of the country's fifth largest steel mill, Antara, by the leading company - Amsteel Mills Sdn. Bhd.

4. Malaysia after the Asian Crisis: An Overview of Labour Market Issues

Shamsulbahriah Ku Ahmad

Discussions of the labour market in Malaysia usually locate labour market issues within the context of the country's colonial history. But debates relating to the earlier British legacy of a labour market segmented by ethnicity and affected by a labour movement malaise have paled in importance since the country's economic transformation following implementation of the New Economic Policy (NEP) in 1971. Thus the impact of the participation of women in the labour force, and the segmentation of the labour market by gender, gained profile over the period up to the 1990s, which was the United Nations decade for the advancement of women.

The high economic growth from the late 1980s into the 1990s also introduced new issues into the labour market agenda, including those surrounding a labour shortage, the position of migrant workers and, most captivating of late, the role of knowledge workers in futuristic Malaysia. The 1997 financial crisis and consequent regional political instability witnessed intensified concerns about the social dimension of regional development, and especially the impact of the crisis on vulnerable groups. Questions over the provision of social safety nets and other protection of workers captured national and international attention. Given the changed economic and social circumstances in the new century, the future direction of Malaysia's labour market, and especially the relationship between the production-based and knowledge-based economies with the implications of this for labour, require examination.

This chapter first reviews the characteristics of the Malaysian labour market, as a backdrop to analysing selected contemporary labour market issues. It then addresses the development path of Malaysia and other Asian economies. It next scrutinizes the position of the Malaysian economy, and the impact on employment of the recent financial crisis. It finally presents some conclusions concerning the relative needs of the knowledge and production components of the Malaysian economy.

LABOUR MARKET CHARACTERISTICS

One fundamental feature of the Malaysian labour market not often highlighted in neo-classical descriptions is the fact that the biggest single group of Malaysians in this market are working class, located at the lowest level of the employment hierarchy (Table 4.1). A recognition of this is essential in assessing the impact of ongoing economic developments on labour, and is irrespective of race and gender. The people in this class mainly comprise workers in routine manual tasks, in industry, and in agriculture.

But although the term 'labour' by definition implies wage earners employed in the bottom part of the employment pyramid, the importance of work as a source of income means that the salaried middle class cannot be excluded from the analysis of this chapter. The middle class in Malaysia is highly differentiated by education, and includes the 'professional-managerial class', 'technicians' and 'routine non-manual workers'. Figures of the shares and numbers in 1991 of the working, middle and other class groups in Peninsular Malaysia are given in Table 4.1.

Juxtaposing the working class and salaried middle class in the employment hierarchy also serves to demonstrate the relationship between the 'K-nowledge' and 'P-roduction' economies in Malaysia's development process. Thus the sizes and compositions of the working class and salaried middle class can be used to indicate the relative scopes of these two economies. It should also be noted that there are in the Malaysian workforce the other significant classes of so-called 'petite bourgeoisie' (small employers and self-employed) and 'farmers' (Table 4.1). These latter components are not dealt with in depth in this chapter, however, with the focus being on wage earners.

The Working Class

The members of this group are sellers of manual labour power, and are employed for a wage. Further information about the features of labourers in the major sub-groups of the working class is given in Table 4.2, which denotes their relatively low level of education. One sub-group included in this table are workers on plantations, who in common with other agricultural labourers do not own property or land, and are employed by farmers or estate owners. They are free to abandon their places of employment, and to move into other unskilled occupations such as construction or general labouring.

The working class is probably the least contentious group in the analysis of the Malaysian class structure, with the main questions arising over the distinction between skilled and unskilled components. These questions spring from problems encountered with the concept of skill itself, where some authors use gradations in this to justify the existence of what they call a 'labour aristocracy'. The term aristocracy in this context is often used to distinguish divisions between skilled and unskilled members of the manual working class, and has been subjected to much debate.

Table 4.1 Class Structure and Gender Distribution in the Peninsular Malaysian Workforce, 1970 - 1991*

Class	1970 Share in Workforce (%)	1980 Share in Workforce (%)	1991 Total Workers
Petite Bourgeoise	*14.6*	*15.2*	*713.886 [14.1]*
Small Employers	2.6	3.2	155,771 (19.3)** [3.1]***
Self-Employed (including family)	12.0	12.0	558,115 (21.2) [11.0]
Farmers	*33.4*	*22.6*	*873.951 (27.4) [17.2]*
Small Farmers (with employees)	1.2	0.6	23,524 (29.9) [0.5]
Self-Employed (farmers & family)	32.2	22.0	850,427 (27.3) [16.7]
Salaried Middle Class	*16.8*	*24.3*	*1,502,454 [29.6]*
Professional-Managerial	2.3	2.6	144,264 (19.6) [2.8]
Technicians	7.2	9.8	533,402 (31.9) [10.5]
Routine Non-Manual	7.4	11.9	824,788 (39.0) [16.3]
Working Class	*35.2*	*37.9*	*1,980,950 [39.1]*
Routine Manual	1.9	2.3	-
Transport & Mail Workers	-	-	42,388 (15.4) [0.8]
Domestic Workers & Cleaners	-	-	82,637 (80.8) [1.6]
Skilled Industrial Workers	4.6	8.0	428,903 (42.4) [8.5]
Unskilled Industrial Workers	11.6	15.3	754,274 (21.2) [14.9]
Agricultural Workers	17.0	12.3	672,748 (47.2) [13.3]
Total	100.0	100.0	5,071,241 [100.0]

Source: Shamsulbahriah (1996).
Notes: * Data to derive this table was obtained from the 2 per cent sample tapes of the Malaysian Population
Census for 1970, 1980 and 1991.
** Figures in parentheses are the proportions of women in this class and sub-group of the workforce.
*** Figures in brackets are the proportions of this class and sub-group and in the total workforce.

Table 4.2 Characteristics of Labourers in Major Occupational Groups of the Working Class, Malaysia, 1991

Occupational Group	General Skill Characteristics	Educational Requirements	Occupational Classification	Income Range, 1991 (RM/month)
Manufacturing	Skilled/unskilled/ semi-skilled	Lower secondary, skill training certificate, computer literacy etc	Production workers Machinery fitters, Electrical and electronics assemblers	369 - 1874 324 - 884
Construction	Skilled/unskilled	Primary, skilled crafts	Construction workers (bricklayers, carpenters and general construction workers)	369 - 1874
Plantations	Unskilled	Primary, ability	Agricultural workers (general plantation and farm workers)	324 - 884
Domestics and other Services	Unskilled	Primary, lower secondary (variations)	Service workers (cooks, maids, cleaners, house-keepers, bartenders)	324 - 1115

The notion of 'skill' used to differentiate Malaysian workers in this chapter is rather limited. It refers to the level of education defined by years of schooling. Those classified as 'skilled' generally hold secondary level education (nine to eleven years' education in total) while the educational attainment of 'unskilled' workers is basically elementary or primary education (six years). The notion does not, however, imply a simplistic positive relationship between years of schooling and skill, for the latter is substantially affected by the level of industrial training or competence obtained through specific apprenticeship courses. Data on the level of training acquired through apprenticeships are not directly available, although skilled industrial workers may be required to possess additional certificates from training institutions depending on areas of specialization. The argument underlying the notion of skill employed here is that a minimum educational level is required at the point of entry into skilled occupations, and that this level may then allow on-the-job training in order to obtain apprenticeship status.

The proportion of 'skilled industrial' labourers in the total workforce increased from 4.6 per cent to 8.0 per cent between 1970 and 1980, and rose slightly again to 8.5 per cent in 1991 (Table 4.1). Yet the proportion of 'unskilled industrial' workers in the workforce also rose from 11.6 per cent in 1970 to 14.9 per cent in 1991. The latter was possible because the share of agricultural workers in the total workforce dropped from 17.0 per cent in 1970 to 13.3 per cent in 1991. The working class as a whole remained large, at close to 40 per cent of the total workforce in 1991.

The changing shares of the sub-groups and main workforce classes followed development trends in the Malaysian economy as a whole over the decades. The first decade of the New Economic Policy from 1970 was marked by rapid industrialization, and accounted for the substantial creation of an urban proletariat. There was also a changing production dynamics characterized by the application of new technologies requiring a more skilled workforce and accounting for the rise in skilled industrial labourers cited above. But the subsequent almost stagnating share of skilled industrial workers, which continued into the 1990s, reflected both the shortage of such workers and the substitution of capital for labour as the economy moved towards a more advanced capitalist mode.

The big decline up to 1980 in the share of agricultural workers in the workforce (Table 4.1) reflected the economic restructuring from agriculture to industry, while the subsequent apparent increase in the share of these workers during the 1980s was probably due to the inflow of migrants to overcome emerging problems of labour shortage. The huge fall between 1990 and 2000 in the share of *all* agricultural 'workers' (including self-employed farmers and persons involved in forestry and fishing) is emphasized in Table 4.3. The fact that the working class remained the largest single element in the Malaysian class structure in the 1990s and into the new century signified the continuing high importance of the production economy and production workers in Malaysian society.

Table 4.3 Employment by Sector in Malaysia, 1990 - 2000

Sector	1990 Total Workers ('000 persons)	1995 Total Workers ('000 persons)	2000 Total Workers* ('000 persons)	Growth 1990 - 1995 (%)	Growth 1995 - 2000 (%)
Agriculture, Forestry, Livestock, Fishing	1738.0 (26.0)**	1428.7 (18.0)	1187.7 (13.1)	-17.9	-16.9
Mining and Quarrying	37.0 (0.6)	40.7 (0.5)	44.5 (0.5)	10.0	9..3
Manufacturing	13390.0 (19.9)	2051.6 (25.9)	2616.3 (28.9)	54.2	27.5
Construction	424.0 (6.3)	659.4 (8.3)	845.4 (9.3)	55.2	28.2
Electricity, Gas & Water	47.0 (0.7)	69.1 (0.9)	84.0 (0.9)	47.0	21.6
Transport, Storage & Communication	302.0 (4.5)	395.2 (5.0)	506.9 (5.6)	30.9	28.3
Wholesale and Retail, Restaurants and Hotels	1218.0 (18.2)	1327.8 (16.8)	1469.6 (16.2)	9.0	10.7
Finance, Insurance, Real Estate & Business Services	258.0 (3.9)	378.5 (4.8)	479.0 (5.3)	46.7	26.6
Government Services	850.0 (12.7)	872.2 (11.0)	894.2 (9.9)	2.6	2.5
Other Services	479.0 (7.2)	692.2 (8.7)	938.6 (10.4)	44.5	35.6
Total	6686.0 (100)	7915 (100)	9066.2 (100)	18.4	14.5
Total Labour Force	7042.0	8140.0	9327.1	10.3	14.1
Local (%)	96	92	92		
Foreign (%)	4	8	8		

Source: Malaysia. Ministry of Human Resources (1997, p. 20).
Notes: * Estimates only for this year.
** Figures in parentheses are percentages of the workforce in this sector.

Women workers occupied an important part of the Peninsular Malaysian working class in 1991 (Table 4.1), being dominant amongst the 'domestic workers and cleaners' component of routine manual workers, and also being quite significant amongst agricultural workers and skilled industrial workers. Unfortunately, data on the changing shares of women in the workforce are not available.

The Salaried Middle Class

The growth of a 'propertyless' white-collar salariat enjoying conditions and opportunities denied to the working class serves to further obfuscate the understanding of the nature of the middle class as a whole. The term 'new middle class' has often been used to refer to the rapid growth of a wide range of clerical, supervisory, sales, service, administrative and managerial occupations. It is accepted that the characteristics of these occupations are somewhat distinct from those of both the working class and the old middle class or petite bourgeoisie. Central to the debate on identifying the nature, composition and dynamics of formation of this class, is the issue of proletarianisation: this is the likelihood of the group being absorbed into the working class as a result of de-skilling.

Who are the 'knowledge workers' within the salaried middle class? The literature contains no rigorous attempt to define such workers, and more often than not the term is used to refer to those employed in 'knowledge-driven' organizations and using information technology. The range of skills identified includes the ability to collect data, analyse information and communicate knowledge. Apart from basic skills such as reading, writing, and interpersonal competence, technology-related expertise is emphasized and computer-related proficiency ranks high. In terms of occupational identity, one sub-group of knowledge workers is often referred to as 'professionals' - doctors, accountants, engineers and senior managers - who have acquired specialist skills in their trade. More generally, this rather small component of the middle class is recognized as comprising highly trained professionals with good credentials. These concepts of knowledge workers illustrate the manifold dichotomy amongst labour market actors.

The use of the terminology 'knowledge workers' in Malaysia refers to those falling within the above framework. Indeed, knowledge workers in Malaysia are mainly within the major occupational categories based on the International Standard Occupational Classification of 'professional, technical and related workers' and 'administrative and managerial workers' (Shamsulbahriah 1996). Most of these people are respectively inside the 'professional-managerial' and 'technicians' sub-groups of the salaried middle class in Table 4.1. These two sub-groups together constituted 13.4 per cent of the Peninsular Malaysian workforce of 5.1 million persons in 1991, and were projected to increase to over 15 per cent by the year 2000.

The two sub-groups were in fact differentiated by their knowledge content, defined according to education, training and skills. The professional-managerial class was at the top, and included engineers, accountants, lawyers, doctors, actuaries, university lecturers, and high-level administrators and managers. Their knowledge content was distinguished by the completion of tertiary education or equivalent professional qualifications. The share of this sub-group in the workforce did not increase much over the two decades to 1991 (Table 4.1). The technician sub-group possessed a rather lower level of training, and performed somewhat more straightforward service functions.

The Peninsular Malaysian domestic workforce is hence shown to be highly polarized into one extreme of a highly knowledgeable, highly paid, and highly empowered 2 to 3 per cent of the workforce, *vis-à-vis* another extreme of a far lower paid and highly alienated routine manual, unskilled industrial and agricultural worker component of just over 30 per cent (Table 4.1). This polarization, which is also judged broadly true of East Malaysia, again emphasizes the importance of the production economy, which is still the major single contributor to Malaysian gross domestic product.

Women members of the Peninsular Malaysian working middle class in 1991 were especially significant amongst the 'technician' category, but for the middle class as a whole occupied some one-sixth of all workers. Women also comprised just over one-fifth of the working members of the petite bourgeoisie and over one-quarter of farmers. Women could not in general be seen to be of major significance amongst the high-knowledge elite, although there is no doubt that their importance at the upper levels of the middle class increased considerably through the 1990s and into the new century.

THE DEVELOPMENT PATH AND EMPLOYMENT

Malaysia in common with many other Asian 'miracle' economies performed very well in terms of growth in gross domestic product before the onset of the Asian financial and economic crisis (see Table 2.1). The crisis then brought negative growth, which was nonetheless followed in Malaysia by subsequent recovery. The measure of gross domestic product has often been used in Malaysia and other countries to mean development, with economic growth models being popular among policy makers and constituting a key feature of development vocabularies in what is considered the mainstream approach. Indeed, many economies in the developing world, and especially those influenced by the World Bank and the International Monetary Fund, have adopted a development path focusing on growth in an effort to achieve 'progress'.

Gross domestic product figures measure the total market value, at purchasers' prices, of final goods and services produced by factors of production within a particular country, plus taxes and net of subsidies and intermediate inputs (World Bank 1999, pp. 234 - 240). Such a measure however, does not indicate the 'welfare' status of a nation's population, and also does not fully reflect the impact of what is often a considerable 'informal' economy where much production is consumed at home or not sold for a price. It is really only useful as a housekeeping tool, and as a broad guide to total economic progress. This comment also applies to the further measure of gross national product, although that additionally embraces net receipts of primary income from non-resident sources. While both measures when broken into their components provide a picture of a country's structure of production, this must be treated with even more caution owing to constraints imposed by the availability of reliable data.

That said, the components of Malaysia's gross domestic product reveal a definite shift in her economic structure from an agricultural base to one of manufacturing and services. The consequent switches in numbers and shares of those employed in each sector in Malaysia as a whole are presented in Table 4.3. Agriculture remained a more major employer in Indonesia, the Philippines, Thailand and Vietnam, on the other hand, while the share of self-employed and unpaid family workers stayed large in Indonesia especially. It should be noted that along with these changes in Malaysia and the alterations discussed in the working and middle classes, the further groups of small employers and self-employed persons in both agriculture and the petite bourgeoisie continued to be very significant. These latter groups still comprised 31.3 per cent of the workforce of Peninsular Malaysia in 1991 (Table 4.1), with little sign of diminution in the 1990s. Given that the Asian crisis has to quite an extent been a financial setback affecting the corporate sector, it might be concluded that the 'real economy' involving the latter groups is also important to consider in analysing the impact of the crisis on labour.

The Asian Development Dynamic

There was some similarity in the chosen development 'models' of the ASEAN economies, Malaysia, Singapore, Thailand and Indonesia. All four countries chose industrialization as a strategy to achieve economic development, with a high premium placed on growth and an assumption that the benefits of growth in industry and other sectors would 'trickle-down' to the rest of the population. There were two distinct phases of industrialization strategies, with the first phase involving import-substitution and the second phase export-oriented industrialization, and with both being led by the manufacturing sector and being dependent on foreign direct investment. It is therefore not surprising that foreign direct investment in these ASEAN economies was very significant compared to other countries such as Taiwan and Korea, where such investment played a more complementary role. A strong correlation has been suggested between the incentives and policies of countries and their success in attracting the inflow of foreign capital (Rasiah 1995).

Manufacturing became the main engine of growth in the four ASEAN economies just mentioned from the 1970s, being dominated by textiles and electronics. Competition for foreign capital was active, and measures to attract foreign investment included ensuring political stability, supplying a docile and cheap labour force, providing infrastructural support services, giving a series of incentives and tax holidays and in later years promising to make available a highly skilled workforce. Countries which could fulfil these aspects became magnets for foreign direct investment. The fast growing 'new industrial economies' of South Korea, Taiwan, Hong Kong and Singapore were most successful in attracting foreign capital within the developing world (Rasiah 1998), but Malaysia, Thailand, and Indonesia as well as the Philippines took similar measures in attempts to achieve a more industrialized status.

The attraction of foreign direct investment to these economies assisted the main objective of their first phase of import-substituting industrialization, which was to create employment for a fast expanding population. This phase therefore saw the expansion of 'unskilled labour-intensive' manufacturing. The second phase of export-oriented industrialization then represented a clear effort to shift to more 'skill-intensive' manufacturing.

The attraction of foreign direct investment to these countries matches the observation that 'footloose' capital moves to countries that offer the most favourable conditions for investment (Lim and Fong 1991). Rising wage costs, shortages of skilled labour and inadequate infrastructural support have frequently induced companies to relocate. Thus Japan, Korea and Taiwan have moved much of their production to ASEAN countries due to price and cost differentials, exchange rate factors and other economic and non-economic variables. Japanese companies have subsequently been relocated for a third time from Singapore into Malaysia, where Singapore's high-wage policy of 1979 - 1981 undermined the city-state's competitiveness *vis-à-vis* other industrializing centres.

The Impact on Labour of Foreign Direct Investment and Manufacturing-led Growth

There is an important implication to be drawn concerning the structure of production and employment in countries like Malaysia that have pursued development strategies dependent on foreign direct investment-led growth. This is with regard to the class bias of the second phase of industrialization emphasizing export-oriented production, which entails expanding a highly skilled workforce and creating a sizeable 'middle class'. In this phase, the bulk of foreign direct investment in the industrializing Asian economies was channelled into the production of automobiles, electrical and electronic goods, textiles and garments. Many of these were arguably consumer durables, fulfilling a large market geared to the taste and demands of the expanding middle class for quality cars, designer clothes, computers, mobile phones and other sophisticated electronic gadgets. This group, which even including elements of the petite bourgeoisie and richer farmers is little larger than the working class and already advantaged in terms of family background and access to education, continues to benefit from such a development strategy. The largely unskilled and poorly educated 'working class' continues to be disadvantaged, however.

The class-bias nature of the foreign direct investment-led growth strategy also has an impact on the structure of production and employment. Thus it has been observed that a shift in emphasis occurs to capital-intensive industrialization as developing economies move towards newly industrializing economy status. There is greater emphasis on capital-intensive high-technology industries, partly to break the cycle of dependency on low-skill, low-wage, and labour-intensive manufacturing and reduce reliance on foreign labour. The class-bias thrust attempts too to create a sizeable middle class, which is considered desirable as an adjunct to the higher skilled workforce. The skilled 'elite', although relatively small, is given priority in terms of education and training, while the needs of unskilled labour are not given due recognition.

THE MALAYSIAN CASE OF A LABOUR-SHORT ECONOMY

The Malaysian foreign direct investment and manufacturing-led development strategy created a full employment economy, operating under a tight labour market which was dependent on foreign labour. The focus on industrial development resulted in sectoral and regional imbalances, a rapid pace of urbanization, rural-urban migration and labour shortages in both the industrial and agricultural sectors. Hence Table 4.3 shows how manufacturing emerged as a major employer in Malaysia in the 1990s, followed by wholesale and retail trade. Agriculture declined to third place,[1] and was followed by other services and construction.

The availability of a 'mobile surplus' of unskilled working class from certain Asian nations has helped sustain labour-intensive industrialization in various ASEAN countries. This is under circumstances where the bulk of labour demand by labour-importing countries has been for unskilled positions in manufacturing and the agriculture/plantation sector. The cases of Malaysia and Indonesia as respective labour importers and exporters clearly illustrate this scenario.

The large presence of foreign workers in Malaysia has become a major cause for concern since the start of the economic crisis. The ratios of legal foreign to local workers in certain main sectors in 1998 are detailed in Table 4.4, while these and other figures indicate an average ratio for *all* sectors of about 1:8. While there are disagreements over these figures, they are often used to reinforce the belief that Malaysia is highly dependent on foreign workers. One key aspect in the controversy over foreign workers is their impact on employment opportunities for local labour, with the associated issue of job competition between local and foreign workers.

Table 4.4 also shows that legal foreign workers were concentrated in manufacturing, plantations and construction, and to a lesser extent in the subsectors of domestic servants and services and catering. It should be noted that there were in addition numerous illegal workers, especially in plantations and construction. It is necessary in addressing the issue of job competition to examine the characteristics of employment in occupations with foreign workers. Thus there is evidence that such occupations were unskilled, requiring low educational attainment and providing low remuneration (Table 4.2). These occupations were likewise those experiencing labour shortages.

*Table 4.4 Distribution of Legal Foreign Workers by Occupational Group,
Malaysia, March 1998*

Occupational Group	Estimated Total Workers	Ratio of Local to Foreign Workers
Manufacturing	280,000	1:8.3
Plantations	265,000	1:3.4
Construction	220,000	1:2.8
Domestic Servants	129,000	-
Services	118,000	1:6.9
Others	21,000	-
Total	1,033,000	1:4.4

Sources: Malaysia. Ministry of Human Resources (1997, p. 20); Malaysia. Ministry of Internal Affairs (1998).

According to the *Seventh Malaysia Plan* (Malaysia 1996), the agricultural sector in the future will continue to require a steady supply of labour to support its growth. An enduring labour shortage along with the slow process of mechanization and reluctance of young locals to work in agriculture due to harsh working conditions and low pay promises to perpetuate this problem. The use of foreign workers in this sector is accordingly expected to persist, albeit on a discriminating basis with the long-term aim of reducing the number of unskilled foreign personnel. Measures to reduce dependence on foreign workers are being taken, and include strategies geared to increasing the land-labour ratio through research and development and to accelerating the mechanization of production and processing. Agriculture apart, a similar continuing demand for unskilled workers is likely to characterize manufacturing and construction in particular.

Employment following the Financial Crisis

The Malaysian sectors most affected by the crisis in terms of immediate losses in employment were manufacturing, wholesale and retail activity, construction and financial services, insurance and trade (Malaysia. Ministry of Human Resources 1999a). Manufacturing was the worst hit in terms of retrenchment, with 26,372 persons being reported as affected in this way from January 1997 to June 1998. Less people were affected in other sectors, with the grand total number of individuals officially recorded as retrenched over the period being 41,790. While other adjustments to the crisis were also made in terms of shorter working hours, as detailed in Chapter 6, this grand total constituted only a tiny proportion of Malaysia's seven to eight million workforce in 1997 - 1998. Given the subsequent recovery and an estimated unemployment rate in the new century of 2.6 per cent, it appears that Malaysia is still operating under a tight labour market.

Data on retrenchment by gender reveal that more men (48 per cent local and 6 per cent foreign) than women (44 per cent local and 1 per cent foreign) were retrenched during the same period (Malaysia. Ministry of Human Resources 1999b), although more women in the manufacturing sector, 52 per cent, lost their jobs. Most men retrenched were employed in traditional male occupations such as construction, transport, storage and communications. The overall number of foreign workers retrenched during the crisis was again quite small, totalling about 6 per cent of total retrenchments.

Respecting the recent period of economic recovery from the crisis, it is judged that the pattern of labour vacancies evident before the crisis is unlikely to have altered much, although the degree of scarcity in each occupational group is probably less. Moreover, foreign workers in very large numbers are still needed to help fill vacancies. Assuming that the total number of foreign workers in Malaysia in the early 2000s remains at the figure of just over one million in 1998 (Table 4.4), such workers comprise about 17 per cent of the six million workers in the agriculture, mining and quarrying, manufacturing, construction and other services sectors (Table 4.3). The ratio of foreign to local workers in those sectors will then be around 1:6.

The most acute shortage based on numbers of unfilled vacancies was observed to be in the category of 'production and related workers, transport equipment operators and labourers', which accounted in 1996 before the economic crisis for about 65 per cent of all Malaysian vacancies (Table 4.5). The two major components in this occupational group were production line workers in the electrical and electronics sector of manufacturing and workers in construction. The other occupational group facing an acute labour shortage in 1996 was that of 'clerical workers', where unfilled vacancies comprised just over 20 per cent of the total for that year. In contrast, the occupational group of 'professional, technical and related workers' only accounted for 5.6 per cent of vacancies, while vacancies amongst service and agricultural workers were even less.

Table 4.5 Vacancies by Occupational Group, 1992 - 1996

Occupational Group	Total Numbers of Vacancies				
	1992	1993	1994	1995	1996
Professional, Technical and Related Workers	2584 (3.1)*	3036 (3.9)	3773 (6.6)	3380 (5.8)	3234 (5.6)
Administrative and Managerial Workers	383 (0.5)	453 (0.6)	655 (1.1)	666 (1.1)	349 (0.6)
Clerical Workers	9960 (12.0)	10165 (13.2)	11472 (20.0)	12327 (21.1)	11785 (20.5)
Sales Workers	1469 (1.8)	1417 (1.8)	1947 (3.4)	1472 (2.5)	1432 (2.5)
Service Workers	1927 (2.3)	1869 (2.4)	1823 (3.2)	2391 (4.1)	2334 (4.1)
Agricultural, Animal Husbandry and Forestry Workers, Fisher-persons and Hunters	2334 (4.1)	2657 (3.4)	4598 (8.0)	1207 (2.1)	1105 (1.9)
Production and Related Workers, Transport Equipment Operators and Labourers	57281(68.8)	57434 (74.6)	33142 (57.7)	36969 (63.3)	37300 (64.8)
Total	83300 (100.0)	77031 (100.0)	57410 (100.0)	58412 (100.0)	57539 (100.0)

Source: Malaysia. Ministry of Human Resources (1997).
Notes: * Figures in parentheses are percentages of total number of vacancies in all occupational groups.

It is clear that the many production jobs in 'secondary'[2] occupations, which basically meet so-called '3D'[3] characteristics, provide continuing opportunities for impoverished migrant workers to earn a living, and that the absence of 'barriers' defined by skills offers reasonably easy entry to the 'mobile surplus' from the Asian region. It thus appears fallacious to conclude that any real competition exists between locals and foreigners for these occupations where there are so many vacancies.

CONCLUSIONS

Despite the shift in Malaysia's economic structure from an agricultural base to one of manufacturing and services, there is still a major demand in the labour market for unskilled labour, which is provided by both a domestic working class and migrant workers. But at the same time there has been growth of a salaried middle class, most of whose members have special skills and a few of whom are highly paid professionals with specific expertise. This middle class along with self-employed petite bourgeoisie and farmers now constitute over 60 per cent of the Malaysian workforce in the new century. But the balance of 40 per cent largely unskilled labourers reflects the continuing importance in the country of a production as opposed to a knowledge economy.

The development path chosen by Malaysian policy makers and putting emphasis on foreign direct investment and manufacturing-led growth made the economy particularly susceptible to the regional financial crisis of the late 1990s. But it also led during periods of economic growth to a tight labour market, and to a demand for workers that could not be satisfied by the local Malaysian population. Although there was some retrenchment of foreigners as a result of the crisis it appears to have been minimal, and Malaysia still relies on large numbers of migrants to sustain its production economy. These people comprise some 8 per cent of the total workforce in the new century.

There appears to be an undoubted class bias in terms of the emphasis in Malaysia on educating and training a skilled 'elite' for the knowledge economy. But it seems important that this effort should not be undertaken at the expense of catering for the continuing large needs of 'unskilled' labour in the production economy. There is no evidence of de-skilling amongst the middle class, with trends in expertise being in the opposite direction. The difficult and low-paid working conditions in agriculture in particular, as well as the ongoing requirements for unskilled workers in manufacturing and other occupations, mean that much more attention should be paid by the authorities to ways of sustaining these crucial contributions to the Malaysian economy.

NOTES
1.   The proportion of foreign workers in agriculture *per se* is an underestimation, since the figure in Table 4.3 is calculated as a proportion of workers in forestry and fishing as well.

2. The term 'secondary' jobs has been popularized in the literature on labour market segmentation. It refers to employment in low-paid occupations where working conditions are poor. 'Primary' jobs on the other hand, offer the reverse, and are often associated with higher credentials and qualification.

3. The nature of jobs undertaken by migrant workers are commonly described in Malaysia as '3-Ds', which refers to their being 'dirty', 'dangerous' and 'difficult'.

5. The Financial Crisis and its Social Implications

Ishak Shari

This chapter discusses the implications of the 1997 - 1998 financial and economic crisis for the social and political stability of Malaysia. As an introduction, the country's socio-economic progress over the 27 years prior to the crisis is discussed, and the social impact of the crisis is assessed.

With this background, the chapter addresses three related questions. First, why did the crisis appear to have a lesser negative impact in Malaysia than in other affected countries? Second, why despite this lesser impact was there a sea change in the Malaysian political scenario, ultimately resulting in a big decline in Malay support for the United Malays National Organization (UMNO) in the November 1999 election? Third, how was a multi-ethnic Malaysia able to maintain social stability despite significant changes in the country's political landscape?

ECONOMIC GROWTH AND SOCIAL DEVELOPMENT, 1970 - 1997

The rapid growth and structural transformation of the Malaysian economy, together with deliberate government affirmative measures to improve the position of *Bumiputera* and other disadvantaged groups, resulted in significant progress in social development. The incidence of absolute poverty was reduced from 52.4 per cent in 1970 to 6.8 per cent in 1997.[1] The number of poor households decreased from 1,100,000 to 346,000 over the same period (Malaysia, 1999a, p. 63). These changes were accompanied by a reduction in income inequality from the end of the 1970s, with the value of the gini coefficient which measures inequality dropping from 0.529 in 1976 to 0.480 in 1984 and 0.446 in 1990. Again over the period from 1970, income gaps between urban and rural households and between major ethnic groups, particularly *Bumiputera* households on the one hand and Chinese and Indian households on the other, also narrowed (Table 5.1).

There was too declining unemployment from 1971 to 1997, and by the latter year Malaysia had a rate of 2.5 per cent. In fact, the labour shortages faced by some subsectors during the 1990s meant the Malaysian economy increasingly relied on foreign labour. Thus one official estimate indicated there were 1.7 million foreign migrant workers in Malaysia in 1997, 560,000 of whom were unregistered (Bank Negara Malaysia 1999, p. 63). More detail is given in Chapter 4.

Table 5.1 Measures of Income Inequality in Malaysia, 1970 - 1997

	1970	*1980*	*1990*	*1997*
Household Income Disparity Ratios:				
Urban: Rural	2.14	1.77	1.70	2.04
Chinese : *Bumiputera*	2.29	1.90	1.74	1.83
Indian: *Bumiputera*	1.77	1.29	1.29	1.46
Gini coefficient	0.501	0.493	0.446	0.470

Source: Derived and calculated from data in Malaysia (1989, 1991b and 1999a).

Despite these achievements, however, several negative trends had emerged to challenge social policies even before the crisis. First, relatively high incidences of poverty persisted in the least developed states of Sabah (22.1 per cent), Kelantan (19.5 per cent) and Terengganu (17.3 per cent), compared to 6.8 per cent for the country as a whole (Malaysia 1999a, p. 64). Second, income inequality trends reversed after 1990, where although mean household incomes increased in both rural and urban areas as well as among major ethnic groups, differential rates of income growth among income groups and between strata resulted in widening income disparities. The Gini coefficient for Malaysia hence increased from 0.446 in 1990 to 0.470 in 1997 (Table 5.1).

Third, Malaysian households still had few formal mechanisms to protect themselves from risks associated with job losses, disabilities, and ageing. Where such formal mechanisms existed, the coverage remained limited though it increased over the years. For example, the number of contributors to the Employees Provident Fund (EPF)[2] in 1997 was only 61.8 per cent of the working population (Malaysia, 1998b).

THE SOCIAL IMPACT OF THE CRISIS

The contraction of the real economy from 1997 reduced employment opportunities, especially in construction (with a decline of 16.9 per cent in 1998) but to a lesser extent in manufacturing (with a decline of 3.6 per cent). Consequently, the number of unemployed rose from 233,100 in 1997 to 343,200 in 1998, an increase of 47.2 per cent.[3] Some of these trends are discussed in Chapter 3.

However, in a crisis situation it is difficult to estimate unemployment and retrenchment figures. This was especially so in the construction sector, where over 80 per cent of the workforce comprised migrant workers of whom a significant proportion were unregistered. Reverse migration took place among foreign workers in Malaysia in 1997 - 1998, most noticeably among illegal foreign workers. Official figures showed that a total of 383,946 foreign workers and their dependants had returned to their respective countries by the end of 1998. Retrenchment of locals in the informal sector also occurred, although the total numbers were not captured in official statistics. Press reports indicated that many small businesses went bankrupt due to falling demand and rising costs, resulting in employees losing their sources of livelihood.

There were also firms which reacted to the crisis not by laying off workers but by cutting wages or lowering or freezing pay increases. For example, in the car assembling industry where unions existed, workers had to accept a 25 per cent wage reduction to avoid retrenchment. But some employers in non-unionized sectors imposed excessive pay cuts of 30 to 50 per cent.

In the aftermath of the crisis, most workers in both private and public sectors no longer worked overtime as they had previously. According to a sample survey among 2,065 workers in six industries in the Klang Valley and Penang conducted in April-July 1999, 51.4 per cent reported that their overtime work was reduced or stopped completely.[4] In some industries, workers were under-employed (working less than 40 hours per week) and forced to take pay cuts. Some companies also defaulted in paying wages and retrenchment benefits to workers. Due to problems of cash flow, the number of employers defaulting on contributions to the Employees Provident Fund increased. All told, workers' wages significantly declined during 1998, reversing the trend of rising real wages since the early 1990s.

Owing to these various developments, the Department of Statistics in its Monthly Survey of Manufacturing Industries reported wages increasing at a slower rate of 5.6 per cent in 1998, compared with 10.2 per cent in 1997 (Bank Negara Malaysia 1999, p. 78). Again, estimates in the Ministry of Finance's *Economic Report 1998 - 1999* suggested that real wages per worker declined by 9.9 per cent during the first seven months of 1998 compared to an increase of 18.9 per cent during the corresponding period in 1997 (Malaysia 1998a, pp. 73 - 74). The fall in real wages was higher in some subsectors, including that of electrical, electronics and machinery industries

While the 1997 - 1998 crisis hit the urban workforce in the formal sector hardest, those engaged in the informal sector and some aspects of rural activity were not spared. Taxi drivers were adversely affected, although some worked longer hours following the crisis. Transportation lorry drivers were influenced, since they had fewer trips to make. The *batik* (traditional textile) industry in the east coast state of Kelantan was also hit due to the rising price of imported white linen and competition from Indonesia and Thailand. Hawkers and petty traders were not spared either. Many workers interviewed in a rapid assessment study in October-November 1998 reported they had either to stop sending remittances to parents in rural areas altogether or reduce the quantum (Ishak Shari and Abdul Rahman Embong 1999). This surely depressed the incomes of rural peoples, as remittances from children working in urban areas constituted a substantial proportion of their incomes.

Rising Prices of Consumer Goods

Every section of the Malaysian population was adversely affected by rising prices of goods and services, including basic essentials. These rises largely reflected the impact of ringgit depreciation on the prices of imported food, which additionally caused increases in prices of locally produced exportable commodities such as palm oil. The official consumer price index (CPI) increased by 5.3 per cent in 1998, as compared to 2.7 per cent in 1997 and 3.5 per cent in 1996. However, price increases in several essential commodities such as rice, flour, sugar, milk and cooking oil were much higher than the CPI average, and had particularly large effects on monthly household expenditures. Hence food items rose by 8.9 per cent in 1998 as compared to increases of 4.1 per cent in 1997 and 5.7 per cent in 1996 (Malaysia 1999b, p. 44).

The burden of higher prices fell heavily upon some of the rural population, who also experienced big declines in their incomes. Unlike oil palm smallholders who benefited from sharp increases in the price of palm oil, rubber smallholders were also badly affected by falling rubber prices. The price of coagulated rubber was reported to have dropped from RM1.60 per kg to RM0.70 - RM0.80 per kg in 1998, resulting in many rubber smallholders earning only RM200 - RM450 per month. The rising food prices meant that many such people found it increasingly difficult to meet daily basic needs, including the educational expenses of their families. Consumers were forced to adjust their consumption patterns to cope with falling incomes, often by reducing purchases of 'quality foods' (such as meat, chicken, eggs and milk). This undermined the satisfaction of dietary needs, especially amongst growing children. These phenomena were reported by all groups covered by the rapid assessment study of late 1998 (Ishak Shari and Abdul Rahman Embong 1999).

Impact on Vulnerable Groups

The crisis appears to have had more serious adverse impacts on certain vulnerable groups in Malaysia, amongst whom were women workers, rubber estate workers, the urban poor and aboriginal people.

While women workers formed 42.3 per cent of total retrenched workers in 1998, they comprised a higher proportion of retrenched workers in manufacturing. These workers had in fact accounted for a greater share of the total workforce in the various manufacturing subsectors prior to the crisis. Women being mainly responsible for domestic budgeting had, following the crisis, to juggle reduced incomes and rising prices in efforts to feed their husbands and children and maintain normal family life. This task was not only physically taxing for working mothers in particular, but also a mental and psychological burden. As a result, women workers had less time to spend with their children, and were usually too tired to enjoy a family life.

The findings of a pilot study of the consequences of the 1997 - 1998 crisis for 50 women in Penang, for example, revealed not only a sharp drop in workers' incomes but also a drift towards activities in the informal sector, particularly vendoring, food-catering and direct-selling. With increasing pressure to supplement family incomes, both parents also tended to spend less time on child minding and parenting (Wazir Johan Karim 1998). Falling incomes also seriously affected the wellbeing of single mothers and female-headed households and especially those with many young children, making them a segment of the new poor.

Rubber estate labourers are among the most poorly paid workers in Malaysia. They were in the early 2000s still daily-rated, and not paid if foul weather or the 'wintering of trees' prevented them from working. Poor housing and medical facilities as well as inadequate educational opportunities for their children characterized the industry. In the 1980s and 1990s, there was an exodus especially of the young from the estates to the urban and industrial areas in search of alternative employment opportunities. Foreign workers were recruited to replace them, and came to predominate on the estates alongside older local workers. Many foreign workers were immediately retrenched as a result of the crisis, invariably without benefits, and only local workers continued to be employed. Although this was a buffer of sorts, the latter were also affected by the crisis.

According to the Consumers' Association of Penang, rubber estate workers found it hard to make ends meet during the crisis.[4] Given the low incomes of rubber estate families and increased living costs due to the economic crisis, existing social problems associated with employment in the industry became even more acute. For instance, malnutrition among estate children worsened, thereby further affecting their education. It is probable that this led to a worsening of the already high dropout rate among estate school-going children, who mainly attended Tamil schools. The opportunity for social mobility via education, already very limited under normal circumstances, was likely to have been further confounded by the crisis.

Another group affected were the urban poor largely involved in the informal sector, who to make ends meet previously depended on cheap housing in the urban centres. Alas, even as the crisis was breaking, the federal government pushed ahead with plans to repeal the Rent Control Act, which since the end of the Second World War had depressed rentals of urban properties. The purpose of this Act had been to house the poor - in part an acknowledgement by the authorities that they had been unable to provide adequate cheap housing for such people.

Although agreement for an interim cap on rental increases was reached between property owners, tenants and local authorities, conceivably on account of upcoming general elections scheduled for 1999, many tenants still could not afford the increases made. There were accordingly widespread evictions and sometimes conflicts, especially in Georgetown on the island of Penang. The problem became especially acute after the one year extension of the interim agreement expired on 1 January 2000, which coincidentally followed the general elections in November 1999.

The aboriginal people or *Orang asli* were another of the poorest most marginalized groups in the country. It is important for understanding the impact of the economic crisis on these people to appreciate their situation and the context of their poverty. Thus official statistics revealed that in the late 1990s 80.8 per cent of *Orang asli* lived below the poverty line (compared to 8.5 per cent nationally), and that 49.9 per cent of people in this group were among the 'very poor' (compared to 2.5 per cent nationally). The crisis impacted most severely upon aborigines in 'fringe' areas, who were those with less access to forest resources or whose forest had been destroyed or lost to others. Such individuals depended on regular cash incomes, contrasting with *orang asli* who because their level of subsistence was higher depended less on the general economy. This latter category withstood the crisis better.

Impact on Poverty and Human Development

Investigations of the impact of the crisis on poverty are severely limited by lack of data. But the Finance Minister's Budget Speech in February 2000 indicated that the incidence of poverty increased from 6.7 per cent in 1997 to 8.5 per cent in 1998 (Malaysia. Ministry of Finance, 2000). The absolute number of households in poverty was thought to have increased by 22 per cent, from 346,000 in 1997 to 448,500 in 1998.

As in other affected countries, the financial and economic crisis in Malaysia discouraged household investments in human development, particularly in education, fertility, health and nutrition. There were several reasons for this. First, although social services were subsidized, households still incurred direct or associated costs in trying to gain access to them. Reduced incomes and higher prices (for medicines and schooling expenses, for instance) meant that poor and low-income households tended to consume less than what was individually and socially optimal.

Second, the quality and quantity of certain public services were likely to have been affected by the budget constraints and big shifts of clients from private to public providers - as from expensive private hospitals to public institutions charging only a nominal sum. The earlier public perception was that private providers supplied better services than their public equivalents, with a consequent preference to seek private facilities if they could be afforded. Third, as households tried to maintain levels of consumption, they probably reduced human capital investment. It would be useful to secure information on such crisis-induced welfare declines as well as on falling investments in human development, but data limitations again mean that only certain issues can be discussed.

Thus it seems that the initially tight fiscal measures implemented by the Malaysian government affected some ongoing programmes for the poor. Although the big budget cut early in the crisis was compensated for in 1998 by additionally allocating RM3.7 billion to assist vulnerable groups adversely affected by the crisis and by expanding government programmes to assist the poorest households, some non-government organizations (NGOs) supported by the federal and state governments had to significantly reduce their activities with such groups.

Again, while the Budget allocation for public health and medical services was increased from RM3.5 billion in 1998 to RM4.5 billion in 1999, Malaysia's national health expenditure as a percentage of gross domestic product (GDP) continued to fall in a trend evident since the mid-1980s.[5] Consequently, although the World Health Organization recommends that 5 per cent of GDP be allocated towards health and medical services in a middle-income country, only 2 per cent was actually allocated to these services in Malaysia in the early 2000s.

The fact that following the crisis many patients previously patronizing private clinics turned to government hospitals led to overcrowding and an increased workload for public doctors and staff. Although the health ministry devised strategies to avoid compromising the quality of health care in government hospitals, these strategies were undercut by shortages of personnel. Official figures denoted there were 4,719 doctors in the government service in 1997, compared to 6,051 registered private practitioners in 1997. The cost of health care has continued to rise, where this is only due partly to the depreciated ringgit following the crisis. There is indeed increasing concern over whether government will continue to bear the heavy burden of providing healthcare to the majority.

The depreciation of the ringgit and rising cost of overseas education have reduced numbers of students studying overseas. Thus the number of Malaysian students enrolled in British tertiary-level institutions dropped by about 44 per cent between 1997 and 1998, from 18,000 to 10,000, and local Malaysian institutions of higher learning were pressured to absorb more students. But given the limited resources available, not all students desiring to continue their education could be absorbed. Hence 112,000 high school students applied to enter public tertiary education in 1998, but only 40,220 or 35.9 per cent managed to secure a place. Some students enrolled in local private universities and colleges instead.

However, while students securing places in public and private universities were and are eligible to apply for government study loans, those joining private colleges are not. Consequently, many who might be deemed eligible to continue their education still cannot afford to do so. Moreover, due apparently to the corporatization of public universities in the late 1990s, fees for professional and postgraduate courses have increased and created a disincentive to potential applicants. These trends, if unchecked, will eventually affect Malaysia's ability to produce the needed manpower for R&D activities that can propel the economy forward in the future.

POLITICAL REPERCUSSIONS OF THE CRISIS

Although the crisis had less social impact in Malaysia than in other East Asian countries, it nonetheless helped trigger a sea change in political scenario whose seeds had been sown previously. Significantly, this political shift appeared to largely involve the Malay community. It had much to do with the expectations of the community towards the UMNO-led government and its post-New Economic Policy (NEP) policies, relating specifically to whether some form of affirmative action might be continued and whom among the *Bumiputera* might benefit from that policy.

Following an earlier economic crisis in the mid-1980s, the Malaysian government implemented a range of policy measures to induce economic liberalization and deregulation. These moves progressively narrowed the role of the public sector in its traditional responsibilities, including education, health and defence. Subsidies were curtailed, with a tighter focus on the hard-core poor. These policies were consolidated from 1991 under the National Development Policy succeeding the NEP, wherein the private sector was regarded as the new engine of economic growth. This change in policy was criticized by various groups including the opposition, some NGOs and even certain sections of UMNO.

There consequently developed from the early 1990s much concern over the uneven ethnic distribution of benefits of rapid economic growth, with this feeling being particularly prominent amongst *Bumiputera*. Such concerns were not without reason. A recent study on income distribution based on 1997 data revealed that *Bumiputera* households made up 70.2 per cent of all households in the income class representing the bottom 40 per cent of the Malaysian society (Table 5.2). On the other hand, such households only constituted 12.9 per cent of households in the top income class (Table 5.3). Other data from the study also revealed a widening income gap within the *Bumiputera* community itself.

The adverse impact of the crisis on *Bumiputera* especially, as well as a leadership style in crisis adjustment perceived by many as focused on bailing out a few rich *Bumiputera* while ignoring the plight of the majority, caused widespread unease. The expulsion of Anwar Ibrahim as deputy prime minister in 1998 was then the catalyst for enhanced activism. There was increased momentum in the campaign for greater transparency, more political freedom and abolition of the Internal Security Act which permitted detention without trial. Among youth, the 'Anwar saga' helped raise political consciousness to a degree not seen since the 1960s and 1970s. This aspect is explored further in Chapter 9.

Table 5.2 Distribution of Households within Income Classes by Ethnicity,
1997

Ethnic Groups	Bottom 40%	Middle 40%	Top 20%
Bumiputera	70.2	55.6	37.3
Chinese	14.4	33.1	47.3
Indians	5.3	8.7	8.8
Others	10.1	2.6	6.5
Average Monthly Income (RM)	840	2202	7006

Source: Samsudin Hitam (1999).

Table 5.3 Distribution of Households within Ethnic Groups by Income Class,
1997

Income Groups	Bumiputera	Chinese	Indians
Top 20%	12.9	33.2	24.1
Middle 40%	38.5	46.5	47.3
Bottom 40%	48.6	20.3	28.6

Source: Samsudin Hitam (1999).

It can indeed be argued that the seeds of the social and political crisis had been sown well before the economic crisis. In the years prior to his dismissal, Anwar Ibrahim was seen to have gone out of his way to promote social justice and develop a liberal philosophy wherein human rights were respected and political, religious and racial differences tolerated. Furthermore, as the country became more affluent and globalization began to affect a generation of young urban Malays, they began questioning whether the government under the existing leadership was desirable. This scepticism grew after the regional economic downturn. *Reformasi* became the most expedient vehicle for such social expression, and although at the beginning the movement simply focused on Anwar's plight and demanded Anwar's reinstatement in UMNO and the government, justice and freedom were later added to its agenda.

MALAYSIA WEATHERING THE STORM

The social impact of the financial and economic crisis in Malaysia may be seen as both widespread and potentially long lasting. If the impact of the crisis on foreign workers is also taken into consideration, the situation had become even more precarious. It will in fact take time to achieve complete recovery from the setbacks described.

But while the crisis triggered unprecedented Malaysian political developments, these were of much smaller magnitude than those in Indonesia.

True, there were street protests and discontent at the grassroots after the dramatic dismissal of Anwar Ibrahim, especially among the young. Yet there was relative peace, and social strife between ethnic groups did not take place. How is that the multi-ethnic society in Malaysia was not torn apart with the worsening of the crisis, as occurred in Indonesia?

First, as argued elsewhere (Ishak Shari 2000; Rasiah and Ishak Shari 1997), the Malaysian state gave high priority to distributional issues in implementing the NEP, particularly in eradicating poverty and reducing economic disparities between major ethnic groups. Malaysia from 1970 allocated substantial budgetary resources for poverty reduction programmes as well as for social services. It appears too that the state was committed to mitigating the short-term adverse effects on vulnerable groups of the recent economic slowdown. The government accordingly ensured that budget shares for social services in 1998 would remain approximately at their 1997 levels, particularly for health and education, and that public expenditures on major anti-poverty programmes would be protected in real terms despite a reduced total development expenditure. These measures may well have minimized the adverse impact of the crisis on the poor, and hence prevented a bigger increase in the incidence of poverty and income disparities.

The state policies and programmes since 1970 may also have influenced the country's political orientation. Despite its interventionist policies, the Malaysian government did not discard the free enterprise doctrine during the NEP period. While the government facilitated the emergence and consolidation of the Malay business and professional classes, non-Malay and foreign interests were also encouraged to expand. In fact, despite restrictions on Chinese capital, the Chinese business class also grew and reaped indirect benefits during the NEP period. Some sections of Chinese business perceived the NEP to be a necessary mechanism to expand Malay capital, thereby correcting the inter-ethnic imbalance and securing stable socio-political conditions. The state liberalization and deregulation of economic policies in the late 1980s further satisfied the Chinese and Indian business and middle classes.

Second, Malaysia's rapid economic growth during the 27 years from 1970 to the crisis produced a large middle class (see Chapter 4) that was multi-ethnic in composition, with the *Bumiputera* segment becoming very conspicuous and politically important. It has been argued that the characteristics of this growing middle class in Malaysia, and in particular the attitude among significant sections of acceptance and acquiescence *vis-à-vis* the state and political leadership, contributed to maintaining the status quo (Abdul Rahman Embong 2000). Such support accompanied by a general satisfaction found highest expression in the results of the 1995 elections in which the ruling coalition won a massive victory. This is not to deny there was increasing resentment on the part especially of the *Bumiputera* middle class regarding liberalization and deregulation measures which reversed some achievements of the NEP.

Indeed, the swing against UMNO in the 1999 election was also related to the growing disenchantment with government economic policies among Malays. The government's privatization policies, which created opportunities for politically-connected corporate leaders to make huge profits but often led to increased financial burdens for ordinary people, also led to further discontent. Such burdens were expressed, for example, in higher rates for public utilities and increased highway toll charges. Yet, significantly, this discontent still did not developed into inter-ethnic conflict on the Indonesian pattern.

Third, the long period of rapid growth which resulted in labour shortages and the employment of large number of foreign workers before the crisis also played a fairly important role in lessening the adverse effects on Malaysian workers. With an unemployment rate in the late 1990s of 2.6 per cent and the presence of more than one million foreign workers in the country, the impact of the crisis on employment opportunities for locals was relatively moderate. By sending back retrenched foreign labour during the crisis, Malaysia was able to 'export back' its social cost. The restrained attitude of the unions and workers' willingness to suffer a decline in real wages rather than face retrenchment also contributed to a situation where relatively few locals lost their jobs.

The enforcement during the crisis of legal provisions protecting workers' interests, with retrenchment being undertaken in accordance with the law, was also very important. According to the Employment Act 1955 (Section 69), retrenched workers must be paid lay-off benefits or compensation. Although some firms had not yet paid such benefits, a labour report for the period ending 3 October 1998 showed that severance pay and retrenchment benefits had been remitted to affected workers in 81 per cent of cases.[4] This helped to cushion the adverse impacts of the crisis on workers, and to ameliorate their conditions.

Fourth, while the medium and long-term impacts of the capital control measures introduced in early September 1998 need further detailed study, their short-term macro-economic impact seemed favourable in mitigating adverse impacts of the crisis. Chapter 2 gives further detail of this aspect. Malaysia's refusal to seek a bailout package from the International Monetary Fund also possibly explained the lesser social impact, as elaborated by Stiglitz (2000). Moreover, the introduction of selective capital controls and pegging of the ringgit to the US dollar enabled many firms to access cheaper loans and avoid bankruptcy, while permitting the government to adopt an expansionary fiscal policy in reviving the economy.

CONCLUSION

The available information does not allow a carefully considered assessment of the welfare consequences of the crisis, in Malaysia or elsewhere. While some analysts have quickly jumped to the conclusion that the crisis has proven the failure of the 'Asian development model', the discussion has shown the issue to be more complex. It must be admitted, however, that the crisis has illustrated the truth of the allegation that this development model encourages corruption and nepotism, with that being particularly true of Indonesia. Yet perhaps there is a larger truth that needs to be discovered.

The International Monetary Fund and World Bank have long been advocating the liberalization of capital markets, including the establishment of stock markets and markets for other derivative financial instruments, largely ignoring the arguments for financial repression and restraint advocated by some specialists in information economics (see, for example, Fitzgerald 1998). There is indeed a significant body of persuasive literature raising serious doubts about the nature and contribution of equity financing to late industrialization.

As the recent financial crisis experience shows, unregulated finance capital ends up largely in short-term and speculative ventures, which in the long run debilitate growth together with efforts to eradicate poverty and reduce income inequality. Consequently, there is now greater appreciation among governments of the dangers of exposing their financial systems to fast liberalization, especially when they lack experience in dealing with the international capital market and their banking regulations and supervision are inadequate. Governments are now more willing to discipline not only the purveyors of labour but also of finance.

Social crises as consequences of economic upheavals are by no means a new feature of the international scene. Those that occur today are but a mirror of the contradictions pervading the lives of new emerging modern countries not certain about the extent to which they wish to integrate with the new global economic order. In this new order alternative effective control mechanisms are sought but not fully established, while the old order is only partially repudiated.

Meanwhile in Malaysia, the contradictions still persist between the residual political culture of the 1970s and the new one becoming more prominent amidst the economic crisis and characterized by demands for transparency, justice, rule of law, etc. Although the economic recovery of the early 2000s may bring relief to the majority, the undercurrent of social discontent will not be blown away by increasingly favourable economic winds. The government's reputation has been damaged and may only be restored by reconstructing institutions characteristic of a modern democratic society.

Furthermore, in a world in which powerful international organizations and transnational corporations, as well as states in advanced industrial countries, are devoted to maximizing the freedom of financial capital around the globe, states in developing countries need to assert social control and continue to pursue redistributive policies. These are policies that could change the hitherto disadvantageous impact of the globalization process on their peoples. A fundamentally different alternative approach which differs from that previously taken, and which involves the democratization of the state and the economy, has to be considered. Inevitably, this entails challenging the national and international structures of power.

In this regard, the proposal of Higgot (1999, pp.12 - 13) for a 'third way', involving a 'middle' ground in which the regulatory role of governments is revitalized, greater attention is given to social issues, and the need is pursued for more 'national' or possibly 'regional' approaches to post-crisis economic management, is worthy of further consideration.

NOTES

1. The government has generally viewed poverty in absolute rather than relative terms. The Poverty Line Income (PLI) used by the government was made public for the first time in the *Mid-Term Review of the Fifth Malaysia Plan* (Malaysia 1989, p. 45). The PLI is defined on the basis of a minimum expenditure level needed to secure a certain standard of living, and is updated annually using the Consumer Price Index to reflect changes in price levels. In 1989, the PLI was determined to be RM350 per month for a household of 5.14 persons in Peninsula Malaysia.

2. The EPF was established in 1951, with the initial goal of providing some retirement security to workers earning low wages. Today in the early 2000s, nearly all employees outside the government's pension scheme are required to contribute to the EPF regardless of salary size. Currently, employees contribute 11 per cent of their salary, while employers are supposed to provide another 12 per cent. Often, however, the latter fail to remit their contributions.

3. While a proportion of those retrenched found new jobs - between January and December 1998, 74,610 job vacancies were available in various industries. Many of these vacancies were either in lower-paid categories or demanding certain levels of skill, and thus not conducive in facilitating labour mobility. Of 43,102 workers retrenched between June and December, 1998, 11,498 found new jobs, 5,615 did not, 4,120 ventured into new spheres such as petty trading, and another 21,869 workers could not be traced (Malaysia 1999b).

4. Unfortunately, the citations for this and certain other studies reported in the chapter were not available in Professor Dr Ishak Shari's notes, and the original materials cannot be traced.

5. Indeed, government expenditure on most social services - including education, health and housing - also declined over the same period.

6. Malaysia's Security Environment and Strategic Responses

Russ Swinnerton

Malaysia's security outlook has been influenced by a history of colonization, a communist insurgency, a limited war with Indonesia, a fear of Vietnamese invasion, an ambition to control its sea environment and, lately, by a sharp economic downturn. These factors have encouraged a pragmatic and independent foreign policy and strategic positioning, and modest but regionally capable armed forces structured for deterrence and conventional war.

This chapter provides a history of the development of Malaysia's security policies and armed forces, and describes the security outlook, threat perceptions, and strategic orientation of the forces. It is felt that barring terrorist threats the current environment is relatively benign, where challenges are largely maritime and particularly in the South China Sea.

BACKGROUND

The history of an independent Malaysian strategic outlook is relatively short, due largely to the circumstance of unchallenged British control over external defence and foreign policy that existed until Malayan Independence in 1957. Nonetheless, the foundations for all three services of the Malaysian armed forces were laid in the 1930s, although their development was to be interrupted by the Second World War. Pressures for establishment of these services came from the traditional rulers rather than from the colonizing power. However, for a variety of reasons, there was no significant arming of the population in Malaya before the war (Tregonning 1964, p. 29).

Even after independence, Malaya continued to depend on British Commonwealth connections for its external defence, and a Defence Agreement was ratified by parliament in 1957. According to Tregonning (1964, p. 87):

> The main provisions of this treaty were that Great Britain would afford military aid if requested. In return for this guarantee, it was permitted to retain in Malaya troops and installations in order that it could meet its many international obligations. This Agreement has been of mutual satisfaction. The British Armed Forces were of great assistance from 1957...in the internal war against the communists...The close cooperation between the Malaysian and British Governments on defence matters also...assisted in the maintenance of a steady, unbroken training pattern of the Malay regiments that constitute the major armed force of the new Malaysia.

DEVELOPMENT OF THE MALAYSIAN ARMED FORCES

The development of the Malaysian armed forces (MAF) since independence can be roughly divided into four periods, each characterized by distinct strategic perspectives and resultant arms acquisitions:[1]

1. The post-Independence period to 1973, when Malaysia had to contend with internal insurgencies and problems associated with the creation of the Federation of Malaysia in 1963 and the British withdrawal East of Suez in 1971.
2. The 1979 to 1984 period, when the MAF responded rapidly to a perceived overland threat from Vietnam.
3. The maritime period, which began in 1985 and continued for about ten years as Malaysia sought to acquire forces to deal with perceived threats following the signing of the United Nations Convention on the Law of the Sea.
4. The 'no threat' present period from the late 1990s into the early 2000s, when non-military dangers are perceived to prevail. The primacy of economic threats was emphasised by the severe financial crisis of 1997 - 98.

When Malaya was granted its independence in 1957, it negotiated with the United Kingdom not only the Anglo-Malayan Agreement on External Defence and Mutual Assistance for external defence of the new nation, but requested that the governments of 'Britain, Australia and New Zealand...continue to make their forces available for Emergency operations' (Hawkins 1972, p. 16). The country then had neither the need, nor indeed the resources, to establish conventional armed forces for external defence. The immediate and real danger to the regime was the ongoing 'emergency' against communist guerrillas, which required the Malaysian government to acquire a substantial counter-insurgency capability. The latter requirement continued until the 1980s, and resulted in the MAF developing into 'an unbalanced force with an infantry-biased structure' (Abdul Razak 1992, p. 305).

This was the main reason why the army came to dominate Malaysian defence planning in terms of force structure, role and acquisitions for almost 30 years. The other reason was history: the royal patronage and the tradition of the British regimental system were perpetuated by the officers of the Royal Malay Regiment after independence, and that regiment ensured not only that the army became the senior service in the MAF, but that its officers would dominate the entire top hierarchy of those forces.

The Emergency and Confrontation[2] both accelerated and distorted the development of the MAF. They also indirectly affected those forces by draining the resources of Britain and hastening the withdrawal of British troops East of Suez. The Malaysian army's strength at that time was only 13,000 persons, so considerable reliance continued to be placed on British

Commonwealth forces (Mohd Noor 1996, p. 3). The Malaysian air force and navy continued to provide support to the army's counter-insurgency war, but both also began to develop embryo capabilities that would continue to develop despite the absence of a coherent policy. The Anglo-Malayan Agreement on External Defence was terminated in 1971, to be replaced by the looser Five-Power Defence Arrangements[3] which provided the framework within which Malaysia would develop a more self-reliant defence force.

The second major phase in the MAF's development and modernization followed the Vietnamese invasion of Cambodia in December 1978. In terms of acquisitions, this period was a heady one for the army. There had been unease in Kuala Lumpur when the United States-backed Saigon regime fell in 1975. The invasion finally convinced the Malaysian government that there was a real possibility of an overland attack by Vietnam, reinforcing the communist threat of the Emergency. Malaysia therefore quickly drew up an ambitious plan for the expansion of the MAF, known by the Malay acronym PERISTA or *Pembesaran Istemewa Tentera* ('armed forces special expansion programme'). This aimed to turn the MAF as rapidly as possible into a conventional warfare force, in order to be able to block a possible Vietnamese thrust across Thailand and down the Malay Peninsula. Apparently, 'Nowhere in the region ha[d] the shift from counter-insurgency to conventional preparedness been more dramatic than in Malaysia' (Weatherbee, 1987, p. 203).

While in retrospect the fears may have been unfounded, the Malaysian government took the Vietnamese overland threat seriously at the time. That the threat was seen as mainly overland, however, could have been because the military hierarchy was still dominated by British-trained officers. These were all keenly conscious of the 1941 Malayan campaign of the Second World War, when the Japanese marched down the peninsula.

Unfavourable international economic conditions in the early 1980s, the economic downturn of 1985, and the growing strains in the government's budgetary position around the same period put acquisitions on hold, and this was to have far-reaching consequences for the army. No one knew at that time how long the economic slowdown would last. An effective 'freeze' was put on all planned purchases until the economy recovered. This pause gave the government time to review the overall strategic situation and the MAF's modernization programme. By this time, Vietnam's failure to completely control Cambodia made Malaysia realise that fears of a Vietnamese attack across Thailand and down the Malay Peninsula were totally unfounded. What made the threat even less likely to materialize was the fact that the Soviet Union was economically over-stretched, and could not afford to underwrite any Vietnamese adventurism.

A second factor which undermined army dominance at that time was the December 1989 truce between Malaysia and the Communist Party of Malaya, officially marking the end of the Emergency.[4] The truce implied that the Malaysian army had lost the primary role of maintaining the integrity of the state against communist subversion. Malaysia in fact moved away from a defence posture targeted specifically at a potential enemy to more general 'capability and affordability' defence planning. Thus a number of ambitious projects under PERISTA - the acquisition of medium battle tanks, additional air defence fighters, the Gong Kedak air base, and the Combat Training Centre in Gemas - were all deferred to a later date.

Nonetheless, the Malaysian army had expanded rapidly from about 53,000 persons in the early 1970s to more than 100,000 by 1989. Its numbers had been bloated by the sudden influx of recruits under the PERISTA programme. But in 1989, for the first time in its post-independence history, it was decided to cut the strength of the standing army from a high of 110,000 to 90,000 by the year 2000 (*Jane's Defence Weekly* 1989). In line with the move towards acquiring a general deterrence posture, the MAF:

> shifted the basis for planning force-level requirements from a threat focus to the defence of national interests, which were defined in terms of the core-area (the territory of Malaysia); the immediate vicinity (which includes the Straits of Malacca, Straits of Singapore, the line of communication between peninsular Malaysia and Sabah/Sarawak, the South China Sea, and the Andaman Islands); and the neighbouring countries (Alagappa 1987 p. 189).

Henceforth, the operational concept of the MAF was based on deterrence and forward defence. This meant that the Royal Malaysian Navy would become the service on which prime responsibility of defending Malaysia's core interests would fall.

The emphasis on the defence of national interests in the face of an economic recession was of particular significance in this new outlook. That was because the economic and national interests of Malaysia were in more ways than one tied up with the nation's maritime interests. Thus, Malaysia was one nation in the Association of South East Asian Nations (ASEAN) which showed an early appreciation of its potential offshore wealth, and in fact was already extracting oil from the South China Sea even before the 1982 United Nations Convention on the Law of the Sea.[5]

This Convention assisted in codifying what had largely become state practice with respect to resource issues and limits of jurisdiction, but also exacerbated territorial disputes by creating potential overlapping jurisdictions and proclaiming fishing zones in common areas. It delivered two particular outcomes which affected Malaysia: first, it legitimized exclusive economic zone and continental shelf (sea-bed) claims out to 200 nautical miles, and second, it allowed recognition of archipelagic waters and associated transit regimes. The latter was of particular interest to Malaysia, with two archipelagic states - Indonesia and the Philippines - as neighbours. Malaysia's maritime focus resulted in its planning for capabilities to assist in fighting a maritime war. Decisions were made to acquire MiG29 air defence aircraft, F/A 18 planes for maritime strikes, the LEKIU-class frigates, and a large class of offshore patrol vessels. Some of these platforms were still on the way in the early 2000s.

The division between this period of maritime rearmament and the present is difficult to define precisely. Certainly at the start of the new century, the threat of Chinese aggression in the Spratly Islands in the South China Sea was still paramount. In an interview with *Jane's Defence Weekly* as early as 1992, the Malaysian chief of defence force noted that: 'In the immediate term...the biggest problem to regional stability will be the settling of the claims in the Spratly and Paracel Islands and whether China will want to pursue its claims militarily' (cited in Acharaya 1995, p. 6). But in 1995, Dr Mahathir Mohamad, Malaysia's prime minister announced that to treat China as a threat was to risk the self-fulfilling prophecy:

> Malaysia has always seen the Peoples' Republic of China as a long-term threat. However, today, Malaysia's perception has somewhat changed, driven by a more pragmatic assessment. ... Malaysia now sees Beijing as a friend and a potential trade partner (Abdul Razak 1995, p. 15).

This shift in perception serves as a good delineator between the maritime rearmament period and that obtaining in the early 2000s.

THE EARLY 2000s

Since the end of the cold war, Malaysia and its surrounding Southeast Asian region have faced a multipolar security structure, without an underlying rigid concert of powers or power balance. This has created an environment of some uncertainty, exacerbated by a region-wide economic slow-down which has tended to focus national attention on immediate economic threats, rather than distant, hypothetical, military threats. Hence the Malaysian government's avowed position is that 'the ASEAN way'[6] will defuse any territorial or border dispute, and prevent any national disagreement from developing into a military contest. Given Southeast Asia's history, it should not be surprising that several points of contention exist, in both the maritime and land environments.

The key area of dispute respecting sea bed exclusive economic zones is of course the Spratly Islands. The experience of the Philippines in 1995 over Mischief Reef in the Spratlys[7] brought the islands into sharp relief for Malaysia. Given China's overwhelming superiority in conventional maritime arms, all the ASEAN claimants of rights in the Spratlys (Brunei, Malaysia, the Philippines and Vietnam) require an ability to influence affairs at sea. This is against China, not for sea assertion or sea denial, but for 'sea credibility' or deterrence. While not suggesting that sovereignty disputes themselves could be influential in causing armed conflict between ASEAN members, their existence exacerbates tensions arising over other difficulties. In this regard an analyst of ASEAN strategic affairs has commented:

> While ASEAN member-states have been reticent about threats emanating to members from within the ASEAN organisation, the foreign and defence policies of the member-states, as well as the pattern of arms procurement, would tend to indicate that more often than not the enemy the ASEAN states are trying to overcome comes from within the organisation rather than without, even though this is never openly stated or identified (Singh 1993, p. 217).

Even fishing remains a continuing source of friction in the region, particularly between neighbours. Actions against illegal fishing occasionally result in loss of life. Recent engagements between Thai fishermen and Malaysian patrol forces are illustrative. The realities of exclusive economic zone dominion combined with a diminishing resource and an increasing demand will ensure that fishing remains a key point of concern, and a justification for the acquisition of maritime surveillance, patrol and response forces at the lower end of the capability spectrum. In particular, the rapid rate of increase of China's fishing catch should be noted. At present, this has not brought it into conflict with the littoral states around the South China Sea, partly because, excepting Thailand, most are not distant-water fishing nations. But as the domestic fisheries of these other states become depleted, they too will start to fish more widely in the region, with greater potential for harmful interaction.

The recognition of two regional states (Indonesia and the Philippines) as archipelagic, and the new status of their archipelagic waters, has further created a potential for misunderstanding on issues of sea lanes. The latter may now be determined for reasons other than those of navigational safety or convenience. In Malaysia's case, the direct route between East and West Malaysia passes through Indonesia's declared archipelagic waters, and a bilateral agreement has been reached to assure Malaysia of passage.

The arguments surrounding the regulation of straits have been similarly amplified by recognition of a 12 nautical mile territorial sea. This has had the effect of completely 'closing' several traditional straits, turning areas which were high seas prior to the United Nations Convention on the Law of the Sea into unbroken territorial waters over which a coastal state may normally have jurisdiction to suspend innocent passage.

The recognition of pre-existing passage rights, through the regime of non-suspendable transit passage in the normal mode of high seas operations, was intended to satisfy maritime states while allowing greater control by coastal states. However the potential for misunderstanding remains. And Malaysia's recognition of the Malacca Straits between it and Sumatra as one of its four major threat areas confirms the potential for this issue to create friction with maritime user-states.

The recognition of coastal states' rights to control economic matters out to 200 nautical miles from their coastlines has resonated with those states concerned at the carriage of dangerous cargoes past their shores, including Malaysia. The transport of plutonium from Europe to Japan since 1992 has brought the issue into sharp focus. Malaysia can be expected to insist on its ability to control access of dangerous cargoes into its economic zone and proximate straits.

The continued existence of piracy[8] provides a challenge to shipping passing through the region, with particularly emotional overtones. Although piracy provides a useful justification for mounting cooperative patrols, very few pirates are caught at sea. In fact, cross-border raids on isolated settlements in East Malaysia by sea-borne bandits have also occurred recently - with the Abu Sayyaf's hostage-taking at Sipadan in 2000 being the latest, most public, but not necessarily the worst, example.[9] These raids are very difficult to defend against, and will continue to provide an important justification for mobile light patrol forces.

By comparison, life on Malaysia's land borders with Thailand, Brunei and Indonesia has been relatively benign over the past decade, with responsibility for security in the hands of the police. Army assistance has been provided for anti-smuggling and illegal immigration operations from time to time, but this remains a relatively minor activity for land forces.

External Interest and Intervention

In the past, the interests in Southeast Asia of outside countries turned on the same questions in the Soviet Union-United States balance preoccupying the rest of the world during the cold war. With an inward-looking former Soviet Union no longer being such an active participant in the region, and with the United States at least until the attack on the World Trade Center in September, 2001, perceived to be disengaging, the security environment in the region is seen to be less certain and predictable.

The alliances and interplays between China, the Soviet Union and Vietnam in particular were clearly of key importance to the emergence and development of ASEAN. The conclusion of the earlier ideological conflict and Vietnam's entry into ASEAN is a clear marker of the extent of change that has occurred. However, the emergence of China as an economic, political and strategic power, as well as a potential superpower, has led to a situation where China preoccupies current strategic analysis - and threatens to hijack the opportunities for dialogue. But other large players, principally the United States and Japan, but also India and Korea, are also involved in the region. This is for a variety of reasons, with only one of these being the formation of 'ASEAN + 3'.[10]

Regarding the ASEAN perception of United States disengagement from the region, two prominent Australian strategic analysts have commented:

the original cold war ideological and geopolitical rationales for United States forward presence and for American alliances in the region have lost most of their force. Not surprisingly, the prospect of continued long-term American commitment to the region seems increasingly questionable to some regional defence planners.... [US withdrawal] is thus a 'worst-case' which regional defence planners *must* take seriously (Mack and Ball 1992, p. 204).

We might consider how these judgements have changed since the terrorist attacks in New York and Washington on 11 September 2001, and the commencement of the US-led 'war on terrorism'. Certainly, the immediate aftermath has been characterised by intensive alliance-building and renewed US interest, including through the presence of military advisers in the Southern Philippines. But the presence will probably be focused on land, with police-style anti-terrorist objectives, and will not promise any major changes to strategic power balances or interests. Although the United States remains forward deployed, the possibility of a less-intensive US presence at sea will continue to encourage Southeast Asian countries in the early 2000s to increase their own capabilities. The interests of large external powers, however, continue to be felt in the region, particularly over issues including:

1. The importance of sea lines of communication through the region to Japan, Korea, Taiwan and (increasingly) to China, and their significance for continued economic development.
2. The interests of US and multinational oil companies prospecting in the Spratlys.
3. The existence of considerable markets for military hardware, which introduces more distant players such as South Africa, Germany, Sweden and, in a new context, Russia.

The enduring feature marking the interest of external powers in the region, in the absence of the paradoxically stabilizing element of cold war interest and attention, is the perception that the strategic security environment of the region is less certain and less secure. In the face of such uncertainty, local countries must take appropriate measures to acquire suitable capabilities for self-defence and protection of their vital interests.

The Official Threat Assessment

The Malaysian defence policy paper *Malaysian Defence*, published in 1997, assesses four main threats in the region of that country, none of which have an overt military dimension:

1. Overlapping claims and territorial disputes.
2. Pollution and congestion in Straits of Malacca.

3. Piracy.
4. Illegal immigrants.

This list of course does not declare any potential threat from Malaysia's ASEAN neighbours, other than in the context of overlapping claims, nor from any other proximate country against whom, one supposes, the nation's strategy of preparing for conventional warfare might be directed. In this way the list serves one of the implicit purposes of a policy paper which is confidence-building. This is done by denying the existence of credible threats from neighbours, and by implying that, apart from border disputation issues, threats to security will largely arise from non-traditional, or small 's' security sources.

Since *Malaysian Defence* was prepared, the situation in Indonesia has raised some concern in Malaysia about the prospects for increased instability. Certainly, Malaysia would expect to receive the first wave of displaced persons as a result of a major breakdown in security or widespread communal violence. These are threats that are very difficult to plan against and counter.

Singapore's regionally impressive capability improvements over the past ten years have attracted critical attention, with the suggestion that they have spurred competitive capability acquisitions in Malaysia. But while some capability matching has occurred, there has been no systematic evaluation of the threat posed by Singapore and a similarly systematic acquisition of countermeasures. War with Singapore is an impossible scenario for Malaysia, but at the same time Malaysia would not wish the capability gap with that country to grow too large.

Notwithstanding the absence of an official threat from neighbours, however, there is a regional pattern of capability acquisition in response to the acquisitions of other regional countries. Hence the purchase of tanks for one country's armed forces encourages anti-tank systems for a neighbour. Again, submarines encourage the development of anti-submarine warfare capabilities (including submarines), and so on. But these 'simultaneous' acquisitions are not significant when balanced against an armed forces' overall capabilities. And with relatively small armed forces, it is also good practice to maintain nuclei of expertise in a range of capabilities, in order to shorten acquisition times when unforeseen threats emerge.

A further factor encouraging the benign official assessment is the way security is viewed by the government. Malaysia is not alone in ASEAN, or indeed in the world, in seeing economic threats as more proximate and pressing than more distant military threats. In his keynote address at the opening ceremony of a Regional Roundtable held in Kuala Lumpur in 1999, Malaysia's deputy prime minister, Dato'Abdullah Ahmad Badawi, declared that the Asia-Pacific region must shift from a narrow preoccupation with military security to that which encompassed the security of all the fundamental needs, core values and vital interests of the individual, society and state. Dato' Abdullah stated:

I would think that at this very moment the greatest threat to the national security of a particular state in north-east Asia is hunger and starvation. For the millions of the acutely poor in Asia too, their gravest security problem is scarcity of food, clothing, shelter and health, while in some South-East Asian countries it could be the haze from forest fires as well as the AIDS virus or the abuse of basic civil and political liberties (*The Star* 1999).

Dato' Abdullah further cited the financial crisis as the most serious security problem facing some countries in the region including Malaysia. Although all countries in Southeast Asia have responded positively to the need for unilateral action and multilateral cooperation to defeat the threat of global terrorism, the potential terrorist threat to Malaysia does not have the same resonance as it does for the US. Thus it remains a problem for attention of the police rather than the armed forces.

Foreign Policy Positioning

Despite the pressures of external power interest in the region, Malaysia's foreign policy position has been remarkably consistent since Independence, and has substantially influenced its strategic outlook and policies in several respects.

Thus Malaysia has always maintained an *opposition to imperialism,* in both its colonial and economic varieties. Malaysia supported Indonesia's efforts to displace the Netherlands in Irian Jaya or West Papua. It now presents the downside of globalism as an emerging form of the old colonial spectre. Malaysia has also constantly *supported the United Nations,* doing this initially as a vehicle to demonstrate the country's independence and equality. Malaysia was one of the first countries into the Congo in 1960, and has maintained its involvement in many operations since then. More than 16,500 Malaysian service personnel, the majority from the army, have taken part in peacekeeping operations since the first contingent went to the Congo. Malaysia provided the first Southeast Asian commander of a major United Nations military operation, in Somalia in 1994, complementing its substantial contribution of combat forces. Malaysia also made major contributions to United Nations forces for operations in ex-Yugoslavia.

Excepting the Five-Power Defence Arrangements, Malaysia has *resisted multilateral security treaties that depend on extra-regional and Western-led membership.* Thus the country did not participate in the South East Asian Treaty Organization.[11] Malaysia has also *encouraged regional groupings that are recognizably Asian,* ranging from the Association of South East Asia to ASEAN, the ASEAN Regional Forum[12], and ASEAN +3. Hence when Dr Mahathir addressed the topic of an East Asian security arrangement at a maritime and aerospace exhibition in Langkawi in 1999, he did not include the participation of non-Asian elements (Mahathir 1999). But neither did he provide a road map of how Asian countries might combine to bolster their security.

There have been recent suggestions from Tony Tan, Singapore's defence minister, as well as from others, that multilateral activity is inevitable if the region is to deal with globalization and modern cross-border threats. This is under circumstances where the latter often come from non-state players and particularly terrorist groups. But there seems to be considerable distance to travel before ASEAN develops an overt security dimension. This is other than through its pursuit of that dimension through the ASEAN Regional Forum - wherein ASEAN remains in control of the process.

Malaysia has avoided great-power alignment and alliances, although it has recognized the benefits of low-key diplomacy and dialogue where its record of consultation with the United States is especially noteworthy. It is an active member of the Non-Aligned Movement, to which it arguably provides intellectual leadership. It is also a champion of South-South alignment among developing countries, partly as a means of diluting the neo-imperialist influence of the developed world. Finally, Malaysia is *pro-Islam* and values its membership of the Organization of the Islamic Conference. The latter became especially topical after it hosted the Conference's foreign ministers' meeting in Kuala Lumpur in 2000. Malaysia's Islamic outlook is a factor in its strategic positioning, and as one example drove its participation in, and public diplomacy regarding, the problems in Bosnia.

Defence Policy and Strategy

Malaysia's 1997 defence policy paper expresses the national strategy as follows:

> Malaysia's defence policy is a manifestation of its goal for the protection of its national strategic interests and the preservation of national security. The defence policy outlines three basic fundamentals, namely national strategic interests, principles of defence and the concept of defence. It emphasises the need for the maintenance of a stable and peaceful environment in the immediate areas of its strategic interests (Malaysia. Ministry of Defence 1997, p. 21).

What follows in the defence paper is essentially an expression of the importance of deterrence and, if that fails, the necessity of having a credible set of capabilities to defeat an indeterminate threat, with external assistance if necessary. The paper also emphasizes the principle of self-reliance, as follows:

> Malaysia's defence revolves around the fundamental principles of *Self-Reliance, Regional Cooperation and External Assistance*. Being an independent and sovereign state, Malaysia has realised that the preservation of its national interest and security is best attained through the pursuit of self-reliance which is the core of its defence policy. This principle emphasises Armed Forces self-reliance within a structure of

national self-reliance. It involves not only combat forces but also logistical support network of military-industrial cooperation in line with the country's development priorities. Self-reliance in this regard should ...also involve all relevant agencies of the government and the people. However, taking into account its limitations, Malaysia's self-reliance capabilities can be drawn from two premises. These are firstly, having the capability to act independently without the need for foreign assistance in matters concerning internal security and secondly, having the capability to act independently protecting its territorial integrity and security interests within the immediate vicinity from low and medium level external threats (*Ibid.*, pp. 21 - 22).

The Five Power Defence Arrangements

In the context of the sometimes vitriolic expressions of Malaysia's geo-strategic priorities from prime minister Mahathir, these Defence Arrangements sit somewhat anachronistically at the top of the list of opportunities for 'external assistance'. There is no doubt that they have delivered the secure environment necessary for Malaysia's armed forces to develop the self-reliant capabilities allowing them to deter regional threats. And it is also clear that the loose structure of the Arrangements, which are obligation-based but with an obligation simply to consult, has delivered such benefits to its members that it continues to be useful for them all.

For Malaysia, the Arrangements still deliver the kinds of operational benefits that allow exercising at all levels, including the strategic, well in advance of the tactical-level activity associated with ad hoc bilateral exercises. The very ambiguity of the Arrangements, whereby they remain an opaque factor in a potential adversary's contingency planning, also helps them act as a strategic underpinning for Malaysia's armed forces. But if the Arrangements did not exist, they could not be created now.

The *Malaysian Defence* paper of 1997 further explained that:

To complement regional cooperation, Malaysia also acknowledges the need for external assistance from countries outside the region...Hence, despite its commitment to ZOPFAN (the Zone of Peace, Freedom and Neutrality), the reality of the situation should not allow Malaysia to preclude the need to request assistance from sources outside the region. This is especially so when the level of threat is of a proportion that goes beyond the capability of the local force.

Malaysia regards the Five Power Defence Arrangement (FPDA)...as an avenue for external assistance...At the time of its inception, Malaysia realised that self-reliance could only be achieved over a period of time. The FPDA thus became the mechanism through which it could develop its defence capabilities with the assistance of traditional allies...Malaysia firmly remains committed to the continued relevance of the FPDA. Nevertheless, in view of the present strategic scenario and the enhanced capabilities of the Malaysian Armed Forces (MAF), the role of the FPDA has been streamlined to meet the current needs (Ibid., pp. 23 - 24).

Procurement and Confidence-Building Measures

Given the perceived threats and Malaysia's prescription for dealing with them, does the armed forces' shopping list reflect coherent strategic priorities? In the early 2000s the shopping list was short, but the economy was on the rise and could be expected to return to pre-1998 levels within a couple of years. But even then, other factors would affect the equipment that Malaysia acquired.

The end of the cold war was of course a factor in the increased availability of modern weapons systems and delivery platforms, at a time when economic growth in the region allowed an increasing amount to be spent on arms. The 1997 economic slowdown resulted in a freeze on many of Malaysia's new purchases, although existing contracts were honoured and some hardware delivered. Renewed progress in 2000 allowed stalled projects to resume. Yet there is an additional dynamic associated with acquisitions, which is that of technology transfer. New state-of-the-art systems bring with them a tail of technology which can be transferred into non-military applications. In this regard, some acquisitions remain sound investments in the future, perhaps especially when the country is seeking to recover from the effects of recession.

Factors other than technology are also at play in determining capability acquisition plans and priorities. Anecdotal information suggests that, as in the rest of the world, prestige, pecuniary interest, and political factors also have some bearing on weapons acquisitions. In this situation, decisions are not always based on a rigorous evaluation of strategic imperatives and capability shortfalls (Singh 1993, p. 223).

The general trend in the region in the early 2000s is towards the acquisition of maritime weapon systems, principally for a sea denial role. This includes maritime surveillance, patrol and response capabilities, as well as those for surface strike from surface, sub-surface and air platforms. Long-distance replenishment and logistic forces are not on the current acquisition lists, meaning that power projection beyond the South China Sea is not physically possible. Some air-to-air refuelling capability is being considered, but this is in the context of fairly limited fighter aircraft ranges, and serves to improve time-on-task rather than increasing the radius of action.

Delivering the keynote address at a maritime seminar about confidence-building measures in Kuala Lumpur in 1994, the Malaysian defence minister publicly welcomed the ASEAN Regional Forum as 'beginning the process of institutionalising CBMs' (Mohd Najib b. Abdul Razak 1994). That process has continued through several subsequent meetings of the Forum, and has led to the framing of a comprehensive plan for the development of confidence-building measures, as well of preventative diplomacy and conflict-resolution mechanisms. The processes of dialogue that derive from the Forums are probably underestimated outside the region, but it is difficult to envisage the current engagement of China in the South China Sea Code of Conduct process if the Forums had not gone before.

CONCLUSION

Despite a difficult history of insurgency and actual and perceived threats across its land borders, Malaysia in the early 2000s is positioned as a state intent on safeguarding its maritime interests in an uncertain maritime region. Historically, its outlook has been non-aligned but pro-regional and selectively supportive of collective arrangements that promote security, and this outlook continues. Decisive police action to disrupt potential terrorist groups within its borders has also allowed it to face the post-September 11 world with confidence.

Malaysia remains committed to the United Nations, ASEAN, the Non-Aligned Movement and the Organization of the Islamic Conference, while continuing to benefit from membership of more narrowly focused security organizations such as the Five Power Defence Arrangements. But this is within an overall national strategic context that views economic threats more seriously than military ones.

If anything, Malaysia at the start of the new century may be too optimistic about the absence of external threats, and too preoccupied with economic and unconventional threats to security excepting terrorism. But as resources permit, it is continuing to safeguard its position with a conventional deterrent force that gives it credibility with any potential aggressor.

NOTES
1.   This description of the first three phases of MAF development derives from the analysis of Mak (2001).
2.   The Emergency was an internal war against communists from 1948 to 1960, while Confrontation was an undeclared war with Indonesia from 1963 to 1966. The impact of the latter on Malaysia's security policy is covered in Mak (1993, pp. 123 - 126)
3.   This agreement committed Australia, Malaysia, New Zealand, Singapore and the United Kingdom to consult on the security of Malaysia and Singapore.
4.   The Emergency or Insurgency was officially over in 1960, but mopping up operations were conducted along the Malaysia-Thai border until December, 1989, when a truce was signed between Malaysia and the Communist Party of Malaya. For details of the last stages of the struggle see Stubbs (1977) and Sebastian (1991).
5.   The first offshore oilfield was found along the Sarawak coast in 1962. In 1968, the West Lutong oilfield off Sarawak came on stream. By 1973, Malaysia had 19 oilfields, nearly all of them offshore. More details are provided by Foo and Ramasamy (1991).
6.   ASEAN prides itself on its ability to resolve differences and maintain good relations through consultation and consensus-building, within principles of mutual respect and non-interference in domestic affairs.
7.   China's 1995 occupation of Mischief Reef ended several years of restraint in the occupation of new features. The construction of 'fishermen's shelters' on the reef occurred without Philippine knowledge or opposition, largely because of the poor surveillance and maritime defence capabilities of the Philippine Armed Forces.
8.   Piracy is more correctly termed sea robbery in Southeast Asia, because it mainly occurs within territorial or archipelagic waters.
9.   The kidnapping in April, 2000, of 21 people (nine Malaysians and 12 mainly European foreigners, who were diving resort guests) from Sipadan Island, off the coast of Sabah in East

Malaysia, earned considerable notoriety for the Abu Sayyaf Group. The hostages were released after four and a half months, following ransom payments.

10.   ASEAN+3 engages ASEAN with China, Japan and the Republic of Korea in a formal mechanism of cooperation.

11.   SEATO comprised US, UK, France, Thailand, Philippines, Pakistan, Australia and New Zealand. SEATO was formed in 1954, when the Malaysian territories were still under British control. But Malaysia did not join the Western-led group after independence, given the leadership role played by ex-colonial powers. A contemporary account of Malaysia's indifference to the group is provided by Tregonning (1964).

12.   The ASEAN Regional Forum is a security forum, with ASEAN rotational chairing, which engages regional countries including the US, China, the Koreas and India in regular security dialogue. The Forum first met in 1994.

PART III

Politics and Other Aspects

7. A New Politics in Malaysia: Ferment and Fragmentation

Francis Loh Kok Wah

Ethnicity remains a very salient aspect of Malaysian politics. However, whereas ethnicism[1] previously dominated the discourse and practice of Malaysian politics and posed limits on democracy, it no longer does so to the same predictable extent. Recent developments, especially those that occurred since 1998, suggest that a new discourse and practice of participatory democracy has gained ground among Malaysians and particularly among Malays. The reference here is specifically to the *reformasi* movement. This comprised the formation of an opposition coalition that made the 1999 general elections uncharacteristically meaningful by offering a real choice to the voters, and a cacophony of new voices demanding justice, accountability, popular participation and an autonomous public sphere.

But in spite of the ferment, the democratic impulse does not yet prevail in Malaysia. Some observers have continued to resort to ethnic factors to explain this lag between Malaysia and certain Southeast and East Asian countries where regime changes have occurred recently. The argument is that it is not ethnicism but 'developmentalism', the cultural by-product of an economic *dirigisme* successfully undertaken by a developmental state since the 1970s, which is principally responsible for limiting democratization in present day Malaysia. However, the fact that democratic ferment is occurring while ethnicism still appeals among certain groups suggests that Malaysia's political culture has become fragmented. In other words, there are contestations between the discourses and practices of ethnicism, participatory democracy *and* developmentalism.

The contestations occur not only between the state and particular individuals and groups in civil society, or *between* the *Barisan Nasional* (National Front) (BN) and the opposition coalition, but *within* the state, the political parties, the groups, the communities and probably amongst individuals too. Nor are these the only discourses. They are simply the major ones involving all the ethnic groups and peoples of all classes, ages and sexes. The distinctions between the different discourses are used in these discussions as heuristic devices. For in the real situation they overlap with one another and are not mutually exclusive.

In this chapter the recent democratic ferment is first elaborated, and the rise of developmentalism which held sway over a majority of Malaysians and allowed the BN to consolidate its rule during the early 1990s is then addressed. The 1999 electoral results are next analysed to show that although the BN triumphed, a new era of post-NEP (New Economic Policy) politics has nonetheless opened in Malaysia, one that is characterized by ferment and fragmentation.

REFORMASI AND THE DEMOCRATIC FERMENT

The 1997 financial crisis brought differences between prime minister, Dr Mahathir Mohamad, and his deputy, Anwar Ibrahim, to a head, particularly over how the crisis should be managed. Anwar, who was then finance minister, severely cut government expenditure and allowed interest rates to float upwards. Privatized 'mega projects' like the Bakun hydro-electric project in Sarawak and a railway linking the Central Station in Kuala Lumpur to the International Airport in Sepang were shelved. Calls to bail out Malaysian companies facing bankruptcies were rejected.

Yet Dr Mahathir considered these and related measures by Anwar to miss the point. They were no different from the International Monetary Fund's response to the crisis and, to his mind, failed to recognize that the crisis was caused not by domestic shortcomings but by international currency speculators and hedge fund managers. By refusing to assist the Malaysian, and especially *Bumiputera,* corporations, Anwar was allowing gains secured under the National Economic Policy (NEP) to become unstuck. Consequently, a different set of policies focusing attention on how to deal with foreign manipulation of the Malaysian economy and on rescuing Malaysian corporations - via restructuring, debt relief and access to new credit - was proposed by the National Economic Action Council headed by former finance minister and Mahathir confidante, Daim Zainuddin. In June 1998 when the UMNO (United Malays National Organization) youth leader associated with Anwar launched an attack on cronyism at that party's annual general assembly, Mahathir hit back openly at Anwar. With this turn of events, Anwar's position in government became untenable. By 2 September, 1998 he had been ousted.[2]

Anwar's sacking from government, expulsion from UMNO, subsequent arrest, prosecution, sentencing to imprisonment, and beating by the Inspector-General of Police while detained, galvanized his supporters inside and outside UMNO, as well as opposition parties and non-government organizations (NGOs), into a mass movement. Public rallies and street demonstrations in support of Anwar were organized. The regime's abuse of power was widely criticized in publications, cassettes, video-tapes and numerous websites. The demands of the movement quickly moved beyond concern for Anwar's well-being to issues such as those of the 'rule of law', 'participatory democracy' and 'justice for all'. They also called for the repeal of coercive laws, for curbs on 'corruption, cronyism and nepotism', and ultimately for Dr Mahathir's resignation. The leaders of the *reformasi* movement first formed the party ADIL, and subsequently the *Parti Keadilan Nasional* (National Justice Party*),* led by Dr Wan Azizah Ismail, Anwar's wife.

In anticipation of the general elections, *Keadilan* and three opposition parties - the Malay-based *Parti Islam SeMalaysia* (Malaysian Islamic Party) (PAS), the Chinese-based Democratic Action Party (DAP) and the small multi-ethnic and socialist-inclined *Parti Rakyat Malaysia* (Malaysian Peoples' Party) (PRM) - formed a new opposition coalition, the *Barisan Alternatif* (Alternative Front) (BA) in mid-1999. The discourse of participatory democracy, previously the purview of small groups of middle-class activists, especially those involved in NGOs, now evolved into a significant counter-discourse also involving the opposition parties.

The opposition parties did not lose their former ethnic-religious spots and stripes completely. Many in the PAS continued to maintain a literalist-fundamentalist notion of Islam, and to understand the party's goals in terms of furthering Islamic laws and ultimately establishing an Islamic state. They rejected democracy as a Western legacy and as an extension of secularism. There were also many PAS leaders and supporters who were narrowly ethnic in outlook, in contrast to Islamic preachings of universalism. However, there were PAS leaders who believed Islam is not incompatible with democracy, and this latter group steered PAS towards championing Anwar's plight, *reformasi* and the formation of the *Barisan Alternatif*.

The DAP, while advocating the deepening of democracy, apparently conducted its internal party affairs in high-handed fashion. In 1998 - 1999, several party stalwarts who accused Lim Kit Siang of authoritarianism and nepotism were suspended or expelled. Some within the party also harboured strong anti-Islamic sentiments, and opposed the national leadership's decision to form the *Barisan Alternatif* and cooperate with PAS in the elections. As well, some former UMNO leaders now in *Keadilan* not surprisingly displayed evidences of UMNO-style exclusivist ethnic politics. For instance, some leaders reportedly had misgivings about the BA's more accommodative stances *vis-à-vis* non-Malay issues, including support for Chinese schools and proposals for more cultural liberalization.

At any rate, the formation of the BA was not merely a 'marriage of convenience', and enough leaders and members of the four parties subscribed to the democratic discourse. Through extended debate and considerable give and take, they reached agreement on the distribution of electoral seats,[3] on the contents of a joint manifesto 'For a Just Malaysia' (see Chapter 12), and even on a 'people-friendly' alternative budget which proposed increased public spending for social programmes.

A related development was the proliferation of NGOs and other independent groups which also made their voices heard in the run-up to the elections. Although it appeared that they were critical of the BN and its policies, these NGOs and new groups were also addressing their concerns to the BA and, indeed, to whomsoever wished to rule the country. They included:

1. The 'Women's Agenda for Change' which demanded that the laws be enforced to protect women's rights, and that these rights be furthered through new legislation;
2. The 'Citizens Health Initiative', which mobilized Malaysians from all walks of life to oppose the corporatization of general hospitals and other health services;
3. The 'People are the Boss' campaign involving Chinese youths who championed the original meaning of democracy;
4. The 17-Point 'Election Appeals' (*Suqiu*), which focused on issues of justice and democracy rather than specific Chinese issues, and was endorsed by more than 2000 Chinese associations;
5. The Election Watch or *Pemantau* organized by 'Budi', a new NGO, which rallied 40-odd non-government organizations to jointly monitor the electoral campaign and prepare a report of its findings;
6. A petition with about 50,000 signatories demanding a monthly wage scheme and better working conditions for plantation workers, several busloads of whom converged on the doorstep of Parliament to deliver their petition;
7. A coalition of NGOs, principally Indian-based, which called for an enquiry into the killing by the police on two separate occasions of eighteen Indians (including a pregnant woman), whom the police had suspected were criminals;
8. An unprecedented march through the streets of Kuala Lumpur in December, 1998, by some 300 lawyers in support of a colleague found guilty of 'contempt of court' for remarks uttered while defending Anwar Ibrahim;
9. Environmentalists who protested the continued resettlement of Sarawak natives despite the shelving of the Bakun hydro-electric project, as well as the proposed construction of the Selangor Dam which threatened the destruction of pristine forests and required eviction of indigenous peoples living in its area;
10 A mass campaign led by consumer organizations to encourage parliamentarians to pass the Consumers' Protection Act;
11. Artistes who parodied the unfolding events and protested against injustices through their compositions and songs, artworks and installations, performances and skits, verses, and (in one instance) an entire novel;
12. Many groups of ordinary Malaysians whose investments in housing development projects were now stalled on account of the economic crisis, and who now protested collectively against the developers and pressured the government to investigate their plight.

Most of the groups and initiatives mentioned above were not associated with the opposition coalition or directly concerned with the outcome of the election. But their emergence alongside the *reformasi* movement and the formation of the BA indicated that Malaysia was in political ferment. The impulses towards democracy demonstrated by them paralleled the burgeoning popular movement in the mid-1980s, which similarly called for 'rule of law', 'participatory democracy', 'accountability', etc., during an earlier period of economic recession. The latter momentum was nipped in the bud when more than 100 activists from opposition parties, educational bodies and NGOs were arrested under the Internal Security Act (ISA) during the so-called *Operasi Lalang* in October 1987 (Saravanamuttu 1992; and Loh 2000). Indeed, some of the demands for justice and democracy were foreshadowed in the struggles of the radical wing of the independence movement in the 1940s and 1950s, and of the leftist opposition in the 1960s.

Nonetheless, there was a significant difference between the previous democratic movements and that which emerged in the late 1990s. For the first time on this latter occasion, significant numbers of the Malay middle classes were involved. Previously supporters of the BN-UMNO government, these Malays now considered that government *zalim* (cruel) and *tak adil* (unjust) and expressed their anger openly. This change in attitude and orientation had everything to do with Anwar's unjust treatment, which for many Malay dissidents was considered to have breached 'traditional' norms and practices (Philip Khoo 1999). Since these dissidents had contact with the grassroots through organisations like ABIM (the Malaysian Islamic Youth Movement) and JIM (the Malaysian Reform Movement), they drew in lower-class Malay support too. Consequently, expectations ran high for a change of government in the forthcoming polls.

However, that change did not occur. The BN as the 14-party ruling coalition led by UMNO won 148 out of 193 parliamentary seats in the November 1999 general elections. Its two-thirds' majority in Parliament was maintained. In the face of the ferment, how does one explain the BN's triumph?

DEVELOPMENTALISM AND THE LIMITS OF DEMOCRATIZATION

Some analysts have resorted to the usual politics of ethnicism, and there is no doubt that ethnic sentiments were fanned, and ethnic separateness emphasized, by the ethnic-based component parties of the BN. There is much evidence of this in the *Barisan Nasional's* electoral campaign. As ethnic tensions heightened, the BN projected itself as the only proven and credible coalition capable of catering to the disparate needs and interests of Malaysia's multi-ethnic and multi-religious society. Accordingly, the new coalition, also composed of ethnic-based partners, was depicted as incapable of ruling Malaysia. In fact, ethnicism was only one of several factors behind the BN's electoral success, which was principally because of developmentalism.

With the end of the NEP in 1990, and with global trends towards privatization and economic deregulation, the private sector replaced the public as the engine of growth under the auspices of 'Malaysia, Inc.', and the National Development Plan, 1991 - 2000. The rapid economic growth rates registered in the early 1990s, and the resultant 'trickle down' provided new jobs and opportunities as well as improved living standards for most Malaysians, and this lasted until the 1997 financial crisis set in. The discourse of developmentalism came into its own amidst this economic growth. It coincided with the consolidation of Malaysia's middle classes involving all ethnic groups (Abdul Rahman Embong 1995).

Embraced by the middle classes, the new political culture places value on sustained economic growth that facilitates an improvement in material standards of living while also resulting in the spread of consumerist habits. Its corollary is an appreciation of the value of political stability, which many Malaysians believed could only be guaranteed by a strong BN-governed state even when authoritarian means were resorted to (Loh 2001a). Developmentalism, therefore, is the cultural consequence of the *dirigiste* developmental state when citizens begin to enjoy improved living conditions as a result of the economic growth the state has fostered. This developmentalism increasingly displaced the ethnic political discourse and practice in the 1990s. Two other related occurrences, namely, cultural liberalization and the consolidation of a politics of public works and services, further facilitated the displacement of ethnicism.

CULTURAL LIBERALIZATION AND UTILITARIAN GOALS IN THE 1990s

Largely for utilitarian reasons, various measures of 'cultural liberalization' were introduced to enhance economic growth in the early 1990s, especially when viewed from the perspective of non-Malays,. Specifically, UMNO leaders began to de-emphasize or redefine the most important emblems of Malay identity - the Malay rulers, Malay language and culture, and Islam - hitherto considered central attributes in defining the Malaysian nation-state (Loh 2001a).

The symbolic and actual powers of the Malay rulers were curtailed as a result of UMNO's challenges to the rulers in 1983 - 1984 and again in 1994. These challenges received widespread support from middle-class Malays. While reaffirming the status of Malay as the national language, Dr Mahathir's government also promoted use of the English language on utilitarian grounds, especially with the onslaught of globalization. For instance, English was promoted as the medium of instruction for certain technical subjects in the universities, a move partially reversing the policy introduced in 1971 of using Malay as the sole medium. In fact, the new Education Act 1996 formally empowered the education minister to exempt the use of Malay as the medium of instruction for certain purposes deemed necessary, even in secondary schools.

By introducing other Acts and amending existing ones pertaining to higher education, the government further facilitated the corporatization of public universities and establishment of private universities and branch campuses of foreign universities in Malaysia. Together with the expansion of the public universities, opportunities were made available to more Malaysians to pursue tertiary-level education, thereby alleviating the previously intense ethnic competition for limited places. The changes further allowed students enrolled in 'twinning colleges' attached to foreign universities to complete their entire university education locally, thereby allowing parents to save money. Other notable aspects of cultural liberalization were the promotion of non-Malay cultures by the Ministry of Culture, Arts and Tourism as a means of attracting the tourist dollar, and the increasing use of English in the mass media especially by privatized radio and television stations. With the introduction of cable and satellite television, pluralization of the mass media also occurred, and now offered choices to Malaysian audiences.

In response to Islamic resurgence, the BN government introduced various Islamization policies of its own, beginning from the 1980s. But it also distinguished itself by advocating a more liberal interpretation of Islam which emphasized the promotion of Islamic values in administration and society *writ large*, rather than the establishment of the Islamic state which PAS and other Muslim radicals advocated. The new policies hence appeared to stress a more inclusive notion of Malaysian nationhood. They also offered choices in the cultural realm, as a result of globalization and deregulation. Middle class Malaysians, and especially non-Malays, welcomed this cultural liberalization.

DELIVERING PUBLIC WORKS AND SERVICES

Coincidentally during this period of economic growth, the non-Malay BN parties disengaged themselves from 'sensitive' ethnic and cultural issues. They also de-emphasized political education and mobilization. Instead, they recast themselves as purveyors of development and providers of social services, the corollary of which was a redefinition of the meaning of politics itself.

Put simply, the non-Malay BN parties transformed themselves into extensions and instruments of the state, so as to assist in maintaining the status quo and in supplementing the delivery of public works and services. The major Chinese-based BN party - the Malaysian Chinese Association (MCA) - even established its own college, namely the Kolej Tunku Abdul Rahman, whose five campuses provided tertiary level education for some 20,000 students annually. Its Langkawi Project catered for the educational needs of primary school children by organizing tuition classes and supplying books and other resources, especially in Chinese new villages. Fundraising was also conducted on behalf of independent Chinese secondary schools during the 1990s while Kojadi, the MCA's savings cooperative, provided low-interest loans for children of cooperative members to attend universities and colleges (Loh 2001b).

The BN parties further established 'service centres' and complaints bureaus throughout the country. These were partially financed by the constituency development funds allocated by the government to elected politicians belonging to the BN. Lower-class Malaysians in particular turned to these centres instead of relevant government agencies in resolving their everyday problems and needs. The latter included applying for official documents, enrolling their children into schools of choice, acquiring business licences, repairing roads and drains, etc. In contrast to the perceived discrimination and neglect during the NEP years, there emerged via the efforts of the non-Malay BN parties a way in which ordinary non-Malays could receive benefits and identify positively, in many instances for the first time, with the BN government (Loh 2001b).

The BN parties as well as politicians also ventured into business activities in a major way, leading to many conflicts of interest. For through their connections, individuals and companies associated with BN parties successfully won privatization projects and benefited from the government's largesse. The end result was a deepening of patronage politics, nepotism and corruption (Gomez and Jomo 1997). In summary therefore, the BN political parties assumed new roles related to developmentalism. Ironically, BN rule was consolidated as the parties progressively disengaged from politics. This relates specifically to the BN's spectacular victory in the 1995 elections, when it polled more than 65 per cent of the popular vote and won four-fifths of all parliamentary seats. Just prior to those elections, the Islamic Movement *Darul Arqam* that had been banned in 1994, was successfully disbanded, while in October 1996, Semangat 46, the Malay opposition party created during the UMNO crisis of 1987/88, voted to dissolve itself. Its leader Tengku Razaleigh was reabsorbed into UMNO. Earlier in 1994, the BN had reversed its fortune in Sabah when it replaced the opposition *Parti Bersatu Sabah* which had ruled the state for the nine preceding years. Finally the *Parti Bangsa Dayak Sarawak* (PBDS), which had quit the Barisan coalition in Sarawak in 1987, returned to the BN fold in 1994 (Loh 2000).

Viewed from the perspective of these successes, the BN suffered a setback in 1999, although it triumphed in the election of that year. More than that, a closer look at the 1999 electoral results suggests that a major change might have occurred.

INTERPRETING THE 1999 ELECTORAL RESULTS

The Malays

UMNO's loss of seats in the 1999 polls was severe. The 94 parliamentary seats it previously held were reduced to 72, while the 231 state assembly seats in the peninsula (elections were not conducted for Sabah and Sarawak state seats) were cut to 175. Significantly, the total number of seats that UMNO now holds in Parliament is less than the total held by its BN partners. Hence the old claim to magnanimity - that UMNO can rule on its own but chooses to share power with others - is no longer tenable. Four ministers, several deputy ministers and parliamentary secretaries, and a *menteri besar* (the chief minister of a state) lost their seats. Many well-known UMNO leaders had their winning majorities drastically reduced, among them the education minister and long-standing UMNO vice-president, Najib Tun Razak, who won by a mere 241 votes.

There were in the 1999 elections 58 parliamentary constituencies in the peninsula where Malays accounted for more than two-thirds (66 per cent) of registered voters. UMNO won 27 of these seats, while the opposition won 31 (PAS 26 and Keadilan 5). Although UMNO still received 49 per cent of the popular vote in these constituencies, its share had dropped significantly from the 59 per cent polled in the 55 constituencies with two-thirds Malay majorities in 1995. In fact, UMNO polled even worse in 1999 than in 1990, when it faced a challenge from the PAS-Semangat 46 coalition and won 55 per cent of the vote in the 52 peninsula seats with two-thirds Malay majorities. In contrast, the number of PAS members of Parliament increased from 8 to 27 (including one in a mixed seat). PAS gained control of the Kelantan and Terengganu state assemblies, and won one-third of all state seats in Kedah.

However, the Malays did not desert UMNO altogether, for the latter gained almost half of the popular vote in the 58 constituencies. It also performed especially well in Johore and other southern states, while its percentage of votes in the four Malay heartland states of Kelantan, Terengganu, Kedah and Perlis, although reduced, remained significant. Hence in Kelantan, UMNO won only one of 14 seats, but its overall share of the popular vote was 37 per cent. In Terengganu UMNO failed to win any of the eight parliamentary seats but polled 41 per cent of the popular vote. And although UMNO captured only five seats to the eight won by PAS in Kedah, it in fact split the popular vote 50-50 with PAS (Maznah Mohamad 2001). Due to the first-past-the-post electoral system,[4] the number of seats captured often belied the percentage gained of the popular vote. Thus UMNO continued to enjoy considerable albeit reduced Malay support in 1999. But the Malay community was now clearly split down the middle. This situation was no longer restricted to Kelantan, whose longer-run behaviour in this respect is usually attributed to the state's sense of regionalism or some other peculiarity.

The Chinese

Some analysts have suggested that the BN would not have maintained its two-thirds majority in Parliament had it not been for overwhelming Chinese support. In fact, only about 51 per cent of the Chinese behaved in this manner. The claim that Chinese were not as significant as alleged by some is based on an analysis of the 24 urban constituencies in peninsular Malaysia where

Chinese constituted more than 50 per cent of the voters. Of these, the BN won 15 seats (MCA 12, Gerakan 3) and the opposition DAP nine seats. Moreover, when the six parliamentary seats in the peninsula with more than 80 per cent Chinese voters (namely Tanjung, Ipoh Timur, Batu Gajah, Kepong, Seputeh and Cheras) are examined, the BN only polled 45 per cent of the average popular vote and won one seat. The opposition DAP, on the other hand, polled 53 per cent of the vote and captured the remaining five seats.

That said, there is no denying that the Chinese swung from the DAP towards the BN in the 1995 elections, when the latter won 16 of the 24 Chinese majority seats while the DAP only managed eight. In the 1990 elections when 22 Chinese majority seats were at stake, the DAP won 18 to the BN's four. The statistics also show that the BN polled 53 per cent of the Chinese popular vote in 1995, up from 42 per cent in 1990, but that the share dipped slightly to 51 per cent in 1999. At any rate, it is inaccurate to claim that the 'Chinese factor' facilitated the BN's two-thirds majority win. To understand the voting pattern behind the BN's victory it is necessary to investigate the so-called 'mixed seats'.

The 'Mixed Seats'

In 1999, the 144 seats in peninsular Malaysia comprised 100 Malay majority seats, 24 Chinese majority seats and another 20 seats in which no ethnic group constituted a majority. The 100 Malay majority seats could be sub-divided into 58 with a more than two-thirds Malay majority and another 42 with 50-66 per cent Malay majorities. There was thus an undue apportionment of electoral constituencies, in the sense that the percentage of constituencies with Malay majorities (68.4 per cent) is disproportionate to the percentage of Malay voters in the electoral rolls (56.7 per cent).

In practice, the non Malay parties (whether in the BN or opposition), contested seats in constituencies with a Chinese majority and those where no ethnic group dominated, as well sometimes in Malay majority seats. In 1999, the *Barisan Alternatif* parties distributed the 144 peninsula seats three ways: those seats with a more than two-thirds Malay majority to the PAS, Chinese majority seats and those without any ethnic majority to the DAP, and the remainder - where Malays comprised 50-66 per cent of registered voters - to *Keadilan*. The parties then 'traded seats' among themselves, and also granted several seats to the smaller *Parti Rakyat Malaysia* and a few prominent non-government organization leaders. Ultimately, the PAS contested 60 parliamentary seats, the DAP 36, *Keadilan* 44, and the PRM 4. UMNO contested 92 of the 100 Malay majority seats in the peninsula, while the remaining 52 seats were shared amongst its non-Malay partners. Consequently, UMNO faced off against PAS (and a few *Keadilan* candidates) in constituencies with two-thirds Malay majorities, and contested *Keadilan* (and a few PAS candidates) in constituencies with 50-66 per cent Malay majorities.

The DAP, PRM and some non-Malay *Keadilan* candidates challenged the non-Malay BN candidates in seats with a Chinese majority and those without any ethnic dominance.

Apparently, the BN's past electoral strategy for winning elections was predicated on its capturing 60-70 per cent of those constituencies with two-thirds Malay majorities (it achieved 58 per cent in 1999), 20-30 per cent of Chinese majority seats (62 per cent in 1999), and 80 per cent of 'mixed' seats. These are defined as combining seats in constituencies without ethnic majority and those in constituencies with 50-66 per cent Malay majorities. There were 61 of these mixed seats in 1999, and in that year the BN won 60 of them while the DAP won one. All *Keadilan* candidates fielded in mixed seats lost, and that party's five seats were gained in constituencies with two-thirds Malay majorities. Hence the BN's sweep of mixed seats ensured its overall victory.

It was especially in mixed seats that the BN pushed its access to the '3 Ms' - media, machines and money - to the fullest advantage. In contrast, the recently-formed *Keadilan* had limited funds, no party machine to speak of, and virtually no access to the tightly controlled mainstream media. It was also in these mixed seats that the BN's resort to ethnic and religious propaganda worked best. Thus the BN parties instilled fear among non-Malays that a vote for any BA party amounted to a vote for PAS, and hence an Islamic state. All the cultural liberalization which had taken place would then be negated. Although BN propaganda of this nature was not at all convincing when a non-Malay BA candidate contested with another non-Malay BN candidate in one of the 24 Chinese majority seats, the propaganda apparently worked in mixed seats where non-Malay voters had to choose between two Malay candidates, one representing the BN-UMNO and the other the BA,.

Moreover, developmentalism was also being emphasised by the BN in its campaign. Non-Malays were reminded of the economic growth in the early 1990s with resultant higher standards of living, and of the new modus operandi for sharing development via delivery of services and goods by BN parties. It is likely for all these reasons that a most non-Malays in mixed seats rallied behind the BN. That said, the statistics indicate that the Chinese community, like the Malay one, was also split down the centre in the 1999 polls.

Marginal Seats

Finally, another indicator of the new politics was the increased number of 'marginal seats'. In 1999, 50 parliamentary seats were won narrowly, 26 by less than 5 per cent margins and another 24 by 5-10 per cent margins. In the event the BN won 29 of all these seats. These slim majorities reflected the clear divisions between ethnic groups, with coalitions facing each other in straight fights.

Considering the BN's advantages in terms of the '3 Ms', its access to and unabashed use of government facilities during its campaign, and its right as incumbent to call elections at its convenience as well as to restrict the campaign period to eight days, its victory was not unpredictable. However, if the BA, and in particular *Keadilan* and the DAP, can overturn some of these unfair BN advantages, there is a real possibility that the BN will, in future, be threatened in marginal seats. For with an additional 5 per cent swing in favour of the BA, the elections in the peninsula might have even ended in a dead heat.[5]

CONCLUSION

Prior to 1998, and especially outside the traditional stronghold of PAS in Kelantan, most Malays readily identified with UMNO and the BN government. Apart from cultural identification with the BN's nation-building project, there were goods and services to gain from supporting the government. But the NEP fostered the consolidation of the Malay middle classes, who developed their own interests and visions. The Anwar episode was a catalyst for certain middle-class Malays to break away from UMNO and the BN, where some joined PAS or rallied behind *Keadilan* and some even maintained a non-partisan but critical stance. These people constituted the core of the *reformasi* movement, and contributed towards the democratic ferment. Today the Malay community is more divided than it has ever been, in a situation that cannot be easily reversed.

The non-Malay middle classes had emerged earlier than their Malay counterparts, and been fragmented even longer. During the NEP years, a clear majority of non-Malays were critical of the BN government and voted for the opposition, although the latter did not really cater to their everyday material and ideational needs. However, since the early 1990s, about one-half of Chinese voters have identified themselves with the BN parties. This is a result of developmentalism, which was made tangible to them via increased business, work and educational opportunities, cultural liberalization, and the delivery of public works and services by BN parties. There hence emerged a new rationale for some non-Malays to identify with the BN government.

On account of the BN's 1999 electoral victory, some analysts have suggested that little has altered. But it is argued in this chapter that important changes have occurred. For apart from a considerable drop in the BN's popular vote, the results indicate that the Malays and the Chinese have split their votes between the BN and the BA *right down the middle*. More than one-third of the parliamentary seats in the peninsula were also won narrowly, suggesting that a change in government is a statistical possibility.

It is believed that the peculiarities of the 1999 electoral results mark a *permanent shift* and not merely a *temporary swing* in the pattern of voting behaviour. Accordingly, Malaysia has entered a new era of post-NEP politics. At any rate, the change alluded to is not a permanent displacement of the BN by the BA. Rather it is a shift from a predictable BN victory with a two-thirds majority to a situation wherein the BN might still win but is denied such dominance. An eventuality of this kind opens up the possibility of a change of government in subsequent elections, not just from the BN to the BA, but also from the BA to the BN, as a result of small swings in voting behaviour. It is believed that the contestations between ethnicism, democracy and developmentalism will persist for some time yet and continue to influence voting patterns.

NOTES

1. 'Ethnicism' is taken to mean the consolidation of a discourse and practice of politics which directs exclusive (rather than inclusive) notions of identity and consciousness, social relations and interests, and political representation and leadership, along ethnic lines. As a result ethnic groups in multi-ethnic societies are often pitted against one another, sometimes threatening political stability. Accommodationist or consociational arrangements are therefore required of political elites, who are supposedly more universalistic and even altruistic in their outlook. However, the ethnic tensions or conflicts occurring as a result of ethnicism are not a result of so-called 'primordial attachments'. They arise because identities, interests, mobilization and inter-group relations are constructed through privileging one's own ethnic group while marginalizing or erasing some 'other'.

2. Anwar's dismissal, arrest, prosecution and trial, together with the emergence of the *reformasi* movement and formation of the opposition front, are discussed in Chapters 8, 9 and 12. Khoo (2000) also comprehensively reviews these and related events. The impact of the economic crisis, as well as the contrasting responses by Anwar Ibrahim and Mahathir himself via the National Economic Action Council and the consequences thereof, are addressed in Chapters 2 and 3.

3. A 'seat' refers to the constituency or area for which an elected politician stands in Parliament, and by whose voting population the politician is elected.

4. A 'First-past-the-post electoral system' is one wherein the candidate who gains the highest number of votes in an electoral constituency, regardless of the percentage of votes polled, is proclaimed the winner. Consequently, in a three or four-cornered contest, it is possible that the winning candidate does not enjoy even a simple majority of the voters of his constituency.

5. The situation in Sabah and Sarawak where the democratic ferment has not yet caught on, has not been discussed in this chapter. The different circumstances of these states is partly due to their distinct historical backgrounds and ethnic compositions, as well as to their geographical distance from Kuala Lumpur, and the predominance of developmentalism (Aeria 1997; Loh 1996). Not surprisingly, the BN performed very well in the two Borneo states in 1999, securing 45 of the 48 seats at stake. The democratic ferment must also occur in Sabah and Sarawak if the changes envisioned in this chapter are to occur there as well.

8. Changing Power Configurations in Malaysia

Michael Ong

The view we take is that democratic government is the best and most acceptable form of government. So long as the form is preserved, the substance can be changed to suit the conditions of a particular country (Abdul Razak bin Hussien 1971).

In our democracy, the *rakyat* is in power...because of that, laws which are made by the peoples' representatives must be observed. Whoever ignores laws made by the Government elected by the *rakyat*, he is tantamount to denying democracy (Mahathir Mohamed 1988).

The arrest of former deputy prime minister, Datuk Anwar Ibrahim, has acted as a catalyst in Malaysian politics and resulted in perhaps the *beginnings* of a sea-change. There were street protests and demonstrations (although mainly by Malays), cooperation between many non-government organizations on a variety of public issues, and the formation of a new political party *Parti Keadilan Nasional* (National Justice Party) *(Keadilan)*. It should be noted that these activities occurred mainly around Kuala Lumpur. With the announcement of the November 1999 elections, the hitherto unthinkable, a new opposition coalition, the *Barisan Alternatif* (Alternative Front), which included *Keadilan*, the *Parti Rakyat Malaysia* (Malaysian Peoples' Party), the Democratic Action Party and the *Parti Islam SeMalaysia* (Malaysian Islamic Party) (PAS), was formed. Shamsul (1999, p. 3) has described these activities as signifying the birth of a 'new politics' movement:

> One that is not concerned simply about winning votes and general elections but more about articulating openly differences, plurality and dissent. It was a nationwide 'politics of resistance', a struggle for social justice, freedom of speech and democracy, hence an attempt to transform 'civil society' to 'democratic civility'.

This view, it is suspected, is an overstatement, and mistakes the actions of a part (the activists) as representing the whole (the entire nation). The confluence of these ferments and activities led many activists and observers to think that, for the first time since the 1969 elections, it was possible to deny the ruling *Barisan National* (National Front) (BN) its two-thirds majority. This was not to be.

The aim of this chapter is to explain why this threat to the BN was not really on the cards. It demonstrates that amendments to the Constitution and the introduction or tightening of existing laws by the ruling coalition since Independence in 1957 have severely affected the roles of elections, Parliament, the judiciary and other institutions, as well as the rules for civil participation in the political process. It is argued that these changes continue to limit present calls for reforms and open political discourse. To understand why these changes were made it is necessary to be refreshed with a bit of political history. More background on and a somewhat different interpretation of events described are given in Chapter 11.

THE MALAYAN UNION AND THE *MERDEKA* CONSTITUTION

After the Second World War, the British colonial government attempted to establish a single government, the Malayan Union, in place of the Federated and Unfederated Malay States and Straits Settlements of Penang and Malacca. The Union was strongly opposed by the Malays, on the grounds that it denied their sovereignty and would grant non-Malays equal citizenship rights. The latter was viewed with alarm, since it could result in the Malays becoming a minority. In the face of this opposition, which was led by Dato' Onn Jaafar, the United Malays National Organization (UMNO) was formed. Malay sovereignty was restored and conditions for non-Malays to gain citizenship made more difficult. British negotiations with UMNO, which were conducted in a way which clearly denied representations to the non-Malays at the most important stage of the Constitution making process, resulted in the Federation of Malaya Agreement of 1948.

This Agreement accepted a *quid pro quo* sanctified by the constitutional phrase 'the special interests of the Malays and the legitimate interests of the other communities'. The symbols of the new nation were distinctively Malay. They included a Malay head of state, the *Yang diPertuan Agong, Bahasa Malaysia* (the Malay language) as the national language, and Islam as the official religion, although other communities were permitted to practise their own religions. The political system of the federation was a constitutional monarchy based on the Westminster parliamentary system of government,[1] and, despite being a federation was highly centralized. With the approach of *Merdeka*, the Reid Constitutional Commission, in attempting to reconcile the contradiction between special privileges for the Malays and a common nationality, recommended that the special privileges be reviewed after fifteen years. This was strongly opposed by the Malays and deleted from the final report. Responsibility for underpinning the *quid pro quo* was given to the *Agong* and the Malay rulers who, as constitutional rulers, had to act on the advice of the prime minister and *menteri besar*(s) (the chief ministers of states).

In a nutshell, the Malays claimed that the land was theirs, and that it was on account of their generosity that non-Malays were given the privilege of citizenship. It was therefore assumed that their right to rule was not challengeable. On the other hand, non-Malays were prepared to accept the special provisions, on the assumption that when these were no longer needed, a united nation, based on equality, would be forged. This was one of the key 'ground rules' or *grundnorm*,[2] and attempts to change this Malay privilege rule have been the primary cause for crises and alterations in the political system.

Although part of the ruling Alliance coalition, the Malayan (later Malaysian) Chinese Association tried to obstruct the possibility of UMNO and the other Malay parties gaining a two-thirds majority on their own by demanding that it be allowed to contest 40 of the 104 constituencies in the 1959 elections. This resulted in Tunku Abdul Rahman, the prime minister and president of UMNO, choosing the 31 Association candidates without consulting that body's president, Dr Lim Chong Eu. Excluded from the list, Dr Lim subsequently resigned as president of the MCA. The brief challenge posed by the People's Action Party of Singapore to unite the majority of non-Malay parties, when Singapore was part of Malaysia in 1963 - 1965, was also interpreted as a threat to Malay political supremacy.

The riots of 13 May 1969 following the 1969 elections were seen as 'the growing political encroachment of the immigrant races against certain provisions of the Constitution, which relate to the Malay language and the position of the Malays' (National Operations Council 1969, p. ix). Writing after the events of 1969, Dr Mahathir Mohamed (1970, p. 121) declared:

> This is a basic contention of the Malays which is challenged by the other races. The Malays maintain that Malaya has always been, and still is, their land. If citizenship must be conferred to the other races who have settled down and made their home in Malaya, it is the Malays who must decide the form of citizenship, the privileges and the obligations. *On becoming citizens, the non-Malays share with the Malays not only the ownership of Malaysia, but also the specifications of what it is to be a citizen, what is the condition of citizenship itself, and what is therefore not to be changed by the new citizen* (Italics added).

Following the 1969 elections and subsequent riots a state of emergency was proclaimed, which led to the suspension of parliamentary government for 21 months. In the interim, the country was ruled by the National Operations Council, led by Tun Abdul Razak, the deputy prime minister. By incorporating most erstwhile opposition parties into the ruling coalition, the Alliance was expanded and renamed the *Barisan Nasional.* parliamentary democracy was restored in 1971, with the confidence that the Constitution could be amended to ensure the disaster of riots would never happen again. The amendments made, according to the then prime minister, Tun Haji Abdul Razak bin Dato Husein, had two broad objectives:

> Firstly, these amendments are intended to remove certain sensitive isues from the realm of public discussion so as to ensure a smooth and continuing function of parliamentary democracy in this country. Secondly, they are intended to redress the racial balance in certain sectors of the nation's life in so far as this imbalance can be rectified by legislation. (Abdul Razak bin Hussien 1972, p. 3).

The 'sensitive issues' referred to were citizenship, the national language, Malay special privileges, and the sovereignty of the Malay rulers. The amendments were further entrenched so they could not be altered without the consent of the conference of rulers. Members of Parliament were also deprived of their parliamentary immunity on these issues, although they were able to question the implementation of the provisions as specified by law. The Sedition Act, 1948, was similarly amended. Thus the particular 'ground rule' outlined above could no longer be questioned. Politically, the nature of the coalition and government was also changed from a relatively cooperative alliance dominated by UMNO to one wherein UMNO was supreme. On the day Tun Abdul Razak became the prime minister he said, 'this government is based on UMNO and I surrender its responsibilities to UMNO in order that UMNO shall determine its form, and it must implement policies which are determined by UMNO' (Funston 1980, p. 225).

The fact that there were other parties in the ruling coalition seemed irrelevant. Nevertheless, their role within the BN provided a veneer of non-Malay inputs in the decision and policy-making processes of the government.

THE ELECTORAL SYSTEM

Since independence, Malaysia has conducted ten national elections. With the exception of the 1969 elections, they were conducted without major incidents and the ruling coalition was returned with a two-thirds majority. This impressive record, however, does not reveal the changes in rules of the game since the 1959 elections.

The electoral system of Malaysia is based on the 'first past the post' British model (see note 4, p. 105), and has resulted in an over-representation of seats held by the ruling parties compared to the percentage of votes won by them. Even when the ruling coalition polled only 47.6 per cent of the popular vote in 1969 (its lowest registered), it won 63.2 per cent of the seats. There is also the added factor in the varying number of voters in the constituencies as they reflect rural Malays and urban non-Malays. As the result of various constitutional amendments since the early 1960s and the decline of an independent Election Commission, the electoral advantages of the ruling coalition, in particular of UMNO, have been strengthened.

Under the Constitution, the Election Commission, consisting of a chairperson and three others including one each to represent Sabah and Sarawak, was responsible for conducting elections, keeping electoral rolls and reviewing the delineation of the country into constituencies. The *Agong*, in consultation with the conference of rulers appointed Commission members. Members had tenure of office until the age of sixty-five, subject to Parliament. A member could not be removed, except in like manner to the removal of a judge in the Federal Court.

In the early years of the Commission's life, it was highly regarded by the public. Its first task was to prepare for the 1959 elections. The 104 new constituencies were drawn from the 52 existing ones used to conduct the 1955 pre-independence elections. However, unlike the 1955 constituencies, the rural-urban weightage[3] was reduced from 50 per cent to 15 per cent, as provided by the *Merdeka* Constitution. The delineation was achieved with 'a scrupulous concern for the fairness of division' (Moore, 1960). In the 1959 elections the Alliance coalition, despite the doubling of non-Malay votes, won 74 of the 104 seats compared to 51 of the 52 in 1955. After the elections, the Commission, as required by the Constitution, undertook to redraw the constituencies. Its report on this matter, although seen as producing delineations 'almost perfectly equitable to electors in urban and rural locales' (McDougall 1968), was viewed with alarm by the Alliance coalition. This was because the coalition felt the divisions would adversely affect its future electoral fortunes.

In 1962, the Alliance government decided to amend the Constitution, and rejected the 1960 Delineation Report of the Election Commission. The Constitution (Amendment) Act 1962 reduced both the powers and independence of the Commission. Members' retiring age was now subject to Parliament, which could by law provide for their terms and office in matters other than their remuneration. The Commission's powers to change the boundaries of constituencies was reduced to that of 'recommending' alterations to Parliament which, having been given the amendments, became the final arbiter on the basis of *a simple parliamentary majority*. Rural-urban weightage was restored to the pre-Independence 50 per cent. As noted by Groves (1964), an authority on the Constitution:

> It is apparent that the (1962) amendments as to the elections have converted a formerly independent Election Commission, whose decisions became law and whose members enjoy permanent tenure, into an advisory body of men of no certain tenure whose terms of office, except for remuneration, are subject to the whims of Parliament. The vital power of determining the size of constituencies as well as their boundaries is now taken from the Commission...and has been made completely political by giving this power to a transient majority in Parliament, whose temptation to gerrymander districts and manipulate the varying numerical possibilities between 'rural' and 'urban' constituencies for political advantage is manifest. It is perhaps unworthy of comment that the Constitution does not offer any criteria for the determination of what is 'rural' and what is 'urban.'

Apart from the amendments, the appointments of other members of the Commission were seen as more responsive to the interests of the Alliance than to those of other parties (McDougall 1968).

The role of the Commission was further restricted by the Constitution (Amendment) No. 2, Act 1973. This increased the total number of parliamentary constituencies by ten, and fixed the numbers of both parliamentary and state seats in each state. That meant the Commission could no longer increase the number of seats, unless there was a constitutional amendment. Of crucial importance was the deletion of the rural-urban weightage. The amendment meant that there was enormous disparity in the weightage given to the rural areas, complete without constitutional sanctions, leading to a huge disparity between rural and urban seats. In the 1999 elections the largest constituency was Ampang Jaya in Selangor with 98,527 voters, and the smallest Hulu Rajang in Sarawak with 16,018 voters. The smallest seat in Peninsular Malaysia was Langkawi in Kedah with 23,081 voters.

It should be pointed out that the constituencies with larger numbers of voters are in the urban areas where non-Malay opposition parties are strongest. Where opposition parties have been able to mount a serious electoral challenge, as in 1969, the ruling coalition has not hesitated to dissipate their strength through its ability to amend the Constitution at will. The establishment of the federal territory, carved out from Selangor after the riots of 1969, is a case in point. Voters in the territory could now no longer vote in the Selangor state elections. In 1969, the combined opposition won 14 of the 28 state seats while in 1974, after the creation of the territory, they won only one seat. The Democratic Action Party claimed at the time that one million voters were disenfranchized. It hence appears that through gerrymandering the constituencies the electoral challenges of the non-Malay opposition have continually been checked. The most recent example of gerrymandering is the case of Sabah. Following the delineation exercise in 1995, the opposition *Parti Bersatu Sabah* became increasingly marginalized in the polls.

There have also been regular complaints and allegations of missing and 'phantom' voters in every election. Again, opposition candidates have been disqualified on technicalities on nomination day. The long delay of nine months in the registration of an estimated 680,000 new voters for the 1999 elections, despite the availability of modern technology, meant they could not vote, and was seen too as advantageous to the coalition. These new voters accounted for about 8 per cent of the total electorate, and could perhaps have made a significant difference in a number of the constituencies contested.

There are two outcomes of the amendments and changes discussed. Firstly, they will ensure that the coalition will always win electoral contests, since their unstated aim was to contain the growing electoral challenge of the mainly non-Malay opposition parties in the 1960s and 1970s. The assumption was that in the urban seats the non-Malay, mainly Chinese, votes would be split between the opposition and the non-Malay party of the coalition, and that urban Malays, voting for the coalition, would determine the outcome in those seats. Secondly, apart from pockets in the east and northern parts of Peninsular Malaysia, the smaller rural seats were assumed to be secure, and places where UMNO would always be able to rely on majority Malay support.

The 1999 elections results upset some of these calculations. With a divided UMNO, an increasingly independent Malay middle class, and a resurgent *Parti Islam SeMalaysia*, there occurred some change in Malay voting patterns in both urban and especially rural seats. These developments resulted in significant

PAS victories in the smaller rural seats. Ironically, the urban Chinese voters, previously supporters of the opposition but now perhaps fearful of the establishment of an Islamic state by PAS via its participation in the *Barisan Alternatif,* helped *Barisan National* candidates in the urban seats. More than that it appears that UMNO and the BN generally further relied on non-Malay support for success in semi-rural seats as well. These *volte face,* which are examined in detail in Chapter 7, have reversed previous assumptions about political behaviour in Malaysia.

Finally, other factors also affected the free operation of the electoral system. These were the ban on public rallies, the use of government resources by the ruling coalition candidates, and a shortening of the campaign period - from just over a month before 1969 to just over a week in the 1990, 1995 and 1999 elections. There was as well the role of the mass media, which was particularly hostile to the opposition during elections. Since the 1980s, the mass media were either owned by the government or by companies owned by parties of the ruling coalition, and were also governed by the Printing Presses and Publication Act which, through various amendments, increasingly restricted press freedom. In contrast to providing wide and favorable coverage to the BN campaign and liberally carrying BN advertisements, the mainstream presses only highlighted negative reports of the opposition, and rarely carried their advertisements. Consequently the opposition parties resorted during the electoral campaign period to publishing their own broadsheets and pamphlets, producing and distributing their own audio- and video-cassettes, and increasingly employing the internet. The latter, however, was only available to less than 5 per cent of the population. While in elections prior to 1999 some *pro rata* time was given to political parties by government radio stations depending on the number of seats contested, even this limited access was denied in the elections of that year.

Ultimately, changes in the electoral system and other related curbs have stifled competitive elections and enabled the ruling coalition to consolidate its power. Yet on being elected, elected opposition members are further confronted by a Parliament whose rules and procedures have also been subjected to drastic changes in favour of the coalition.

PARLIAMENT

Parliament in Malaysia consists of the *Yang diPertuan Agong* (the King), the *Dewan Rakyat* (the House of Representatives), and the *Dewan Negara* (the Senate). The Senate has never played an effective role in the affairs of the nation. Most of its members are appointed by the states, and the rest by the *Agong* upon the advice of the prime minister. The *Agong's* role is largely symbolic, and his discretionary powers (as well as those of the sultans) have been curbed as a result of constitutional amendments in 1983 and 1993. The concern here is with the *Dewan Rakyat*.

In considering changes to parliamentary procedures it is necessary to be mindful of Parliament's functions which, amongst others, are to debate and deliberate on proposed laws before their legislation, to authorize finance for government, and to hold the government accountable for its actions and decisions. Given the government's majority, it is inevitable that its proposed legislation will be passed.

The rules and procedures of Parliament are made by the Standing Orders Committee and chaired by the speaker who, since 1964, has not needed to be a member of the House. The membership of the Committee reflects the relative strength of the various parties in the *Dewan Rakyat*. An examination of its reports over the years reveals that it was only during the first Parliament (1959 - 1963) that opposition suggestions were considered. Since then the views of the opposition have rarely been taken into account, while its proposals have been rejected *in toto,* as in 1965 and 1973. Consequently, the Standing Orders Committee's reports were usually challenged to no avail by opposition parties when tabled in Parliament. As a result of effective opposition of this nature, particularly on the part of the Democratic Action Party, the majority of the original Standing Orders were amended in 1972 to 1974 to restrict such activity.

But in general the changes to the Standing Orders have undermined the public accountability of the government. Contrary to Westminster practice, the chairman of the Public Accounts Committee has always been a member of the ruling coalition. Since 1962, individual members (read opposition MPs) of this Committee have no longer been allowed to subpoena witnesses. This ruling also applies to other parliamentary committees.

Other parliamentary means of making the government accountable have also been curbed or 'sabotaged', as has occurred for Question Time, Adjournment Speeches or Urgent Motions. For instance, until the early 1990s parliamentarians were allowed to ask up to 20 oral and five written questions at any one meeting of the *Dewan*. This allowance was reduced to ten oral questions in December 1997. Contrary to past practice when a particular minister was required to be present to answer questions concerning his or her portfolio, nowadays *any* minister or deputy minister may answer on behalf of another minister. Again, Adjournment Speeches, which require the relevant minister to reply, have also been sabotaged through lack of a quorum, with coalition members deliberately leaving the chamber when such speeches are begun by opposition parliamentarians. Urgent motions have rarely been allowed, as rules have been tightened. Opposition motions have likewise rarely seen the light of day.

In practice, the views of the opposition and its proposed amendments are rarely taken into account. Amendments to laws such as the Industrial Co-ordination Act 1975 and the Constitution Amendment Act 1983 have been the result of *external pressures* even though these same issues might have been raised during their legislative process. Conceivably, this is because the legislative process is interpreted as a 'zero-sum game', and any concession to the opposition is seen as a sign of weakness. Moreover, and despite opposition complaints over the years, members are often given limited time to prepare their comments on and debate the government budget while important Bills are often only made available to them at the last minute, just before the first reading. The duration of debate on major legislation such as the budget has also been reduced. Whereas previously ten days was common, by 1997 it was cut to eight days. In 1999, members were further limited to speak for only ten minutes each during the Budget Debate.

Opposition members in the early 2000s were at best tolerated, so as to present a veneer of democracy. Unless there were parliamentary reforms, which were called for by the opposition but ignored by the BN coalition, it was unlikely that a denuded Parliament would be able to look after the interests of the public.

RULE BY LAW

Participation in politics, unless in support of the coalition, is not for the faint-hearted. The ruling coalition since 1959 has used its parliamentary majority to amend the Constitution, and to enact and amend laws to limit the role and participation, not only of the opposition, but also of key groups which potentially could pose a check on governmental power (Rais Yatim 1995). Despite this, there have still been committed individuals and groups prepared to take positions on important issues. In fact there have been cases when pressures from affected interests have modified existing laws.

An instance in point was opposition by non-government organizations to the 1985 amendments to the *Societies Act*. At that time Dr Mahathir had criticized the activities of non-government organizations as 'challenging the authorities and arrogating to themselves powers which did not belong to them' (*New Straits Times* 1985). According to him:

> the reaction of the legitimate authorities to the disruptive challenges to their authority is either to become…more repressive or to retreat from their responsibility. The latter will result in anarchy, which in turn will attract forces keen on a seizure of power. Once this happens, the usurper will discard democracy and resort to repression in order to stay in power. Either way, disruptive challenges to authority in a democracy will lead to repression and the death of democracy.

The problem was that the government decided what activities were 'disruptive'. The possibility of dialogue and negotiations on public issues appeared to be dismissed in the above statement. This was either repression or an abnegation of responsibility. Yet in the *Societies Act* case which threatened to much reduce the potential of non-government organizations, the government was in the end forced to withdraw the amendment, as elaborated below.

It should be recalled that after the restoration of democracy in 1971, the government announced that the country would be guided by the five tenets of the *Rukun Negara*, or National Ideology. Among these tenets was the principle of 'the rule of law', with its normally accepted meaning of fair laws underpinned by a judiciary able to rule on abuses of power. However, in practice, the circumstances in Malaysia have meant increasingly the operation of *rule by law*.

Firstly in relation to this, it should be noted that the emergency powers provided under Article 150 of the Constitution were invoked on four occasions - the 1964 Indonesian Confrontation, the 1966 Sarawak Crisis, the 1969 Emergency Powers and the 1977 Kelantan crisis - and have not been repealed. As noted by Rais Yatim (1995, p. 242):

> Over the years, these powers have grown by leaps and bounds, far exceeding the necessities of any emergency and by 1981 the courts have been totally barred from reviewing the subjective finding of the *Agong...on behalf of the executive* under Article 150. The amendments introduced leave neither residual routes nor opportunities through which to test in a court of law acts of the executive during an emergency rule (italics added).

In addition, there are at least 14 acts of Parliament that grant the government wide discretionary powers which inhibit the operations of a normal democratic society. The legislation involved includes the Internal Security Act (ISA), which was transformed from the British colonial government's Emergency Regulations 1948, drawn up in response to the rebellion led by the Malayan Communist Party. The ISA provides, amongst other things, for detention without trial, and has been used against political opposition and leaders of non-government organizations. It was employed in this way, for example in the *Operasi Lalang* of 1987.[4] In 1988, legislation to amend the ISA was rushed through Parliament and made effective on 14 July to prevent a *habeas corpus* hearing involving the Democratic Action Party's Lim Kit Siang from being heard. The judge said that had it not been for the amendment, the government's action would have been illegal (Rais Yatim 1995, pp. 289 - 290). Under the ISA, the Emergency (Security Cases) Regulations 1975 were introduced to apply to criminal cases with contested procedures. Since 1989 ministerial decisions, except rules and procedures, have been no longer subject to judicial review.

Since the Trade Union Act 1959 was promulgated, trade unionists have been barred from holding party political office, although they can be nominated as party candidates. This Act was clearly aimed at preventing opposition party leaders from developing close ties with the unions. Again, the Universities and Universities Colleges Act 1971 forbids academics and students from political activities, except with the permission of their vice-chancellor. The Societies

Act (1966) requires all societies to be registered with the Registrar of Societies. The amendment of this Act in 1981 further required societies to declare whether they were 'political' or 'friendly', and gave wide powers to the Registrar in examining their foreign contacts. It was in opposition to these amendments that Anwar Ibrahim and the Islamic Youth Movement joined up with other non-government organizations, and when due to the efforts led by Anwar there was a widespread public outcry which led to the removal of some key clauses.

The Sedition Act 1948 is aimed at restricting the scope of discussion of political matters. Following the 1969 riots, the Act was amended, widening the scope of sedition to cover 'sensitive issues'. It was under this Act that the former opposition MP and Democratic Action Party youth leader, Lim Guan Eng, was charged and convicted in 1997. The Legal Profession (Amendment) Act 1984 removed the clause enabling the Bar Council to advise the government in certain areas. Nowadays rules made by the Council have to be approved by the attorney general, who is empowered to amend the rules even after they have been passed by the Council. Apparently, the amendments to the Legal Profession Act were made without the knowledge of the Council.

The Official Secrets Act 1972 and its amendments in 1983 were seen by Lim Kit Siang of the Democratic Action Party as including a 'super catch all clause' as an instrument to cow and curb press freedom. Under the Act, any information held by an official is deemed to be a secret, and breaches involve a mandatory custodial sentence.

Freedom of the press, which is not listed in the section of the Constitution on fundamental liberties, is subject to parliamentary restrictions and is controlled under the Printing Presses and Publication Act 1984. This Act requires the printers and publishers of all publications to apply for an annual permit for these materials, where this may be cancelled at any time if the publication breaches conditions set by the minister. Ministerial action, according to deputy prime minister Abdullah Badawi in explaining recent actions taken against the *Parti Islam SeMalaysia* publication, *Harakah*, is based on the law and not on the political beliefs involved. Over the years a number of local publications (*Sin Chew Jit Poh*, The Star, *Watan*, *Thootan*, The Rocket, and recently *Detik*, *Wasilah*, *Eksklusif* and *Tamadun*) have been banned for a period, or faced delays in acquiring their annual permits.

The mass media of press, radio and television are either owned by the government or by companies owned by the coalition parties. Their veracity has declined, and is viewed with distrust by increasing numbers of Malaysians. Even mainstream media journalists have grown more and more concerned with their own role. In a recent memorandum to the deputy prime minister calling for the establishment of a press council, these journalists stated that questions had been raised about the media's credibility, not just by the opposition parties and long-time critics of the government but by ordinary members of the public. They added that 'troubling still are accusations that local journalists are merely a part of the government's propaganda machine' (Malaysiakini.com 2000). According to the journalists, this had resulted in the public's turning to other sources - the foreign press, the internet and opposition newspapers such as *Harakah* - for news.

The Printing Presses and Publication Act also allows the Minister to ban foreign publications deemed to be prejudicial to public order, and his decisions are not subject to judicial review. Since August 1999 foreign journalists have been required to apply for a press card from the police. The police have meantime established a unit to monitor contents of sites and newsgroups for information and messages which could affect public security. With the help of the Malaysian Institute of Microelectronics System, an internet provider, four people were arrested for spreading rumours of rioting via the internet.

Rule by Law has thus been growing incrementally, but it was not until the crisis involving the sacking of Tan Sri Salleh Abas, then lord president of the judiciary, and two other senior judges, as well as the promulgation of the Constitutional (Amendment) Act 1988, that the *coup de grace* was made (Rais Yatim 1995, chapter 7). In this situation adverse decisions by the judiciary in a number of cases involving UMNO and the government were to result in the curtailment of its independent powers by Dr Mahathir, whose 'understanding or rather his misunderstanding of the concept of the separation of powers has been quite extraordinary' (Rais Yatim 1995, p. 309).

In this regard, an international report has noted that:

> the central problem appears to lie in the actions of the various branches of an extremely powerful executive, which has not acted with due regard for the other essential elements of a free and democratic society based on the just rule of law. Such due regard requires both a clear grasp of the concept of the separation of powers and also an element of restraint by all branches of the executive. These have not always been evident. There must be a truly independent judiciary, fully prepared at all times to do justice for all (International Bar Association 2000, p. 77).

For Rais Yatim (1995, p. 206), this unhealthy situation emerged 'through the utilisation of Parliament's law making authority' and consequently 'judicial power is only to be allowed in the form that the executive allows'. The result is that 'the nature of judicial attitude has been one of docility and a general atmosphere of timidity is in the air' (ibid., p. 329). The late Tun Mohamed Suffian, another former lord president, stated just before his death in 2000 that 'the public perception is that the judiciary as a whole can no longer be trusted to honour their oath of office...and I wouldn't like to be tried by today's judges, especially if I am innocent' (Mohamed Suffian 2000).

With restrictive laws and a judiciary which is perceived as being compliant, it is perhaps not a coincidence that multi-million ringgit legal suits are now the order of the day to silence the opposition and critics. The checks and balances of the political system have been severely weakened by restrictive laws, made by a Parliament denuded of its traditional roles, and without an independent judiciary to administer justice.

CONCLUSION

This chapter has shown how the Westminster system of parliamentary democracy, as provided by the *Merdeka* Constitution of 1957, has been so severely modified that only its form remains. Democracy *à la* Malaysia is one that is determined currently by Dr Mahathir, who has built on past restrictions imposed by his predecessors. His views on the subject provide little comfort for those who advocate change towards a more democratic situation.

As shown, the constitutional changes and the introduction and amendments to various laws were initially aimed to limit the challenges and activities of non-Malay opposition to the government. However, once on the statute books it should be noted that they could apply equally to opponents within the ruling coalition and particularly UMNO. The question is whether the system, evolved to deal with communal issues and the entrenchment of UMNO, can be transformed to deal with a changing Malaysian society. The issues of good governance raised by a new generation of Malaysians will not go away. The danger is that, in order to arrest UMNO's weakening support in its traditional areas and on grounds of the need for Malay unity, UMNO may seek to revert to the politics of the past.

It is ironic that the 1999 elections and the BN's strategy of divide and rule saw a united opposition, despite differences in a number of key areas. The *Barisan Alternatif* remained a nascent and fragile plant, and following the elections there were internal centrifugal pressures. Coupling this with a reversion to the politics of the past by a still powerful UMNO, the *Barisan Alternatif* needed committed leaders and discipline of a high order within all parties. This was required to ensure that the sea-change in Malaysian politics was sustained and, ultimately and ironically, achieved the united *Bangsa Malaysia* of Dr Mahathir's dream.

NOTES
1.   This parliamentary system is that operating in the United Kingdom.
2.   The various *grundnorm* are explored further in Chapter 11.
3.   This is the weightage given to rural as opposed to urban constituencies
4.   *Operasi Lalang* or 'Operation Wild Grass' was the code name of a police swoop which resulted in the detention of 118 politicians and activists, many from NGOs (It is interesting to note that *Lalang*, or *Imperata Cylindrica*, is a grass spreading inconspicuously but speedily through a system of underground stems which may only be controlled by very drastic treatment).

9. The Anwar Trial and its Wider Implications

William Case

Malaysian audiences were astonished during 1998 by the fall from grace of the country's deputy prime minister and minister of finance, Anwar Ibrahim. Long identified as successor to the prime ministership, Anwar was abruptly sacked from his government and party positions, arrested and jailed, beaten while in custody, hauled into court on corruption and sexual misconduct charges, then convicted and sentenced to six years in jail. Nor did the recrimination stop even there. Close associates of Anwar were purged systematically from government agencies, corporate boardrooms, and media organizations. Further, those who in late 1998 mounted street protests on his behalf - a broad coalition of Malay youths, middle-class liberals, and Islamicists - were confronted by security forces and often harshly interrogated. Finally, after the government secured Anwar's conviction on the corruption charges but failed to prove sexual misconduct, it ordered a second trial in mid-1999. Anwar was this time convicted on all counts, thus supplementing his initial sentence with an additional nine years and greatly extending his time in Malaysia's political wilderness. To be sure, his fate continues at some level to galvanize reformist and Islamicist sentiments. But with his trials concluded and his public appearances now limited, Anwar's political role would seem to have been diminished.

This chapter begins by providing some brief background to the case of Anwar Ibrahim. Its main aim, however, is to examine the role of the judiciary in Anwar's downfall, especially with respect to his first trial. How did disputes over the government's economic policy, culminating finally in Anwar's 'testing' Mahathir's leadership, filter into Malaysia's judiciary? Did the judiciary then deal impartially with Anwar, giving legitimacy to his removal from office? Or was the institution itself debased by the nature of its proceedings? In answering these questions, this chapter considers some assessments made by critical journalists and international observers. But it gives most attention to the written summation of the presiding judge, Augustine Paul. The chapter also briefly recounts Anwar's second trial, while noting his several appeal actions. It concludes by briefly exploring some of the broader political implications for Malaysia's political stability and development.

BACKGROUND TO THE ANWAR TRIAL

Malaysia, like many countries in East Asia, was gravely affected by the economic crisis that hit the region in 1997, and by the consequent contraction in 1998 of the country's economy (Jomo 1998). Accordingly, prime minister Mahathir's socio-economic policies, long geared to rapidly industrializing while 'breeding' indigenous Malay capitalists, now encountered great setbacks. He thus roundly denounced international currency traders, speculative investors, and the International Monetary Fund (IMF) for running his small economy down (*Far Eastern Economic Review* 1997).

Moreover, in attempting to keep Malay business people afloat, Mahathir met resistance from his deputy prime minister and finance minister, Anwar Ibrahim. In brief, where Mahathir saw a necessary promotion of Malay business people so as to better distribute wealth across ethnic lines, Anwar saw favouritism and corrupt practices. And where Mahathir now undertook to 'assist' Malay businesses in coping with the crisis, Anwar feared cronyist 'bail-outs'. In this context, some of Mahathir's expansionary measures were countermanded by Anwar, introducing an austerity more attuned to the preferences of the International Monetary Fund, even if Malaysia avoided the Fund's formal embrace (*Business Week* 1998, p. 26). Of course, in imposing austerity on an already contracting economy, Anwar may have exacerbated the crisis, tipping Malaysia's economy more swiftly into recession in much the same way as the Fund had in Indonesia, Thailand, and South Korea (Sachs 1999, p. 11). But the measures also enabled Anwar to enhance his standing before Western governments and financial institutions, augmenting the already extensive personal and Islamic contacts he had established throughout Southeast Asia and the Muslim world. One notes too that Anwar solidified these relationships with great personal charm, contrasting sharply on the global scene with the irascibility of Mahathir.

The prime minister thus brooded, seeming to fear that his deputy was eclipsing him. Anwar, in turn, encouraged by his reformist views and personal ambitions, then tested Mahathir's leadership - although he avoided a full challenge. Nonetheless, in making his probe, Anwar acted in one of the most critical arenas of Malaysian politics, namely, the annual general assembly of the country's dominant political party, the United Malays National Organization (UMNO) (Case 1999, pp. 4 - 5). Specifically, at the June 1998 meeting, Anwar's supporters criticized Mahathir openly for his opaque distributions of state contracts and special share issues. Indeed, they invoked the idioms of *korupsi, kolusi, dan nepotism* (corruption, collusion and nepotism), coined during the Indonesian struggle, and thus drew stark parallels between Mahathir and Suharto. However, Mahathir had evidently been forewarned, enabling him to respond the next day by unveiling some lists at the assembly of those who had received government favours. Prominent among the names were some of Anwar's family members and closest allies. Thus, a chastened Anwar pledged his support for Mahathir's continued leadership in his final address. He also promised to help reflate the economy through a new fiscal stimulus package of housing construction and infrastructure.

Mahathir, though, was unmollified. He recollected the ways in which Anwar had earlier gained the UMNO deputy presidency - and hence, the deputy prime ministership - at the general assembly in 1993, a year in which party elections had been held. Anwar, after pledging that he would not challenge the incumbent, quietly activated his networks and energized enough grass-roots support that he soon became unstoppable (Case 1994). Mahathir may well have feared that Anwar would do the same to him when the UMNO next held its party elections, scheduled for 1999.

Hence, on 1 September 1998 Mahathir confronted Anwar, demanding that his deputy resign from government or face a campaign of 'humiliation' (*Business Week* 1998, p. 29). Anwar, though, refused 'to go quietly', insisting that their rift be publicly exposed by his formal sacking. Mahathir responded first by imposing new capital controls - pegging the Malaysian ringgit to the United States dollar and blocking the outflow of capital gains - and then by ordering Anwar's removal on the next day. He also pressured the UMNO Supreme Council to expel his deputy from the party. However, while Anwar had probably found greater international favour than Mahathir, the capital controls meant that his ouster exerted no further downward pressure on the ringgit.

Anwar then took to the streets, mobilizing mass followings with reformist and Islamicist appeals. In this way, the largest demonstrations in Kuala Lumpur in recent decades took place round the national mosque and Independence Square - at precisely the moment that Mahathir stood a few kilometres away in the national stadium, presiding alongside Queen Elizabeth over the closing ceremonies of the Commonwealth games. Shortly afterwards, Anwar was detained under the Internal Security Act through a heavy-handed police raid on his official residence.

ANWAR IS CHARGED

During the 1950s, the British introduced the principle of preventive detention in Malaya in order to suppress the communist insurgency. But after the insurgency ended and independence was won, the new government perpetuated this principle, enshrining it in the Internal Security Act which is further addressed in Chapter 11. At first, the Act was mostly deployed against opposition leaders and trade unionists, and those who were identified by the government as fomenting class grievances. But as its use grew more habitual, social activists, Chinese educationists, and even arsonists and forgers were targeted, finally drawing much local and international criticism. Hence, the government began in the 1990s to make greater use of judicial procedures, working through proxies to mount lawsuits against dissident journalists and academics.

Accordingly, the government's reverting to the use of the Internal Security Act against Anwar drew new rounds of international criticism, some of which called into question Mahathir's commitments to the 'open skies' policy associated with the Multimedia Super Corridor, thus alarming investors (see, for example, Toffler 1998). Anwar's detention under the Act was thus quickly rescinded. However, the Attorney-General then laid criminal charges against him, involving five counts of sexual misconduct and five (later reduced to four) of corrupt practices under the Emergency (Essential Powers) Ordinances 2 (1). These charges appeared calculated to tarnish Anwar's image as a reformer and devout Muslim, so disillusioning his followers that he would never again be able to challenge Mahathir. Indeed, there could be no doubt about the political nature of the case against Anwar. As Mahathir himself lamented in an interview with the *Los Angeles Times*, 'He tried to overthrow me. He's the one who turned the issue into a political problem' (Lamb 1999).[1]

But to what extent could the judiciary lend legitimacy to Mahathir's removal of Anwar? On the one hand, Malaysia has rigorously perpetuated the outward forms and procedures of an independent judiciary - equally a legacy of British colonial experience. Judges and lawyers are still frequently trained at London's sundry 'inns' and 'temples'. The capital of Kuala Lumpur abounds in law offices and partnerships, the Bar Council appears well-resourced, an air of professionalism pervades most trial proceedings, and court judgements are scrupulously recorded in staid law journals. At the same time, Malaysia's executive has so tightened its grip over the judiciary that for more than a decade, an important political case has not been won against it. In 1988, and as detailed in Chapter 8, Mahathir's government deposed the then lord president, Tan Sri Salleh Abas, along with a number of Supreme Court judges, thus warding off a challenge to his political paramountcy (Lawyers' Committee on Human Rights 1989).

These removals, firmed by much subsequent judicial reorganization, have since encouraged great pliancy on the bench (Khoo 1999; and Rais 1995). In addition, while Malaysia's judiciary remained credited with a capacity at least to dispense justice in ordinary criminal and commercial cases, even this seemed threatened by the late 1990s. With the stakes in corporate disputes having grown high during a decade of economic boom, suspicions had mounted that powerful litigants sought to influence the selection of courts and judges who would hear their cases.

The background to the case against Anwar begins in August 1997 when Ummi Hafilda, the sister of Anwar's personal secretary, and Azizan Abu Bakar, a former chauffeur for Anwar's family, wrote a letter to prime minister Mahathir asserting that Anwar had sodomised Azizan. Mahathir received the letter, showed it to Anwar, then warned of the kinds of enemies that his deputy faced. Indeed, 'flying letters' had for some years been circulating about

Anwar's alleged pecadilloes, evidently timed to compromise his standing during UMNO general assemblies. These allegations even took the form of a book entitled *50 Reasons Why Anwar Cannot be Prime Minister*, which was distributed to delegates at the assembly in June 1998. However, Mahathir dismissed the letter written by Ummi and Azizan as baseless, and appeared to let the matter rest.

Anwar, though, was said to have grown so concerned about the missive and its effects on his prospects that he contacted the police Special Branch, a powerful security agency that, since its formation by the British during the emergency, has specialized in gathering intelligence and countering subversion. Anwar, however, was alleged to have 'directed' the Special Branch to 'obtain a written confession' from Ummi and Azizan that their allegations were false. The agency claimed then to have obliged Anwar, locating Ummi and Azizan and gaining their retraction. But in September 1988, after Anwar's arrest, Mahathir asserted that there was truth to the allegations after all. He knew this, he said, because he had personally conducted interviews with the persons involved and now possessed incontrovertible evidence (Spaeth 1998, p. 21). And it was upon his discovery that Anwar was a 'homosexual' and 'unfit' for high office that the charges of corruption and misconduct were laid.

THE TRIAL PROCEEDINGS

From the start, misgivings were expressed about the selection of the presiding judge, Augustine Paul. He had spent most of his judicial career in a provincial sessions court, equivalent to a magistrate in the judicial systems of many other Commonwealth countries. He had been promoted to the Kuala Lumpur high court in mid-1998, roughly the same time at which the UMNO general assembly had been held. He served first as a judicial commissioner, and then was transferred to the High Court's criminal division only weeks before Anwar's trial began (Chelvarajah 1999, p. 11). Hence, while Judge Paul was cast as an authority on evidence, concerns were widely expressed over how so junior a figure had been selected to preside in a case of such magnitude.

In contrast, Anwar's defence counsel contained some of Malaysia's best-known lawyers. And in the early stages of the trial, they appeared to make great gains. The mainstay of their defence was to show that allegations of sexual conduct were false, and that Anwar had never used his office corruptly in order to cover them up. They argued that Anwar had instead been the victim of a political conspiracy, one mounted by top politicians and business people whose interests he had threatened. Ummi and Azizan had thus been offered 'benefits' in return for writing their letter to Mahathir.

Anwar's lawyers began by cross-examining the director of the Special Branch. In particular, they inquired about his willingness to lie in court 'if someone higher than the deputy prime minister were to instruct you to'.

Astonishingly, he replied, 'It would depend on the situation. I may or may not lie' (Paul 1999, pp. 79 - 80). Later, the director changed his testimony over whether he had sent a report on the matter to the prime minister, first denying it and later conceding it. The cross-examination of a second officer revealed the harsh techniques used by the Special Branch in order to gain confessions, a process he labelled a 'turning over operation' and elaborated with a Malay neologism, '*me-neutralize*'.

Further, when Azizan, Anwar's former driver, appeared on the stand, his responses caused the prosecution twice to amend the sodomy charges. Anwar had at first been charged with sodomizing Azizan in May 1994. But after Azizan testified that he had not been sodomized after 1992, the date of the offence was hastily changed to May of that year. Then, after defence counsel showed that the condominium in which the sexual misconduct was alleged to have taken place had not yet been completed in 1992, the date was amended once more to between January and March 1993. Amid this confusion, Azizan appeared at one stage even to deny that an encounter had ever taken place.

Ummi proved to be a firmer witness, although defence counsel nevertheless raised doubts about her credibility. During cross-examination, she was unable to remember whether her modest advertising company had attracted government favours, namely a contract for an anti-drug campaign. Further, her claim that her disclosures were motivated by concern for her family were belied by the news that her father had 'disowned' her. And her brother, Anwar's secretary, characterized her on the stand as a 'compulsive liar' (Asiaweek.com 1999).

Finally, a local forensic scientist was summoned by the prosecution to provide advice on a semen sample that had been taken from a mattress allegedly used by Anwar during his trysts. He stated that the sample's DNA matched that of another that had been taken from Anwar. However, under cross-examination, he acknowledged that because there had been no 'unbroken chain of custody' in transporting the samples from the police to the government's chemistry lab, he had only the word of the police that they were genuinely Anwar's.

With doubts over the sexual misconduct charges rapidly mounting, the prosecution requested that Judge Paul permit it once more to amend its case. Specifically, the sexual misconduct charges were to be dropped, while the corruption charges were to be changed from the Special Branch's obtaining a 'confession' to a 'statement'. And with Paul approving the amendments - probably the most controversial phase in the proceedings - the prosecution's task was made much simpler. In short, the prosecution no longer had to show that Anwar's committing sexual misconduct was the motivation for his corruptly deploying the Special Branch against Ummi and Azizan. It could instead show that there was motivation enough simply in the allegations having been made, however baseless. Observers from the International Commission of Jurists who attended the trial, while recognizing the right of the prosecution under Malaysian law to make amendments in this way, doubted nonetheless that the new charges even constituted a crime (Ackland 1999). Indeed, the ordinance on which the charges were based had previously been repealed by the lower house of parliament and was waiting final action in the senate.

In these changed circumstances, though, Judge Paul grew much tougher. During the cross-examination of Anwar, he now ruled that a defence based on political conspiracy was 'irrelevant', because the truth or falsity of the allegations no longer mattered. However, in the view of the Chairman of the Malaysian Bar Council, R.R. Chelvarajah, this effectively prohibited 'the accused from raising every possible and conceivable defence' (Chelvarajah 1999, p. 11). What is more, Judge Paul not only limited the defence options from which Anwar's counsel might choose, but also the witnesses who could be summoned. In particular, he demanded that defence counsel reveal before calling its witnesses what evidence it hoped to adduce, while barring other witnesses as 'irrelevant' or their testimony as 'inadmissable' and 'hearsay' even before their testimony could be heard (Paul 1999, p. 190). Finally, he sentenced one of Anwar's lawyers to a three-month jail term for contempt, while threatening others with the same.

In this situation, Anwar's defence counsel found it difficult to proceed. After yet another ruling from Judge Paul over irrelevance, Anwar lamented during cross-examination, 'Your lordship says I can't go into political conspiracy. I don't know what to do with my defence. It's so inter-related' (Asiaweek.com 1999). At first, Anwar's lawyers attempted to demonstrate that if there was no political conspiracy, there was surely a conspiracy mounted by the police. In brief, Anwar had merely ordered the Special Branch to carry out an investigation of Ummi and Azizan, but the police had on their own gone further in obtaining a statement, an action they now falsely attributed to Anwar. Trial proceedings concluded shortly thereafter.

In his written summation, Judge Paul accepted the Special Branch's contention that 'turning over' was only carried out against security risks - 'communists' and 'religious fanatics' - indicating that someone with high authority must have ordered its unprecedented use against 'ordinary people' like Ummi and Azizan. He then rejected Anwar's claim that as deputy prime minister and finance minister he had no such authority, noting the ways in which Anwar had regularly summoned Special Branch officers for intelligence briefings about popular reactions to government policies - sometimes late at night at the official residence. He also interpreted a statement made by Anwar in court that in August 1997 'he had not decided which branch of the police would conduct the investigations' as further evidence of Anwar's having the power to demand that the Special Branch gain confessions (Paul 1999, p. 220). And when Anwar countered desperately that if he was guilty of directing Special Branch officers to obtain written statements, then they were necessarily 'accomplices', Judge Paul dismissed this as an 'alternative defence' which, while having some merit, weakened Anwar's defence overall (Paul 1999, pp.

219 - 220). Finally, in considering the admission by the director of the Special Branch made early in the trial that he would in some circumstances lie, Judge Paul dismissed this as 'theoretical'. He wrote that the director's changes in testimony were in fact an indicator of reliability, suggesting 'that he has not been coached' (Paul 1999, pp. 80 - 81).

In these circumstances, Judge Paul concluded that Anwar, fearing for his political future, had corruptly used his office in directing the Special Branch to obtain statements from Ummi and Azizan. He suggested too that Anwar had avoided making a police report to the Criminal Investigation Division as per normal procedures, because of the publicity this would generate in the courts and media. Hence, the matter only came to the attention of the Division and the attorney-general, the judge continued, when Anwar later made a report over another set of allegations, finally bringing police investigators into contact with the Special Branch (Paul 1999, p. 229). Thus, after a trial lasting 78 days - Malaysia's longest criminal trial - Anwar was convicted on all four charges of corrupt practice.

In passing sentence, Judge Paul claimed that neither Anwar nor his lawyers had entered any mitigating plea. Rather, Anwar had read a prepared statement, returning to themes of political conspiracy, mounting attacks on the judiciary, and denouncing the verdict as 'stink[ing] to high heaven' (Anwar 1999). In addition, the judge agreed with the prosecution that because Anwar had headed a cabinet committee geared to containing corruption, Anwar must be held accountable to high standards, necessitating a 'deterrent sentence'. On the other hand, Judge Paul claimed to take into account Anwar's very long service to government. He wrote that while he might have sentenced Anwar to 14 years in prison on each charge, he displayed leniency in handing down four terms of six years each, to be served concurrently.

The gallery appeared stunned by what it perceived as the severity of the sentence, however, while police officers in attendance clapped and erupted in cheers. And with a five-year ban on participating in politics added to every jail sentence in Malaysia of more than a year, Anwar appeared now, depending on how the country's politics might unfold, to have effectively been barred from contesting the next three general elections. Meanwhile, Mahathir's position seemed quite impregnable - even as his attempts to gain legitimacy for his actions did more to erode that of the judiciary. Indeed, Mahathir may not yet have finished with the institution. When he was asked in an interview after the trial whether he saw any areas in need of reform, he replied: 'The judiciary, we would like to see the judiciary reformed. The judiciary is very independent. They tend to favour [the opposition] and I hope when I say this it doesn't influence them against me' (*Far Eastern Economic Review* 1999, p. 13).

ANWAR'S SECOND TRIAL

Much scepticism was expressed, both locally and by the foreign media, over the rightfulness of Anwar's conviction. Hence, in a second attempt to lend legitimacy to his jailing, the government again charged Anwar, along with his adopted brother, Sukma Darmawan, of sexual misconduct. The trial in Kuala Lumpur High Court began in June 1999 and ran until August 2000.

In contrast to Augustine Paul, the judge presiding over this second trial, Arifin Jaka, permitted Anwar's counsel much greater scope in developing a defence based on high-level political conspiracy. The prosecution, for its part, stuck steadfastly by the testimony of Azizan Abu Bakar - although it tried now to corroborate Azizan's testimony by presenting a 'confession' made by Sukma while in police custody in September 1998 that he and Anwar had indeed sodomized Azizan. The defence thus responded by arguing that Azizan lacked credibility, that Sukma's confession had been extracted under great duress, and that government officials had fabricated evidence in order to stop Anwar's rise to the prime ministership. Then, to demonstrate conspiracy, the defence subpoenaed Mahathir to appear in court as a witness.

As in the first trial, Anwar's counsel appeared early on to make some gains. During ten days of testimony and cross-examination, Azizan prevaricated so much over the timing of the alleged offence and other matters that even Judge Arifin lost patience, exclaiming: 'This witness is saying one thing today and another thing tomorrow… [H]e refuses to answer even simple questions' (Kim Quek 2000). In September, Azizan's credibility was further diminished when he was arrested by Islamic religious authorities in Melaka for *khalwat* (close proximity) with a young female student, leading to a brief period of detention during which he married her. Meanwhile, the defence focused once more on the prosecution's having changed the date of its charges several times in order to correlate with Azizan's shifting testimony. Further, it appeared to provide reasonable alibis for most of the three-month period in 1993 that the prosecution had settled upon. Finally, when a former director-general of Malaysia's Anti-Corruption Agency was called as a witness, he revealed that during an earlier attempt that had been made to investigate officials in the Economic Planning Unit, housed in the Prime Minister's Department, he had been stopped through the personal intervention of Mahathir. In short, Anwar's second trial, like his first one, began to shed light on the inner workings of Malaysia's state apparatus.

Thereafter, however, proceedings began to turn against Anwar. In September 1999, amid a great uproar, Anwar's supporters claimed that he had been poisoned by arsenic. Judge Arifin immediately permitted Anwar to choose a hospital for further examination. Tests soon demonstrated, however, that Anwar did not suffer from unusually high arsenic levels, casting some doubt on his own credibility. Further, Mahathir refused to honour the subpoena against him, forgoing the chance to present in court the 'incontrovertible' evidence of Anwar's transgressions that he purported to hold. Arifin then sanctioned Mahathir's refusal to appear through a separate ruling in April 2000 - a worrying precedent in that it seemed to enable any witness who might be summonsed to learn in advance what questions might be asked, then dispute their relevance (Asiaweek.com 2000). Nonetheless, Arifin's ruling was upheld by the Court of Appeals in June, and Anwar's further appeal was dismissed by the Federal Court in August. These same courts also dismissed Anwar's appeals against the conviction in his first trial for corruption.

As the proceedings neared their end, Anwar came to view his defence as fruitless. What is more, he was proscribed by Judge Arifin from making his own summary statement, ostensibly because he possessed defence counsel able to do his bidding. Anwar thus responded by dismissing his lawyers. He then used his opportunity to speak not to issue a plea for mitigation, but instead a stinging denunciation of the judiciary (Anwar Ibrahim 2000b) - precisely as the judge had feared. A tempestuous exchange erupted in the courtroom between Arifin and Anwar. Shortly afterward, in handing down his ruling, the judge determined that 'Azizan gave evidence for a total of 10 days and was cross-examined aggressively and extensively. He came out unscathed... Azizan has made five prior consistent statements. This enhances his credibility' (Arifin Jaka 2000, p. 8). Accordingly, Anwar was found guilty as charged, namely, 'carnal intercourse against the order of nature' (Asiwaweek.com 2000). Arifin, in then characterising this 'despicable act' as warranting 'the utmost condemnation', sentenced Anwar to nine years in prison, to be served consecutively with his existing sentence. Sukma was sentenced to six years, reinforced by four lashes of the *rotan*. Observers promptly calculated that Anwar, even allowing for one-third remission for good behaviour, as well as the one year he had already served, faced nine more years in jail. Thus, together with the five-year ban on contesting political office, Anwar would remain on the sidelines for the next fourteen years - surely beyond the time frame of Mahathir's political life.

WIDER IMPLICATIONS

In his recent study of legal structures in East Asia, Jayasuriya (1999) observed that the rule of law, far from protecting society from the state, is oftentimes better understood as an extension of state power (ibid., p. 3). In brief, although judiciaries may take on 'Western' forms, they serve to insulate state autonomy and sanction state policies, rather than defend civil liberties and mediate public complaints. On this count, authoritarian governments in Singapore, Hong Kong, China and Vietnam have in varying degrees encouraged the rule of law in order to rationalize state apparatuses and policies, then further to claim legitimacy from the enhanced performance that such rationalizing can bring. In these instances, Jayasuriya refers to legalism as a 'technique of rule'.

By contrast, some of the region's new democracies have upgraded their judiciaries in an effort to increase political accountability and market efficiencies. For example, as part of its constitutional reform package adopted in 1997, Thailand set up new constitutional and administrative courts, then embraced the doctrine of judicial review. Indonesia has also introduced a range of legal reforms, designed to curb corruption on the bench and enhance the quality of adjudication. It has as well established a specialized bankruptcy court, even if delaying the court's proper functioning.

However, whether the rule of law extends state power or limits it, semi-democratic Malaysia has for more than a decade shunned both sets of imperatives. Instead, the government has reined in the courts, leaving the judiciary a diminished tool of an increasingly paramount prime minister. The parliament and media have been similarly transfigured. Malaysia has thus embarked on an analytically fascinating course that, in hollowing out most formal institutions while personalizing the executive, runs counter to the strategies increasingly deployed in the rest of the region. And in thereby foregoing the rationalization and legitimation valued by authoritarian governments, as well as the accountability and efficiencies countenanced by democratic ones, Malaysia must innovate new practices by which to perpetuate its semi-democratic regime and politicized markets.

To be sure, Malaysia's economic recovery will do much to restore performance legitimacy to a paramount executive. But without such recovery and legitimacy, it is difficult to see what institutions the executive might turn to in order to perpetuate its dominance - except, of course, the security forces. In this situation, one can speculate that the wider implications of the ways in which the judiciary has been transposed, as made clear by the Anwar trial, involve a rise in personalist and arbitrary rule, sustained by varying amounts of performance criticism and coercion.

CONCLUSIONS

For many observers, Mahathir's wanting to banish Anwar from his cabinet, and then from even the UMNO, was quite understandable. Policy differences over recovery strategies, business promotion, and Islamicization, crystallizing in factional alliances and personal rivalries, culminated finally in Mahathir's leadership being tested by his deputy. One also recollects that while Anwar declared himself during the recent economic crisis to be a reformist - ordering investigations and overturning mega-projects - he had long conformed to the demands of UMNO politics by forging business links, gathering patronage resources, propping up supporters, and swaying mass opinion through his control over media outlets (Gomez and Jomo 1997, p. 96). Anwar was hence correctly assessed by Mahathir as politically ambitious and potentially disloyal.

What is troubling, however, is that Mahathir was not content merely to expel Anwar from government. Instead, he sought next to 'humiliate' his deputy through corruption and sexual misconduct charges. By laying these charges, Mahathir's aim was to sever Anwar from his social base, denying his deputy the constituencies by which to mount any serious challenge from outside the government. This was something that Anwar had made plain his willingness to do by mobilizing mass protests during the Commonwealth games, even turning to the national mosque for focal imagery. At the same time, some analysts suggest that by vilifying Anwar, Mahathir could also discredit the revivalist strands of Islam with which Anwar had been partly associated, thereby elevating his own standard of industrializing Islam and even of secular Malay-ness (Maznah 2000, p. 5), Thus, amid Malaysia's Islamic resurgence, quickened during the recent economic crisis, then alloyed by new resentments over the high-level cronyism that the crisis had rendered less tolerable, Mahathir struck hard at his deputy.

Nonetheless, in view of the allegations that Mahathir elected to make - widely assessed as bizarre and unproven - many Malays, rather than being outraged over Anwar's behaviour, grimaced at Mahathir with cultural loathing. As Hari Singh (2000) reminds us, in traditional Malay belief systems, patrons are sooner forgiven for executing disloyal clients than wilfully humiliating them and causing them to lose face. Hari thus observes that if Mahathir's ruthlessness towards Anwar served to intimidate those who might plot to replace him, it has also unleashed a vast undercurrent of contempt (ibid., pp. 530 - 531). However, from the perspective of this chapter, it is the concerns of Malaysians over the erosion of their country's political institutions, in particular, the judiciary, that weigh more heavily. Anwar's final court statement, though, of course, highly partisan, doubtless reflects the suspicions of many Malaysians:

Mahathir could have used the draconian Internal Security Act to imprison me for as long as he wanted, without destroying the judiciary and without sullying the Attorney General's chambers. But he is a coward who would not take responsibility for his own evil. So he uses the courts, and with the same stroke, he completes the destruction of the judiciary (Anwar 2000a, p. 10).

To be sure, Mahathir leaves a complex legacy, including his disregard for organized labour and rural workers, indigenous peoples, the environment, and tactful international diplomacy which are counterpoised by his more benign record on ethnic relations, Third World solidarity, and in some degree, gender equality. Nor can one gainsay his country's rapid industrial progress. But the obduracy with which he has dealt with opposition forces while pursuing these aims - then tapped the country's judiciary so deeply for legitimacy that he has deadened it - forges an odd trajectory in which the country modernizes its industrial base while its political institutions are demeaned. Of course, most analysts suggest that this contradiction cannot be finessed forever: beyond some developmental threshold, industrial modernization demands a sound legal structure. But this day of reckoning, if ever Malaysia reaches it, will likely only come after Mahathir has departed. In the meantime, he might argue that it is precisely because he has bent the rules that Malaysia has made its initial gains.

NOTES

1. In an interview with the *Far Eastern Economic Review*, Mahathir was asked whether Anwar could ever make a comeback. Mahathir replied: 'Not in this case. Because it's not political. Political, we can. We can recant and say I now subscribe to the party's policies and all that. This [the sexual misconduct charges] is something that is not acceptable in Malaysian society' (*Far Eastern Economic Review*, 1999, p. 1).

10. Mahathir, Australia and the Rescue of the Malays

Anthony Milner

Prime minister Mahathir, let us not deny it, has irritated a lot of people in the West, including Australians. His policies and his blunt pronouncements in some cases damage the Australian sense of national interest and self-respect, and contradict values that we hold dearly. It is true that the particular manner in which Australians tend to think about their political leaders means that we can probably tolerate the way Mahathir has insulted both our current and our last prime minister. We are less comfortable, though, when Mahathir calls Australia a 'small nation' and tells us to 'behave like a small nation' (*The Australian* 2000a). It also might have done some damage to Australian self-esteem when, at the time the Keating Labour government of the early 1990s was speaking with enthusiasm about Australia's role in Asia, Mahathir took pains to point out that we were in no real sense a part of the region. 'You cannot just change sides like that', he warned Australians. And then he went on to say that if we did hope eventually to be accepted in Asia, we would need to begin by 'changing (our) attitudes and improving (our) manners' (Mahathir Mohamad and Shintaro Ishihara 1995, p. 85). Mahathir clearly distinguished between bad manners and his own penchant for forthright criticism.

In practical terms, Mahathir's rejection of Australia's aspirations in Asia has involved opposing Australia's participation in a number of important regional processes. It is well known, for instance, that he rejected Australia's involvement in the Europe-Asia, so-called ASEM, meetings. We never expected him to welcome us at the ASEAN + 3[1] meetings. In fact, Mahathir has been vigorous over a number of years in urging the development of a regional organization that would specifically exclude Australia as well as the United States. In a period when Australian governments have worked toward the strengthening of APEC (the Asia-Pacific Economic Community), a body that brings Asian countries together with the United States, Canada, Australia and New Zealand, Mahathir has been urging a more exclusive organization in the Asian region. Mahathir describes APEC as a 'fuzzy concept', and seeks instead to bring together East Asian countries in an East Asian Economic Caucus (Mahathir Mohamad and Shintaro Ishihara 1995, p. 28).[2]

'Asia' (or often 'East Asia') is an important concept and an aspiration for Mahathir. 'We must', he says, 'commit ourselves to ensuring that the history of East Asia will be made in East Asia, for East Asians, and by East Asians' (Ibid., p. 16). Mahathir, of course, seeks to identify certain common Asian values that will help to bond together an international Asian community,[3] and one senses that it may be partly to assist in the process of formulating these common values that he sometimes takes the opportunity to single out Australia as a country that in cultural terms lies outside the region. Whatever Mahathir may observe, however, in many cases it is simply obvious that Australians do not tend to share these so-called Asian values - and, in fact, that these values are further irritants in the Australian-Malaysian relationship. Australians tend to be uneasy, for instance, when Mahathir refers to the 'West's moral degeneration' (Mahathir and Isihara 1995, p. 80), especially when this seems to suggest that Western countries give too much respect to individual freedoms and democracy. When Mahathir praises what he calls 'not-so-liberal democracies' that possess 'Governments that play a major role in the economy' (Mahathir Mohamad and Shintaro Ishihara 1995, p. 83), some Australians may find this attractive, but they are less impressed when they see the implications of support for strong government in the area of press control, civil rights and what Australians tend to see as the undermining of proper legal processes.

Enough has been said, perhaps, to recall the different areas in which the blunt, volatile, determined prime minister Mahathir has unsettled and often outraged Australian public opinion.[4] What is often lost sight of in Australia, however, are his achievements and talent as a leader. To trivialize these achievements, it is hardly necessary to add, can do nothing to assist mutual understanding between Australia and Malaysia. The problem is that even Mahathir's central achievement - the rescue of the Malays - has entailed policies or approaches that run up against values that are deeply held in Australia. There is even reason to believe that the Malay policy he has advocated has been the decisive factor in bringing about the deterioration of Malaysian-Australian relations.

The rescue of the Malays - what Mahathir sometimes has called the 'rehabilitation of the Malays' - has certainly been pivotal in his political life, although this might seem an ironic observation when one considers the 1999 election result in which Mahathir's party lost much support in the Malay community (Zakaria Haji Ahmad et al. 2000). As a young medical student in Singapore fifty years ago, Mahathir wrote newspaper articles which expressed concern about what he termed the 'backwardness of the Malays' compared to other communities in Malaya.[5] Insisting that the Malays had hereditary rights as the indigenous people of Malaysia, he urged the Malays to 'awaken to the danger that they are far behind the Chinese and Indians in education'. In the context of Malay 'backwardness' he warned about the disadvantages of Malay conservatism - of their determination to continue to respect their long-held customs. Mahathir was impatient, too, with Malay royalty, wondering how long feudalism could hold out against the forces of modernity.

Such themes - introduced in these writings of 1948, 1949 and 1950 - were developed and strengthened in his influential book of 1970, *The Malay Dilemma* (Mahathir 1979). Written in the aftermath of the 1969 ethnic rioting, it appeared at a time when the Malay ruling party was debating its future policies and directions. The Malays, it argued, were being held back partly by their physical environment - an environment that was so favourable that it discouraged habits of industry - and partly by hereditary factors. Mahathir wrote confidently about the latter, perhaps on the basis of his medical training, drawing attention in particular to the relative absence of inter-racial marriage in Malay rural areas and the presence of the 'habit of family in-breeding' (ibid., p. 29). Because of their environment and hereditary features, explained Mahathir, the Malays possessed a world view that retarded them in the contest between races in Malaysia. That world view was influenced by the indulgence shown to Malay children by their elders and by the importance in the Malay outlook of politeness, restraint, deference, fatalism, the failure to value time and the inability to understand the 'capacity of money' (Khoo 1996, pp. 32 - 33). Such views and such manners, argued Mahathir, could easily be exploited by the opponents of the Malays and would certainly damage the Malay capacity for commercial enterprise. With such characteristics, he suggested, Malays were little match for the 'industrious and determined immigrants' (Mahathir 1979, p. 25), and had thus lost out in the competition over business, skilled jobs and urban employment.

As in 1950, Mahathir insisted in his 1970 book that the Malays possessed 'inalienable rights' because they were the 'original or indigenous people of Malaya and the only people who can claim Malaysia as their one and only country' (ibid,, p. 133). What the plight of these indigenous people required, he insisted, was 'constructive protection' (Khoo 1996, pp. 28 - 29) and for this reason he defended the limited government policies already in place that aimed to give Malays special economic privileges. He defended, for instance, constitutional provisions for Malay land reserves, scholarships for Malay students, quotas for Malay employment in the civil service and providing assistance for Malays to get into the business world. Malay people, explained Mahathir, were hampered by a lack of experience when they attempted to apply for jobs. 'Any Malay wanting to do business with the Government, or to start a major enterprise like mining or transport, was invariably asked whether he had any experience'. And the demonstrated lack of experience inevitably led to a negative response to the application (Mahathir 1979, p. 40). One of the purposes of the special economic opportunities that had been designed for Malays was to remedy this weakness in employment records.

Such special opportunities, Mahathir proposed, were therefore aimed at reducing not creating inequality. In the case of specific scholarships for Malay students, he argued, they were 'not a manifestation of racial inequality'. Rather, he said, they were a 'means of breaking down the superior position of the non-Malays in the field of education' (ibid., p. 76).

Apart from urging the maintaining and expanding of programmes of 'constructive protection' for the Malay community, *The Malay Dilemma* devotes much attention to the need to change the Malay way of thinking. 'To complete the rehabilitation of the Malays', Mahathir declared, 'there is a need to break away from custom or *adat* and to acquire new thinking and a new system of ideas'. Urbanization, he felt, would assist this process but there also needed to be 'a conscious effort to destroy the old ways and replace them with new ideas and values' (ibid., p. 113).

Once again, this 1970 Mahathir argument recalls a theme established in his earlier 1948 - 1950 writings. 'Traditional politeness', he said in *The Malay Dilemma*, has 'apparently failed' (ibid., p. 172). Malays should be less deferential - less influenced by the code of deference arising from the 'feudal nature of Malay society' (p. 170). They should be far less respectful to foreigners and remember that 'frankness is the order of the day' (p. 171). Self-restraint and the desire not to displease, he complained in *The Malay Dilemma*, does not make for an aggressive society (p. 171). Also, Malays needed to be 'properly motivated' (p. 172), and if they could develop a clearer sense of time, and of the need not to waste time, they would be better workers.

One aspect of the Malay world view, or values, to which Mahathir gave little attention in *The Malay Dilemma*, was religion. But in a later book published in Malay, *The Challenge* (Mahathir 1995), Mahathir responded to the spokespeople of the Islamic resurgence taking place at that time, portraying their doctrines as a further hindrance to Malay progress. It was, he said, 'one of the saddest ironies of recent times' that the faith that had once made its followers 'progressive and powerful' was now being 'invoked to promote retrogression which will bring in its wake weakness and eventual collapse'. In the powerful essays of this book he argued against what he saw as a narrow-minded and divisive interpretation of Islam (ibid., Introduction).

Implicit in this and every other statement that Mahathir has made with respect to world views and values is the assumption that values can indeed be changed, and that leaders have the responsibility and capacity to do so. Leaders, he says, 'can lead the way with the certainty that they will be followed by the masses' (Mahathir 1979, p. 173). As prime minister, we have constantly seen Mahathir in this didactic role - lecturing, hectoring his people: urging them to adopt new values and new attitudes; calling on them to undergo a 'mental revolution and a cultural transformation', to become what he began to term *Melayu Baru,* or new Malays (Khoo 1996, p. 336; and Shamsul 1999).

The Mahathir project of, on the one hand, 'constructive protection of the Malays' and, on the other, of the reform of Malay attitudes, has had the immediate aim of rehabilitating or rescuing the Malay community. But Mahathir (1979, p. 41) has also argued that the Malay policy is 'essential for the stability' of the country as a whole - in a sense a precondition for the advancement of the Malaysian nation. Indeed, he as prime minister has promulgated a Vision 2020 - a vision that assumes the presence of an 'economically resilient and fully competitive' indigenous community (Khoo 1996, p. 334) and, on that basis, anticipates the emergence of a 'united Malaysian nation' made up of one 'Malaysian race' possessing a 'sense of common and shared destiny' (Khoo 1996, p. 331; and Shamsul 1999, pp. 103 - 106).[6]

Even to anticipate the presence of an economically resilient Malay community implies an element of success for Mahathir's Malay project.

Mahathir himself has sometimes spoken proudly of the achievements of the Malays - of the fact that Malays had begun to hold positions as 'heads of departments, scientists, actuaries, nuclear physicists, surgeons, experts in the fields of medicine and aviation, bankers and corporate leaders' (Khoo 1996, p. 337). He has noted, again with some justification, that many of these Malays come from rural backgrounds. In recent times Mahathir has been much less positive, bemoaning the fact that the Malays have made too little of the economic advantages offered them. Economically, he says, 'they have less than half the 30% share that has been allocated to them'. The Malays have tended to 'lean on the crutches of Malay privileges' and are 'not even using the crutches properly' (Mahathir 2002).

To make a full assessment of the success or otherwise of the Malay policies, of course, would require extensive research and analysis. It would be necessary to examine such issues as the degree of independence from government patronage of Malay entrepreneurs; the impact on the middle class of the 1997 - 1998 financial crisis; and the extent to which Mahathir's specific policies may have divided rather than strengthened the Malay community, in a way that contributed to the dramatic decline of Malay support for his own party in the 1999 election.[7] Despite the possibility of such qualifications, however, few commentators would question the claim that over three decades there has been a substantial increase of Malays entering the modern sector in the economy, the modern education system and the urban environment (Crouch 1996, pp. 211 - 212 and pp. 237 - 238; Shamsul 1999, p. 100; and Searle 1999). Moreover, in the words of a former prominent judge, Suffian Hashim, Mahathir has made his people 'more confident of themselves. He's changed their attitudes, which makes them less sensitive to Chinese economic domination'.[8]

The second observation that ought to be made about Mahathir's Malay policy is that it is characterized not so much by originality as by extraordinary determination or tenacity. To stress the point that Mahathir's commitment to, and even his programme for, rescuing the Malays, has historical roots in Malay society is not to take away from his achievement. It reminds us, in fact, of the scale of the challenge he set himself. It can be argued that Malay society over a long period possessed what might be termed an acute sense of insecurity. A saying sometimes attributed to the legendary Malay hero, Hang Tuah - a statement that Mahathir has himself quoted (Mahathir 1995, p. 2)[9] - is that 'the Malays shall not vanish from the face of the earth'. Although such speculation about the possible vanishing of an ethnic group would tend to surprise many people today, it is a reminder of the ethnic fluidity that once existed in much of Southeast Asia. People did shift from one ethnic group to another, and just as there is abundant evidence of non-Malays becoming Malay over the centuries, there is also plenty of indication that in some regions people converted (if that is the best word) out of Malaydom (Milner 1982; Milner et al. 1978). That is to say, not only could kingdoms virtually disappear in the ebb and flow of Malay history, but it was also conceivable that in certain circumstance a people itself might disappear.

Looking back over the Malay past, and remembering the many statements one finds in Malay texts about transience, including the transience of life itself, it is tempting to identify in the Malay community a long-term preoccupation, or anxiety, about the problem of anchoring, or fixing, or giving shape and substance to, the existence of individuals, polities or even the Malay people themselves (Milner 1982, Chapter 6; Milner 1995, pp. 215 - 216). It is an approach to the world, one might suggest, that can only have heightened the concerns that would inevitably be provoked by the influx into the Malay states of large numbers of immigrants from China and elsewhere - immigrants, who, as Mahathir put it, often displayed energy and enterprise.

When such a vast influx did occur - in the context of the nineteenth-century expansion of European power in Asia and the facilitating of migration from China - Malay commentators soon voiced their sense of threat. These commentators were forerunners of Mahathir and other mid-twentieth-century Malay nationalists, and had a good deal in common with them. One of the earliest in the 1830s and 1840s was Munshi Abdullah - 'Munshi' means 'teacher', and Munshi was a teacher of the Malay language to many influential members of the British colonial establishment in Malaysia and Singapore - who wrote vigorously about what he saw as the danger facing Malays as a result of the new forces entering the Malay Peninsula at that time. Like Mahathir, Abdullah came from a family background that had a strong Indian element. Both men thus analysed Malay society from a somewhat ambiguous standpoint, while they possessed the degree of analytical distance that comes from being a partial outsider.

Abdullah warned that the Malays faced tough competition from other races, and were likely to be 'trodden under foot' (Milner 1995, p. 83).[10] He looked to what he called a 'new generation' of Malays (ibid., p. 84) to reform Malay society so that it might face this challenge. Changes had to be made in the Malay royal class and the traditional Malay world view. Many Malay customs and maxims, according to Abdullah, were simply 'foolish' and 'useless'. They discouraged Malays from doing 'anything important', from being ambitious and enterprising (pp. 18 - 19). Malay custom gave no respect, for instance, to private property, and thus no incentive to personal industry (p. 19). Abdullah challenged Malays to embrace modern education - to think of themselves as individuals with ambitions and aspirations (p. 35). He told them that in British-governed territories, persons who worked hard and gained wealth 'can build houses and wear clothes just like rajas' (p. 33). He wanted ordinary Malays to 'think big' in this way (p. 43).

To reinforce the call to 'think big' and be enterprising, Abdullah adopted a writing style possessing an assertiveness, a provocative tone, and a stress on the authorial 'I', that was a radical departure in Malay literature. Recalling Mahathir's own provocative tone, it seems true in both cases that the rhetorical style was deliberately chosen to complement the content of ideas, that is, to reinforce the summons to Malays to become more self-assertive. In the way they present their ideas, both Abdullah and Mahathir seem consciously to be giving Malays a lesson in personal assertiveness.[11]

Abdullah was writing at the beginning of the British colonial period, when the potential challenge to the Malays was first becoming apparent. In 1900, when the British controlled most of the Malay states on the peninsula, the early Malay newspapers spoke with increasing urgency about the plight of the Malays, particularly with respect to the competition presented by the rapidly growing population of Chinese and other immigrants. Malays, said the newspaper, the *Utusan Melayu,* in 1907, were in danger of being driven 'away from their own states by other races' (Milner 1995, p. 119). The Chinese, the paper explained, were feared not only in Malaya, but also in Australia and Canada. These and other foreigners had not come to Malaya at 'our invitation', and now the Malays needed the British to protect them in their competition with Chinese mine owners, European rubber planters and Indian money lenders (ibid., p. 119). Such a request, of course, anticipated 'the constructive protection' which Mahathir was to support many decades later.

This turn-of-the-century Malay paper, the *Utusan Melayu,* also called for Malay reforms, including the adoption of values of hard work, industry, and rational thinking (Milner 1995, p. 124). Particularly when it is stressed that the notion that 'work' involved a new perception of time, one recalls again the writing of Mahathir. Malays, explained the Malay paper, should learn to work 'to the best of their ability every day' and wage labour itself - including the work on plantations that Malays often avoided - could enhance 'the individual's sense of self' and bring 'freedom and happiness' (ibid., p. 124). The paper urged the individual Malay to be more self-assertive, and not merely in economic behaviour. It told them to express themselves on a range of public matters suggesting, for instance, that they send letters to the paper itself. For Mahathir, of course, such assertiveness - entailing as it does, a certain stress on freedom of speech - has had to be balanced against a desire to maintain certain controls on public criticism. It has to be weighed against what might be characterized as the rights of the Malay leader to instruct his people. But the fact remains that Mahathir directly or indirectly has helped to promote the sort of assertiveness in Malay society that makes it increasingly difficult to impose such censorship.

There is no need to continue to work through modern Malay history, identifying those who have spoken with most passion about the dangers to the Malay community, and who have gone to lengths to reform Malay society, and particularly Malay customs and values.[12] Mahathir himself took pains in his *Malay Dilemma* to show ways in which even the British colonial administration created organisations to promote the Malay community, including a 'Rural and Industrial Development Authority' (Mahathir 1979, p. 39) that would provide capital and know-how to help Malays get into business. He saw such British measures as extremely limited, and it is certainly true that in the early years of the independent Malayan state the Malays remained to a large extent in a rural, economic backwater. But the British measures did at least demonstrate that the government, as Mahathir explained it, was not 'going to accept as a matter of course, the exclusion of the Malays from the commercial life of the country' (ibid., p. 41). Such British measures as the Rural and Industrial Development Authority, he argued, helped to establish the 'principle that helping the Malays is not racialism but is actually essential for the stability of the country' (p. 41).

The race riots of May 1969, of course, were interpreted in some quarters of the Malay community as demonstrating that those measures that had been adopted in the past to rescue the Malay community had simply not gone far enough. In 1970, in the aftermath of the riots and long before Mahathir became deputy prime minister or prime minister, the New Economic Policy was introduced with the specific aim of 'accelerating the process of restructuring Malaysian society to correct economic imbalance' - an aim that involved plans for what was called 'the creation of a Malay commercial and industrial community' (Barraclough 1988, p. 60; Crouch 1996, pp. 24 and 27). One particular governmental strategy for the advancement of the Malay community at this time - a strategy that, as we have seen, had been urged by Malay reformists over a longer period - was what the government termed 'the revolutionizing of Malay thinking'. The condemnation of the traditional world view and the new doctrines advocated were spelt out in an influential book, *Revolusi Mental* (Senu Abdul Rahman 1973). Once again, the stress was on becoming more assertive, more imaginative, more ambitious and more capitalistic. This book, in fact, calls attention to a number of prominent entrepreneurs, Western as well as Chinese, offering such figures as John Paul Getty as models for its Malay audience.

Reviewing the way the Malay issue was being handled in the post-1969 riots period, it is clear that it was a renewed effort to protect, promote and reform the Malay community - a policy that was to be implemented in the New Economic Policy - that Mahathir was advocating in 1970 in *The Malay Dilemma*. Going back even further to the early nineteenth century helps to underline the fact that as political leader, deputy prime minister, and finally, prime minister, he confronted a long-standing and massively threatening problem for the Malay community, and that he did so with extraordinary tenacity.

This brings me to the third observation that might be made about Mahathir's Malay policy - that, at least in Australian experience, it is rare to encounter leaders who are committed in this way to long-term, transformative, projects. Perhaps it is a consequence of working with a vigorous liberal democracy, but it would probably be necessary to go back to Alfred Deakin, one of Australia's earliest prime ministers, to find a leader who possessed a comprehensive far-reaching vision and the capacity to implement it (La Nauze 1965; Kelly 1992, pp. 1 - 2). A rigorous comparison between Malaysia and Australia would be likely to lend support to the view that Mahathir (like Lee Kwan Yew) is exceptional in the degree to which he is committed to do more than merely keeping the ship of state afloat. He is a visionary, who has throughout his life promoted, and has had some success in implementing, a grand strategy for the survival of the Malay people. But here it must be admitted that it would be easier to make a case for this being a reason for Australians to respect Mahathir if it were not for the fact that the project of rescuing the Malays is in itself one fundamental reason for the tension that exists between Australia and Malaysia. The role of the Malay policy in damaging Australian-Malaysian relations is in fact the fourth and final observation I will offer.

The point is an important one. It questions a widely held view in Australia today that the continuing Australia-Malaysia tension is due merely to personality differences between our respective leaders or, more bluntly, to the personality of Mahathir himself. It is also true to say that the Malay-first policy of post-1969 Malaysia has not got the recognition it deserves from scholars for being a critical ingredient - not the only ingredient, of course, but just possibly the critical ingredient - in the decline of Malaysia-Australia relations (see, for example, Searle 1996; and Crouch 1998). Where it has been recognized is in a diplomatic memoir published in the early 1990s. In an account of his diplomatic postings in the Asian region, the ambassador and poet, John Rowland, who served as high commissioner to Malaysia from 1969 to 1972, related that he witnessed the turning point in Australian-Malaysian relations. Before the racial rioting of 1969, Australia had a remarkably close diplomatic connection - in fact, the Australian high commissioner of that time, Tom Critchley, had been Tunku Abdul Rahman's 'favourite golf partner' and frequent confidant (Rowland 1992, p. 46). After the riots, Australia's prime minister, John Gorton, had indicated his concern about Malaysian government policy by refusing to provide the Malaysian army with barbed wire and other supplies. He also lectured the Malaysian leaders on race relations (Rowland 1992, p. 44). In other ways, too, Australia began to be seen - sometimes for quite innocent reasons - as being identified with the cause of the non-Malays who were critical of the Malay-first policies of the Malaysian Government. Australia, recalled former high commissioner Rowland, was soon perceived by Malaysia to be an 'unreliable ally' (ibid., p. 44).

In a sense Mahathir himself almost seems to have predicted that his Malay policy would damage relations with Australia. In his *Malay Dilemma* he actually tried to compare the Malay position with that of British Australians – arguing that both have a right to retain the identity of their countries, including a right to insist that immigrants conform to that identity. 'An Australian Chinese', observed Mahathir, 'may not ask that the Chinese language and culture be accepted as the language and culture of Australia' (Mahathir 1979, pp. 122 - 123). If this was an appeal to an Australian audience, however, I suspect it had relatively little success. Perhaps Mahathir's claim that his policy of helping Malays was 'not racialism but is essential to the stability of the country' had the potential to win greater approval - especially when we note his reminder that this was a policy endorsed in earlier years by the British, and when we reflect on how many previous Malay leaders had been committed to a broadly similar approach to protecting the Malays.[13] Having said this, however, I think that prime minister Gorton, as reported by former high commissioner Rowland, was fairly successful in this as in other areas in reflecting the popular view in Australia. For one thing, many European Australians are likely, as fellow immigrants, to express a certain sympathy for the plight of immigrant peoples in Malaysia and other countries. There is in addition a powerful perception in Australia - shaped to a large extent by the liberal ideologies that dominate our political thinking (Milner 1996b) - that all citizens should be treated more or less equally, regardless of race. It is an egalitarian aspiration - one that admittedly can be both hypocritical and self-interested - and tends to make Australians blind to the real merits of the Malay case in Malaysia and, it might be argued, following the dramatic events in Suva in 2000, to any positive aspects of the Fijian case in Fiji.[14] It is a form of egalitarianism also that involves a suspicion of political leaders who hold themselves above their people, instructing them as to how to think; and for that reason makes the rallying, didactic speeches of Mahathir yet another unattractive aspect of his Malay policy and nation building.

The task of identifying critical conflicts of viewpoint between Malaysia and Australia necessarily involves the backgrounding of important areas of agreement. It obscures, for instance, the extent to which there are Malaysians who hold values and perceptions very close to those dominant in Australia, and, by the same token, elements in Australia who argue for ethnicity-based policies (and even economic and international policies) that are close to those advocated by the Mahathir government. A comprehensive examination of the Australian-Malaysian relationship would also need to assess the multiple dimensions of the business, educational, defence and non-government organization relations that - despite all that has been said in this essay about a clash of viewpoints - make this one of Australia's most intimate engagements in the region.

Let me end, however, on the central point of this chapter. It is a mistake to assume that where differences do exist between Malaysia and Australia, they are always superficial or simply personality-based. The fact, and it is a fact that possesses a certain tragic character, is that the great project for which Mahathir deserves real respect as a political leader, the rescue of the Malays, has itself involved policies that do violence to the egalitarian aspirations that are so deeply embedded in Australian society. The only thing I can think of that might help to overcome this impediment to Malaysian-Australian relations is to urge that the history of the Malay policy be discussed openly, and that in such a discussion both sides show a willingness to listen as well as to explain. It is a discussion that would demand some serious reflection on fundamental values operating in both countries. In Australia's case, this might encourage a much-needed re-assessment of the way we balance indigenous rights against democratic rights. It is a balance that Australians need to examine in their approach not only to Malaysia, but also to the struggle taking place in Fiji and other parts of the Pacific and, indeed, to the acutely-troubled, Aboriginal situation that exists within Australia.[15]

NOTES

1.   See note 10 of Chapter 6.
2.   For a more recent statement by Mahathir urging support for such an East Asian organization, see the report of the Malaysia-China Forum, in Ian Stewart 'Mahathir Woos China as a Partner' (*Australian* 1999).
3.   For different views on the Asian Values issue, see Pertierra (1999) and Milner (2000). Mahathir lists 'Asian values' as hard work, respect for authority, discipline, submission to the interest and the good of the majority and filial piety. See his comments at the Third Pacific Dialogue (*Australian* 1996).
4.   For further discussion of elements of tension, and the possible reasons for tension, in the Malaysian-Australian relationship see Crouch (1998), Kessler (1991) and Searle (1996). Also, see Susan Aitken, 'Unrocking Malaysian Relations' (*Canberra Times* 1991), and Paul Kelly, 'Firing from the chip on his shoulder' (*Australian* 2000b).
5.   The following discussion of Mahathir's views in the 1948 to 1950 period is based on Khoo (1996, pp. 81 - 88).
6.   In June 2000, Mahathir went so far as to propose that some day in the future, if Malaysians worked together, 'even a non-Malay might become prime minister' (*Australian* 2000c).
7.   For division in the Malay community, see Crouch (1996), especially chapters 7 and 8; Khoo Kay Jin (1992); and Milner (1991) and (1996a). For a treatment of this in the 1999 election, see Zakaria Haji Ahmad et al. (2000).
8.   See V.G. Kulkarni, S. Jayasankaran and Murray Hiebert, 'A Price to Pay for Growth' (*The Canberra Times* 1996).
9.   For discussion of this statement of Hang Tuah, and the way it is used, see Rehman Rashid (1996).
10. All the following references to Abdullah's writings are taken from this book.
11. I discuss issues of political style in the Mahathir era in Milner (1991).
12. See Ariffin Omar (1993); Shaharuddin Maaruf (1984) and (1998); and Milner (1995) for further discussion of this matter.
13. In a discussion with Greg Sheridan in the *Australian*, Mahathir compared the Malay policy to affirmative action in the United States: 'We are trying to bring up the *Bumis* to the same level (as the non-*Bumis*) not to bring anyone else down' (Sheridan 1997, p. 198).
14. From time to time, the Fijians in Fiji have themselves compared their position with that of the Malays of Malaysia, and have sought inspiration from the Malay policy of the Malaysian government. See, for instance, M.G.G. Pillai, 'Ratu Mara Turns to Malaysia for Advice' (*Australian* 1990). For a recent Australian critique of the role played by race in Mahathir's international policies, see Paul Kelly, 'Firing from the Chip on his Shoulder' (*Australian* 2000b).
15. At certain times, Mahathir has drawn attention to the shortcomings of Australia's Aboriginal policies. See, for example, Ian Stewart, 'Mahathir Blasts Lingering Intolerance of Aboriginals' (*Australian* 1996).

11. Some Aspects of Malaysian Civil Liberties

Rais Yatim

No modern society is completely happy with the state of affairs pertaining to its own set of domestic rights under its constitution. Even in the United Kingdom a human rights expert asserts that 'liberty is ill in Britain...freedom is being curtailed or sacrificed in favour of some other real or supposed advantage...' (Boyle 1988, p. 85). People never appear to have enough of rights under their noses. On the other hand, there are always factions who assert that one's rights are demarcated and the adage is still true: 'My rights begin where the bridge of your nose ends.' And free speech could well claim its bastion from that well-known Voltaire quip, 'I disapprove of what you say, but I will defend to the death your right to say it' (Jay 1996). These are civil rights maxims to the layman, but lawyers will be quick to assert that they are pivotal in discourses on fundamental rights.

A discussion on current Malaysian civil liberties will at once be faced with two opposing assumptions. The first assumption is the tempting generalization of a picture of executive interplay in the inner works of government which renders the Malaysian civil liberty position as being too contrary to the American or European civil liberty yardstick. The second assumption is that the current set of constitutional and statutory limitations imposed on civil liberties in Malaysia has offered a practical set of solutions to Malaysia's needs of domestic social and economic advancement.

If, in the first place, one accepts that the types of rights and freedoms are to be determined democratically by the people of each country, then recognition of a country's public system in terms of what are basic rights must also follow. No other outside force should exercise interference purely on the assumption that 'violations' of human rights have taken place, unless perhaps these acts are of such dimension that mankind sees them as being so atrocious and inhuman that civil life has been replaced by pure dictatorship. Even then, the yardstick which is to be used in a country invokes the question of choice. If, for instance, the choice of a system is determined by the people themselves, then the voice of the majority must be respected however unpalatable that system may be to the outsider. Indeed, the judicial and executive system of a country remains very much a matter of national purview rather than that of a foreign power.

Civil liberties or fundamental rights or human rights on the whole could be said to generate the same notion, i.e. rights that are considered basic and inherent in the daily life of the individual in society. Although lawyers differ in their opinion as to the actual meanings of what constitute civil liberties, generally they agree that certain rights must be present in the overall or generic notion of these liberties. The purist will want to maintain that man is not given these rights - he is born with them and that no one has the right to take away those rights. That is idealism at its best. This assertion may not do well in the midst of changing values in the lives of modern men, since there is no such thing as absolute freedom given the laws and regulations that they have to live with in their life environments.

The generalization may be made, for the sake of ease and broad understanding, that human rights and civil liberties complement each other in terms of ingredients which represent the rights of man. The constitutions of all nations in the world invariably contain provisions for:

> The right to life (Malaysian Constitution, Article 5);
> The right to be heard in a court of law within a specified time when charged with certain crimes (Clause (4) of Article 5);
> The right not to be subject to retrospective criminal laws;
> The rights to be free from forced labour and slavery (Articles (6) and 7);
> Equality before the law, and rights to non-discriminatory treatment (Article 8);
> Prohibition from being banished and freedom of movement;
> The rights to free speech, assembly, and association (Article 10);
> The right to profess any religion of one's choice (Article 11);
> Rights in respect of education (Article 12);
> The rights to own property (Article 13).

Malaysia has in her 43 years as an independent nation recognized rights and liberties that are consonant with the rule of law environment. Of course, some quarters lament that these rights and liberties do not include all those in United Nations' covenants as well as those standardized by the West, arguing that Malaysia must therefore conform to those standards and types of rights. But the Malaysian system has worked, and Malaysians have buttressed their currency and economy despite harsh criticisms from outside. Through limited currency control Malaysia has been able to conserve its arbitrary outflow of funds. The outsider may want to be critical, but Malaysia cannot allow those with the above sentiment to dictate terms to a national government in matters pertaining to national wellbeing. This principle runs parallel to a nation's law on civil liberty.

CONTEXTUAL RIGHTS

The meanings and boundaries of human rights should not be so arcane that they tend to be looked at only from the viewpoint of the Western eye. Rights must extend beyond the precincts of politics, and more importantly beyond the focus of any national or international power. But rights must be realistic *vis-à-vis* personal freedoms and the power of the state. In this respect the definitions and understandings of human rights outside Europe and America have tended to be neglected, and the human rights focus has been more on the rights or freedoms of individuals as spelt out under the Universal Declaration of Human Rights. Whilst this covenant suffices as an international document that binds signatory countries, other areas of human rights, practices and ideals should also be recognized through conventions and usages.

The rights and freedoms of the East are no less significant, at least in so far as a truly universal set of human rights are deemed relevant in this century, and it is unfortunate that the act of 'looking East' has not been performed. In this context the assertion that Asia also has a contribution to make on what is best in terms of human rights was made by Dr Mahathir Mohamad in 1991:

Nobody can claim to have the monopoly of wisdom to determine what is right and proper for all countries and peoples. It would be condescending, to say the least, and suspect for the West, to preach human rights to us in the East' (Mahathir Mohamad 1991).

Human rights or civil liberties ought to be augmented by those age-old values and principles imbued and practised by peoples in the East for centuries. Through Confucianism, Islam, Hinduism, Buddhism and other religions, certain norms have become paramount and formed the bedrock of daily life for the teeming millions. In Malaysia and Indonesia, for instance, there are numerous *adat* (custom) tenets and practices that have moulded life for centuries, yet *adat* is nowhere spelt out to be paramount in constitutional bearing. Freedom *per se* without responsibility is just not relevant in the East.

It is indeed remarkable that even the constitutions of countries in Southeast Asia do not firstly incorporate these other values and principles. An immediate reaction to this lamentation perhaps could lie in the reality that there have in Asia been no writers in the genre of Montesquieu or Tocqueville, who reached the precincts of Western mindset. Moreover, the aftermath of colonization does not seem to resurrect Asian values in governmental work. Instead, the preferred stand is to propagate Western values in the constitutions of India, Pakistan, Sri Lanka, Malaysia and Singapore. This scenario explains why these countries are still saddled with ongoing issues of jurisprudence that appear to be locked into the Western motherboard. Even though Malaysia cut off the Privy Council's umbilical cord in 1975, it cannot get out of the English common law grip of things in many of her legal and judicial premises.

Having said this, the next difficulty is in determining what constitute Eastern values or, for that matter, Asian values, of civil liberties within the framework of human rights? This is no easy task. Perhaps over time the essence of life's philosophy about rights and freedoms could be woven into the constitutional works of eastern countries. For the moment many may want to settle with the satisfaction of including the rights to food and shelter, to have a clean environment that encompasses the elements of nature, to access justice,[1] to have privacy, and to possess a transparent accountable government accompanied by a good system of checks and balances. These rights may then include various other liberties and freedoms that are considered common needs of modern men wherever they happen to live on this globe. They are actual rights of the person, as well as rights of society. Thus contextually while Western elements in concepts of rights as envisaged under the Universal Declaration of Human Rights 1948 are deemed to be the motherboard of all rights and freedoms, the rights of Asian nations drawn from the context of Asia must also be recognized as universal elements of rights and liberties. The past and present wisdoms of Asia must be hinged on to the pan-Asian notions of rights with responsibilities.

As a general rule, Asian societies tend to place more importance on society as a whole rather than the individual *per se*.[2] This is in common with, say, Islam, which emphasizes the rights of the *ummah* (people of the faith) rather than those of the individual although the *Quran* and the *Hadith* are strewn with sanctions relating to rights of the individual person specifically (Haider 1978). That society and not the individual is to be given more importance is consonant with the following viewpoint of Lee Kuan Yew:

> Whether in periods of golden prosperity or in the depths of disorder, Asia has never valued the individual over society. The society has always been more important than the individual. I think that is what has saved Asia from greatest misery (quoted in Burton 1993).

In the interim it is useful to admit that the champions of human rights in Asian countries today, including those in India, Malaysia and Singapore, tend to over-stress the importance of the individual rather than society as a whole.

The accusation of 'authoritarianism' has always been applied to national governments that efficiently defeat the individual person when confronted with risks related to internal security and public order. The conflicts between the power of the State and the rights of individuals have baffled purists in human rights jurisprudence for decades. The questions which naturally emanate and point to the issue of determining to what extent the state can make laws that are counter to basic rights, can only be justified if there is a fair balance between rights and responsibilities. That is to say, where there are rights there are responsibilities to be meted out.

Can the conflict between rule of law and executive power continue unobtrusively for the future without any limitation? One may argue by saying that the power of the State to do this will continue for so long as there are governments and the governed. Violations of basic rights can exist and persist in New York, Peking or Jakarta or in any Asian city. And purists can blame anybody for any mishap or abuse for as long as the need to keep law and order persists. This is also true in Malaysia, as in other emerging democracies that claim to be pegged to democratic systems of government.

Whilst civil liberties have been constant hot pursuits in the West, stemming from domestic dictates of the rule of law as well as international covenants, in Asia civil liberties remain equally relevant when determining the dictates of daily life. But while this is so, domestic governments prefer to safeguard society first followed by the individual, while in the West it is the opposite. At the same time, rights and freedoms constitutionally framed have been known to be meaningless if the populace goes hungry, if the citizenry is overridden by an outside economic force, if a superpower hovers over the realms of a domestic jurisdiction, or when a national government is pushed aside by force or through the might of a superpower.

Colonization in the past encompassed all these aspects and more. When colonization ceases, usually after an affair of tumult and revolt, a large segment of the colonizer's values continue to be imbued and practised in the legal system, the economy and other governmental approaches. But usually the new native fervour and choice slowly takes form, and subsequent to this the native value system takes effect. Rights and freedoms, obligations and responsibilities develop through public as well as private policies and permutations.

RECEPTION OF CIVIL LIBERTY NORMS

It is useful to explore a segment of the Malaysian scene on civil liberties, given that much of the country's legal and judicial structure is fashioned after the common law. Before the commencement of British rule towards the third quarter of the nineteenth century, the Malays administered *adat* (customary tenets) and Islamic norms. The Malays abide by the system of old by following the maxims:

Bulat air kerana pembetung	Water is shaped by its container
Bulat manusia kerana muafakat	Men unite under consensus
Adat bersandar pada Syara'	*Adat* is founded on the Syariah
Syara' bersandar Kitabillah	Syariah is based on the Book (Quran)
Alam beraja, luak berpenghulu	The King rules his kingdom, the Chief his domain
Manusia merancang	Man proposes
Allah menentu	God disposes

Simplistic as it may seem, Malay kingdoms of old - be they in Sumatra or the Malay Peninsula, appeared to have run effective albeit feudalistic governments. R. J. Wilkinson, one of the more ardent students of Malay topics, admitted that were it not for the British intervention, Islamic law or *Syariah* would have held sway in the Malay States (Wilkinson 1922). But because of the British intervention, the common law tradition and a broadly similar court system as first practised in the Straits Settlements had by this time taken root in the various territories, and by the time Malaya received its *Merdeka* (Independence) in 1957 the constituent Malay States had already experienced a long history of their own administration of justice through the conduit of common law. Yet as if steered by the wheel of revival, Islam has had a robust reassertion in present-day Malaysia. Pursuant to a constitutional amendment in 1988, *Syariah* offences are now triable only in the country's *Syariah* court. In an obverse perspective, Wilkinson's postulation on Islamic law appears to emerge in bloom.

Much of what is understood to have been the rule of law prior to *Merdeka* depended on what the English common law brought into the Straits Settlements and the Malay States,[3] all of which came to be directly or indirectly under British rule from the late nineteenth century. Despite the impact of Dicey's elucidation of the rule of law in England in 1885 (Dicey 1987), there had been no particular and direct reference made to the doctrine of the rule of law either by the local courts or the pre-*Merdeka* legislature.

Yet the notion and administration of justice had not been totally overridden by executive priorities, which in the main sprang from the need to quell militant communism in the Malay States, especially from 1948 to 1960.[4] Confronted up to the Japanese Occupation in the early 1940s by problems brought about by foreign labour, namely Chinese and Indians, scuffles for tin on the west coast of the Peninsula, and various types of incursions and social unrest arising from secret societies, Malaya was so preoccupied with its own domestic problems that there was hardly any interval within which the British authorities could nurture a balanced rule of law environment.

At the same time it must be admitted that no colonial government was eager to establish an accountable democratic system, since that exercise would go counter to the interests of the colonial administration. However, a variety of decisions based on common law principles were at hand even before independence, although Malayans came into the shade of fundamental rights only after the coming into force of the *Merdeka* constitution in 1957. This historical backdrop needs to be appreciated when viewing the set-up of basic rights under the Constitution.

Malaysia has achieved much by way of having its share of the common law tradition, although many may want to dispute this fact. More than two decades prior to *Merdeka* the rules of natural justice were already clear and guiding principles in the Malay States. This was evident from the observations of Terrell Ag. CJ in *Motor Emporium v. Arumugam*,[5] who regarding natural justice in the Malay States said that:

> The Courts of the Federated Malay States have on many occasions acted on equitable principles, *not because English rules of equity apply, but because such rules happen to conform to the principles of natural justice* (italics supplied).

There was, however, an irony in the fate of a judge like Terrell who, twenty years later in 1953, had to take action against the Secretary of State for the Colonies for having prematurely dismissed him as a judge on spurious grounds.[6] Terrell's case stands for the proposition that there was no actual independence of the judiciary in the Straits Settlements and Malay States, although through the judgements of the court justice was seen to be done.

With *Merdeka* in 1957, the Malay States experienced for the first time the force of a formal constitution that boasted several tenets of the rule of law, including fundamental rights[7] and a demarcation of powers and functions for the executive,[8] legislature[9] and the judiciary.[10]

The critic, perhaps, should not be too hasty in branding certain shortcomings in Malaysia's rule of law environment if its accompanying history is appreciated. Between the First and Second World Wars leading up to the Malays' rejection of the Malayan Union in 1946, the country had been torn by the various skirmishes recounted above, and then it was hit by militant communist terrorists. In May 1969 the country had to contend with racial riots over political and economic issues, chiefly between Malays and Chinese. That resulted in enhanced security and public order laws. In a way, the phobia against the 'enemy of the state' had helped to develop a perpetuation of sorts in the thrust of colonial laws, with new post-Independence instruments exemplifying a British pattern of colonial laws (Table 11.1). With Independence at hand, it was more than assuring for native authorities to imbue and utilise what had been left behind.

Table 11.1 Legal Instruments Pertaining to Security in Malaysia

Legislation	Brief description
The Restricted Residence Act 1933	Extension from the colonial instrument, Restricted Residence Enactment, 1933. A person may be compelled to be confined to a district or county for a period of time without having recourse to be heard by a court of law.
The Sedition Act 1948	Partial restriction on freedom of speech. It is unlawful to (a) bring into contempt and hatred the government or Rulers (b) raise disaffection among citizenry (c) question citizenship, Malay special rights, or the National Language.

Politics and Other Aspects

Table 11.1 (Continued)

Legislation	Brief description
The Internal Security Act 1960	Re-hashed from the British Emergency Ordinance, 1948. Allows executive detention under s.8 (1) for up to 2 years for breach of national security or public order. Provides for death penalty under s.57 (1) for illegal arms. Judicial review only on technical grounds.
The Police Act 1967	Fashioned after the colonial Police Ordinance, 1951. Main features: police empowered not to issue permit for a meeting in public places, and all political gatherings must obtain a police permit (under s. 27).
The University and University College Act, 1975	Enacted soon after the 1974 student riots in Kuala Lumpur headed by Anwar Ibrahim. Main features: students not allowed to participate in politics; certain activities subject to the approval of university authorities.
Publications and Printing Presses Act 1984	Fashioned after the colonial Publications and Printing Presses Enactment, 1948. Main features: all publications subject to approval of the home minister who may also terminate a publication. No grounds need be given. Ministerial decision not allowed to be challenged in any court. However, the publication of books is not controlled.
The Emergency (Public Order and Prevention of Crime) Ordinance 1969 (EPOPCO)	Somewhat similar to the powers outlined under the Internal Security Act. Aimed mainly at the habitual criminal who threatens public order. Executive detention may be effected by the home minister for up to 2 years each time. No judicial review except on technical grounds.

FUNDAMENTAL RIGHTS IN THE CONSTITUTION

The general arrangement of fundamental liberties under the Malaysian Constitution (the Constitution)[11] is now examined. In its general structure, the earlier *Merdeka* Constitution followed the draft prepared by the Reid Commission, which was entrusted with the duty of proposing a finished constitution for Malaya. In 1963, and pursuant to the formation of Malaysia, the Malaysian Constitution followed closely the *Merdeka* Constitution, apart from certain new provisions relating to the rights of the Borneo States of Sabah and Sarawak (Trindade and Lee 1986). However, what is significant is that the rights the Constitution originally offered under Part II (Articles 5 to 13) were made to undergo various changes through the force of constitutional amendments. Thus what were supposed to be regarded as the ground rules or entrenched freedom provisions – called *grundnorm* in legal terminology - ended up quite differently many years after *Merdeka,* as compared to their original concept.

Many able legal icons have fought hard to establish these *grundnorm* over the years. But one of the underpinning priorities, to which the Malaysian courts have been visibly receptive, is the need to buttress security and public order in light of the experience of militant communism after the Communist Party of Malaya took root in the early 1920s with the advent of mainland China migration to the Malay States. Against this background it has not been an easy task for the Malaysian law lords to be judicially active in their judgements over the years when cases involving fundamental rights were at hand.

The first point to be noted is that not all fundamental rights are treated equally under the Malaysian Constitution. Part II of the Constitution, known as the fundamental liberties, contains certain restricted aspects of human rights. These restrictions started with the Reid Draft. The subsequent alterations made by the Alliance Government to the Reid Draft, and alterations to the Merdeka Constitution itself in later years, sharply reduced the protection of these rights. Nevertheless, some of these liberties enjoyed a higher status by virtue of the fact that it was difficult for ordinary law to abridge them. The scope of these rights and the power of Parliament to limit them are clearly spelt out in the Constitution. The following may be said to represent the 'better protected' rights:

Freedom from slavery and forced labour (Article 6);
Protection against retrospective criminal laws and repeated trials (Article 7A);
Prohibition against banishment of citizens (Article 9);
Freedom to profess and practice a religion (Article 11(1));
Freedom from special but not general taxation to support a religion other than one's own (Article 12);
Freedom of a religious group to manage its own religious affairs and to establish and maintain institutions for religious or charitable purposes (Articles 11(3) and 12(2));

Right to adequate compensation for compulsory acquisition or use of private property (Article 13(2)).

The above rights are better protected, in that they are not subject to exceptions or overriding clauses such as considerations of security, public order or morality. In contrast, the freedoms of movement (Article 9), speech, assembly and association (Article 10), for example, are predicated by such exceptions as security, public order, public health or morality. Article 5, in particular, which provides for the liberty of the person from arbitrary arrest is another proviso that has been much qualified and overridden. That Article is superseded by the dictates of internal security and public order. Certain powers of the immigration authorities also preclude the operation of Article 5.

Other fundamental freedoms under Part II are well guarded against executive arbitrariness, but not as well secured against legislative imperatives. 'The Constitution formulates them more as goals, standards and targets than as real guarantees. Their scope is left undefined and Parliament is given extensive power to regulate them on grounds of security, public interest, public health and morality'(Faruqi 1985). Some of these lesser protected rights are:

The right not to be deprived of life or liberty 'save in accordance with law' (Article 5(1));
Equality before the law (Articles 8 and 12 (1));
Freedom of movement (Articles 9 (2) & 9 (3));
Freedom of speech, assembly and association (Article 10).

A second way to categorize fundamental rights would be to demarcate them according to the treatment received by individuals. Some liberties are conferred on all persons, while others are granted to citizens only. Personal liberty, the right to property, freedom of religion, protection against retrospective criminal laws, and repeated trial and prohibition against slavery and forced labour, are rights within the first category. The second category of rights relate to education, equality before the law, freedom of speech, assembly and association, and prohibition against banishment. A significant matter to be appreciated is that all the liberty provisions, except Clause 4 of Article 10, could be amended easily as allowed under Article 159 of the Constitution.[12]

Thus fundamental rights are not entrenched provisions under the Constitution. Certainly, this state of affairs might kindle fresh interest in the wake of Malaysia's new legislation, the establishment in 1999 by Parliament of a Commission on Human Rights, and the growing awareness among the citizenry of personal liberties.

A third way to categorize the liberties in Part II of the Constitution would be to view them within the perspective and currency of emergency power under Article 150 (6A). This lays down that during an emergency the power of Parliament shall not extend to any matter of Islamic law, the custom of the

Malays (*adat*), native law or custom in the states of Sabah and Sarawak, matters of religion, and citizenship and language. All other rights under Part II are subservient to emergency laws. Thus in view of the power of Parliament under Articles 149[13] and 150 to override most fundamental liberties under the Constitution, 'the only genuinely safeguarded provisions of the Constitution are not those contained in Part II but those given under Article 150 (6A). They enjoy greater sanctity and are more entrenched in the Constitution than any other rights' (Faruqi 1985, p. 8).

It has been said also that the constitution guarantees no more than what are the basic rights of citizens, and that it only manifests the sum total of such rights and liberties before its existence (Dicey 1987, p. 135). The fact that rights are pre-constitutional suggests that they are inalienable. However, this has not proven to be so in the case of Malaysia because these 'rights' were not clearly in existence prior to the adoption of the Constitution in 1957. Prior to Independence in 1957, what were deemed to be basic rights had not been clearly formulated or seen as being concrete and traditional, given the pre-existence of sultanate rule. Looked at from this angle, Part II of the Constitution was a direct import of limited rights and freedoms, exceptions being accorded to the executive to take care of matters pertaining to security and public order. Such rights were not embedded in the Indian Constitution or those like it.

In contrast, what were really regarded as 'traditional elements' of the Constitution were matters like citizenship rights (Part III), the special position of the Malays (Article 153), the National (Malay) Language (Article 152), and the sovereign rights of the Rulers (Article 181) (Mohd Salleh Abas 1986). These may not be amended unless they are supported by at least two-thirds of the total number of members of each House of Parliament and consented to by the Conference of Rulers (Article 159 (5)). Be that as it may, the affairs of 1993 prove that even the Sultans' hitherto sovereign status gave way to certain constitutional amendments that strengthen the rule of law (Rais Yatim 1995).

In the light of these more entrenched provisions, the fundamental liberties appear to occupy secondary importance in the Constitution. Even the Reid Commission did not recommend them to be grouped as entrenched provisions. It could also be discerned that what were finally translated into Part II were matters which were more in the nature of superimposed rather than basic rights. This is one aspect which, at least in theory, sets the Malaysian Constitution apart from the British Westminster model or its Indian counterpart. Another aspect is that while checks and balances are in-built within the Westminster model, particularly by way of a powerful public opinion generated by a free media, under the Malaysian Constitution, equilibrium is determined by the need to keep law and order and the uncompromising need of national security priority. In essence this arrangement is not too distinct from the framework in the Reid Draft, which allows for the maintenance of security and public order.

LIBERTY OF THE PERSON

One of the most trodden upon human rights provisions of the Constitution is Article 5, which guarantees that 'no person shall be deprived of his life or personal liberty save in accordance with law'. The original version of this article in the *Merdeka* Constitution was largely similar to the one recommended by the Reid Commission. Article 5 in the *Merdeka* Constitution read:

1. No person shall be deprived of his life or personal liberty save in accordance with law.
2. Where complaint is made to a High Court or any judge thereof that a person is being unlawfully detained the court shall inquire into the complaint and, unless satisfied that the detention is lawful, shall order him to be produced before the court and release him.
3. Where a person is arrested he shall be informed as soon as may be of the grounds of his arrest and shall be allowed to consult and be defended by a legal practitioner of his choice.
4. Where a person is arrested and not released he shall without unreasonable delay, and in any case within twenty-four hours (excluding the time of any necessary journey) be produced before a magistrate and shall not be further detained in custody without the magistrate's authority.[14]

Thus, on the authority of Clause (1) of Article 5, if Parliament created a law that deprived life consequent upon certain prohibitions, e.g. the trafficking of dangerous drugs, that law would be valid. Thus it is true to say that executive action can freely violate the personal liberties of an individual 'provided it enacts a law to sanction such breaches' (Scoble and Wiseberg 1997).

Handing down a decision on restricted residence in 1977, the presiding judge defined the court's constitutional outlook in respect of rights under the Constitution in the following way:

The Constitution is not a mere collection of pious platitudes. It is the supreme law of the land embodying three basic concepts: One of them is that *the individual has certain fundamental rights upon which not even the power of the State may encroach*. The second is the distribution of sovereign power between the States and the Federation, that the 13 States shall exercise sovereign power in local matters and the nation in matters affecting the country at large. The third is that no single man or body shall exercise complete sovereign power, but that it shall be distributed among the Executive, Legislative and Judicial Branches of government, compendiously expressed in modern terms that we are government of laws, not men[15] (italics supplied).

RESTRICTIONS OF LIBERTY

Liberty or freedom can never be total for man. As in all things, freedom has its own share of exceptions and overrides. In Malaysia, as has been shown, this principle permeates even its most cherished constitutional provisions. Table 11.1 of instruments, true to the tradition of prioritizing public interest first and an individual's rights second, describes a number of tough security and public order laws.

These laws, albeit having been contested in court, have in the finality been rendered constitutional. Thus restriction of movement in the country is allowed under Article 9 (2) for purposes of ensuring security and public order, public health or the punishment of offenders. Freedom of speech, assembly and association under Article 10 also have a host of overrides and exceptions by virtue of Parliament's overall authority to legislate contrary to these rights on the premises of security, friendly relations with other countries, public order or morality. Freedom of speech is restricted, for example, by the Sedition Act, 1948, and by the Publications and Printing Presses Act, 1984. Freedom of assembly is restrained by the Police Act, 1967, the Restricted Residence Act, 1933, and the Public Order Act, 1958. The right to associate is confined in part by the Societies Act, 1966. The Internal Security Act could be invoked on grounds of security, but executive detention has not been effected even in the midst of unruly antagonism in the wake of the Anwar Ibrahim dismissal and trial. This bears testimony to the relenting attitude of the authorities, although oppositional views continue to assert that civil liberties are not sufficiently catered for and nurtured. As signified at the outset of this chapter, the adequacy and insufficiency of rights will always be contentious.

CONSTITUTIONALISM

Constitutionalism, being a legal and judicial concept to balance segments and powers in government, must finally be brought to bear, whether on grounds of fairness and justice or other valid grounds of constitutional force and influence. Whilst constitutionalism is said to thrive on unwritten rules i.e. customs or conventions (De Smith 1963, p. 142), it has proven to be inapplicable in Malaysia for the simple reason that judicial attention to customs or conventions has been negligible. Constitutional conventions are not generally recognized by the courts in Malaysia. Apart from the *adat* which has been accorded a special position of its own in constitutional outlay and interpretation, the courts have not recognized conventions such as the 'concept of basic structures' or 'basic residual rights', both of which have been constitutional safeguards in India and the United States.

The Malaysian law lords, in the main, prefer strict interpretation of the written law, which is not an altogether wrong approach, but this disposition certainly renders dormant any semblance of judicial dynamism. Thus if Parliament wants Article 5 (4) to be overridden by the Restricted Residence Enactment, 1933, so be it. This scenario has been well accepted in the endeavour to establish and perpetuate law and order pursuant to the need to upkeep public order

CONCLUSION

It has been remarked that in Asia the public does not tolerate a weak government (Walsh 1993, p. 16). A local political scientist said, 'Those that govern best are those that govern most' (Ibid., p. 15). Such views no doubt lead to strong governments, albeit by way of some arbitrary power. But recent developments in Kuala Lumpur, specifically the Anwar Ibrahim dismissal and trial, have precipitated certain developments that could compel the re-examination of public order laws. Malaysia believes in contextual liberty which in essence does not rest on pure theoretical rights and freedoms. Liberty must rest on the larger interests of the public.

The emergence of violent street demonstrations subsequent to the Anwar Ibrahim case has compelled the taking of proportionate action by the authorities pursuant to existing laws. Some student bodies had expressed collective concern over certain actions taken by the government.[16] The politics of religion in the country, monopolized and galvanized by the Pan Malaysia Islamic Party, has been seen to thwart multi-racial harmony, the one spinal column of Malaysia's social and political well-being. Islam has of late been abused by this party to suit its political ends, and in the process genuine religious tenets and practice have been compromised. Local civil liberties have been subjugated by this trend, not to mention the danger of uncontrolled zeal in propagating one's religious and political priorities. If unchecked, this tendency will definitely end up as a security and public order problem apart from destroying Muslims' *aqidah* or proper path in the faith.

It could be envisaged that the government will continue to adopt a proactive stand on this development, giving a premium on public safety in a law and order environment. Already there have been strong views from certain Islamic purists to suggest a policy of barring the usage of the name of any religion in any political party, if the situation warrants such a last resort to quell religious bigotry. It must be admitted this line of action will be met by certain difficulties in the area of interpretation and outlook, although the power of Parliament to pass such law is unhindered.

The East-West compartmentalization of the notion of freedom is erroneous, on the score that it grants no leeway to Asia's vast reservoir of social justice.

The continued arm-twisting with the 'fall in line or else' tactic of the big powers will no longer work. For history has a way of judging the success of a nation, although certain international sectors have ways and means of condemning a country's system by attacking its judiciary and administration of justice. The fact that Malaysia has emerged self-reliant and subsisting on its economy and domestic value system gives much assurance for the coming millennium. The 'displeasure' of outside forces in regard to Malaysia's style of doing things must necessarily be regarded as the typical historical baggage of superpower politics, which Malaysia understands but which she cannot and will not accept in the wake of her own national priorities. Those persons who have walked the streets of Kuala Lumpur or Penang or any of Malaysia's big towns during the small hours of the night know that public safety is a matter of course. That feeling is not mutual when a walk is taken in the Bronx in New York or Watts in Los Angeles.

Malaysia will continue to have its own brand of civil liberty and its own style of doing things despite recent activism by the Federal Court, which leans to the objective test when interpreting arrest and detaining powers under the Internal Security Act.[17] But it is also likely that Malaysia will review its respective laws affecting human rights from time to time, given the tremendous changes taking place in its socio-economic environment, not to mention the need to accommodate new thrusts and challenges propelled by the country's swelling educated elite. A *caveat* that goes with this forecast is that whatever changes are anticipated will have to conform to the Malaysian milieu and not to that of outside dictates. Already Malaysia has created a fresh law on human rights - the Human Rights Commission Act, 1999. This legislation singularly ushers in a new dimension in the future of local civil liberties. Although some quarters are not happy with the Act's definition of human rights, at least a milestone development is taking place in a sphere where there were hitherto no provisions. With the power to investigate and make known human rights' violations, the new Act can be expected to contribute substantially to Malaysia's human rights development.

It is envisaged that for the remainder of the new decade Malaysia will continue to galvanize changes in the concept and practice of civil liberty, but again with the *caveat* that it will do so according to the Malaysian way of being just and fair for the larger interests of society.

NOTES
1. Some equate this right with the right to an adequate standard of living (see Sieghart 1988, pp. 71 - 84).
2. Mr Lee Kuan Yew, former prime minister of Singapore, opined this view in 1993 (see Burton 1993, p. 21). The leadership in Malaysia, and until recently in Indonesia, have appeared to subscribe to this view although no direct permeation of ideas *inter parte* is on record.
3. The original Malay States comprised Perlis, Kedah, Kelantan, Terengganu, Perak, Selangor, Negeri Sembilan, Pahang and Johore. Penang and Malacca, formerly part of the Straits

Settlements, joined the Federation of Malaya by virtue of the Federation of Malaya Agreement 1948. The whole political unit was then known as Malaya.

4. The present Internal Security Act, 1960, originated from the Emergency Ordinance, 1948.
5. (1933) MLJ276.
6. *Terrell v. Secretary of State for the Colonies* (1953) 2 QB 482.
7. See Part II of the Constitution.
8. Articles 39 - 43 (Part IV).
9. Articles 44 - 66 (Part IV Chapter 4).
10. Articles 121 - 131 (Part IX).
11. The Malaysian Constitution is officially called the Federal Constitution. It replaced the *Merdeka* Constitution in 1963 with the coming into force of the Malaysia Act 1963 (Act 26/1963) on 16 September 1963.
12. The Constitution can be amended if the amendment '...has been supported on Second and Third Readings by the votes of not less than two-thirds of the total number of members of that House' (see Article 38).
13. Special powers against subversion, organized violence, and acts prejudicial to the public.
14. Clause (4) of Article 5 has undergone 3 amendments since *Merdeka*.
15. (1977) 2 MLJ 187 at 188.
16. Thus on 12 October 1999, a group of student leaders demanded, in the presence of the then new Deputy prime minister, Datuk Seri Abdullah Ahmad Badawi, changes to certain laws - the Internal Security Act and the Universities and University Colleges Act being two of these. Consequently, a student-government parley group was formed to give vent to the students' outcry.
17. See Mohd Ezzam and Others v. Minister of Home Affairs (2002) 4 AMR 4053. Dzaiddin Ismail CJ, Steve Shim FCJ, Abdul Malek Ahmad FCJ, and Siti Norma FCJ held that when the police effect power of arrest and detention under s.73 (1) of the ISA due regard must be had in respect of grounds of arrest and detention; that the police in respect of detention must be seen to be applying reasons based on security; that there is to be no denial of the basic right to counsel during police dentention under s.73 (1).

12. The Challenges of Opposition Politics in Malaysia - Checking Growing Authoritarianism and Ethnic Re-polarization

Lim Kit Siang

Many Malaysians had hoped that the tenth Malaysian general election in November 1999 would be a watershed event - not to topple from power the UMNO-dominated *Barisan Nasional* (BN) coalition but to create a paradigm shift in Malaysian politics by breaking the BN's political hegemony and its uninterrupted two-thirds parliamentary majority. For the first time in Malaysian electoral history, a single multi-ethnic and multi-religious opposition front, the *Barisan Alternatif* (BA) was formed comprising four opposition parties: *Parti Islam SeMalaysia* (PAS), *Parti Keadilan Nasional* (*Keadilan*), *Parti Rakyat Malaysia* and the Democratic Action Party, covering a wide spectrum of political and class interests.

Opposition parties in Malaysia had previously cooperated in general elections. In 1969, for instance, electoral pacts were forged involving the Democratic Action Party, the *Parti Gerakan Rakyat Malaysia* and the People's Progressive Party. In 1990, the formation of *Parti Semangat 46* as a splinter group of UMNO in opposition to Dr Mahathir was the common factor in the formation of two opposition groupings. One with the Democratic Action Party, *Parti Rakyat Malaysia* and other non-Malay parties was labelled GAGASAN, and the other with PAS and other Muslim-based parties was called *Angkatan Perpaduan Ummah* (APU). However, 1999 was the first time that a single opposition front involving PAS and the Democratic Action Party in particular had emerged.

Indeed, until 1998 both PAS and Democratic Action Party leaders generally avoided working and being seen together on the same platform, so that the electorate as well as their own supporters would not be confused. This was because the BN, through its tight control of the mass media, had succeeded over the years in demonizing the two parties and in projecting them as diametrically opposed to one another. On the one hand the Democratic Action Party was portrayed as anti-Malay and anti-Islam, while PAS was portrayed as intolerant, extremist and fanatical.

EMERGENCE OF THE *BARISAN ALTERNATIF*

The political ferment and effervescence unleashed by the Anwar Ibrahim event beginning from September 1998 (see Chapter 9) called into question such demonization of the opposition parties. In fact, the questioning of this baseless and malicious political stereotyping of the opposition parties and personalities had started even earlier, as can be illustrated in the case of the then Democratic Action Party member of parliament (MP), Lim Guan Eng.

Guan Eng was the first prominent political leader in four decades of Malaysian nationhood who crossed ethnic and religious boundaries, not just by his words but also by his deeds. A three-term ethnic Chinese Malaysian MP, Guan Eng stood up in the defence of the rights and dignity of an under-aged Malay girl who was a victim of statutory rape. This led to his arrest and prosecution on a charge of sedition.[1] Although his treatment by the authorities was questioned at home and abroad and he was adopted by Amnesty International as a 'prisoner of conscience', nonetheless he was imprisoned and disqualified as an MP. Guan Eng has since been released after serving his sentence, but by virtue of his imprisonment remains disenfranchized of his full political and civil rights for another five years, until August 2004.

However, it was the Anwar Ibrahim factor which had the greatest catalytic effect. Anwar's sacking, arrest, prosecution and imprisonment created the political conditions for a multi-ethnic and multi-religious opposition front to emerge. For the public was even more outraged at how the second highest political leader in the land, Mahathir's heir-apparent who had virtually been anointed as the incoming fifth prime minister, could overnight be dumped and treated as the most notorious criminal in the country. In the event, all independent organs of government were suborned and decency and fair play thrown overboard, thereby igniting a political awakening and uprising, especially among young Malays. It was a vivid and potent reminder that no Malaysian can be assured of justice, fair play or even common decency so long as the powerful apparatus of government has been subverted to serve, not the interests of the people and nation as it should, but the interests of the powers-that-be and especially the prime minister.

There was another reason why the BA differed from earlier efforts in bringing opposition parties together. It succeeded in formulating a common manifesto, which spelled out the priority concerns and agenda of the opposition coalition.

A COMMON MANIFESTO

Entitled *Towards a Just Malaysia*, the common manifesto of the BA (*Barisan Alternatif* 1999) proclaimed that the 'biggest challenge facing the people of Malaysia is the creation of a just and democratic country'. It focused on the 'political crisis' facing the country, resulting from 'a government which concentrates power in the Executive, in a single individual in particular, thus crippling our system of checks and balances'. The manifesto stated that:

> When power becomes so concentrated and personalised:
> 1. The interests of those in power become paramount, the interests of the people are ignored;
> 2. Those in power determine everything, including what is supposedly the interests of the people;
> 3. The people are paralysed and human rights violations become rampant;
> 4. Those in power do not respect nor consider the differing views of others; instead they are vilified, including with fabricated accusations;
> 5. Blind loyalty to the leadership is expected, even when the leadership is wrong; and
> 6. The principles and practice of public accountability are ignored and in the process institutions are undermined (*Barisan Alternatif* 1999).

The BA pledged to create 'A Just and Democratic Malaysia' with Malaysians of all races and at all levels of society. Together with the people, the Alternative Front sought to usher in a system of governance that:

1. Is honest, dynamic and truly accountable;
2. Has a truly democratic parliamentary system that represents their interests;
3. Has truly independent and clean judicial institutions;
4. Has a police force which is professional and executes its duties in a just and fair manner, according to the tenets of law;
5. Has a mass media that is free and not beholden to those in power;
6. Values accountability and transparency as its fundamental elements;
7. Respects differences of views, using them to correct mistakes arising from human shortcomings; and
8. Supports a dynamic, resilient and just economy, which is also internationally competitive.

The BA stressed that the 'just and democratic society' would be based on the fundamental spiritual and ethical values that are part and parcel of the teachings of Islam as well as of the other great religions practised in Malaysia, so as to provide a bastion against corruption, unbridled greed and moral decay. The BA further committed itself to uphold the fundamental principles of the Malaysian constitution, namely:

1. Constitutional sovereignty;
2. Constitutional monarchy;
3. Parliamentary democracy;
4. Fundamental freedoms;
5. The rule of law;
6. Judicial independence;
7. The rights and responsibilities of citizenship;

8. The position of Islam as the religion of the Federation, coupled with the principle of the freedom of worship;
9. The position of *Bahasa Melayu* as the national language, the language of knowledge and the official language, whilst safeguarding the right to use and learn other languages;
10. The special position of the Malays and the *Bumiputera* of Sabah and Sarawak, and the legitimate rights of other races; and
11. A federal administrative system that fulfils its responsibilities, including protection and respect for the special position of the states of Sabah and Sarawak.

Before spelling out in detail its action plan and programme in the common manifesto, the BA also made further pledges.[2]

The general election of 1999 was therefore the most ambitious and wide-ranging attempt on the part of the opposition parties to usher in a new politics. Through its ability to forge a common manifesto, the opposition presented itself to the people as a coherent and credible united front possessing a common set of goals. Hence, it appeared confident of taking on the BN juggernaut and cutting it down to size.

THE ELECTION CAMPAIGN AND RESULTS

However, the hoped-for result was not to be. The BN secured its usual two-thirds parliamentary majority. Although it won 56 per cent of the national vote, the BN secured 76 per cent of the parliamentary seats - thanks to the undemocratic electoral system. Apart from the gerrymandering of the constituencies, the unfair preparation and revision of the electoral register caused some 680,000 recently registered young voters to be denied their right to vote in the 1999 general election (see Chapter 8). Other electoral abuses included unsupervised postal voting, the existence of 'phantom voters' and the National Front's unfair, perhaps even illegal, access to the '3Ms' - mass media, money politics and government machinery.

Nonetheless, UMNO fared poorly in the general election, emerging as the BN's greatest casualty. For the first time, UMNO won fewer parliamentary seats than did its coalition partners combined. The BN won 148 out of the 193 parliamentary seats contested in 1999, down from 161 in 1995, a 13-seat reduction. UMNO won only 72 seats in 1999 compared to 88 seats in 1995, a 16-seat loss. The state assembly results in the election were even more devastating for UMNO. It not only failed to recapture the state of Kelantan, but also lost Terengganu to the PAS, and narrowly staved off the fall of two other northern states, namely Perlis and Kedah. Overall for Peninsular Malaysia, UMNO captured only 176 state seats in 1999 compared to 231 state seats in 1995, a drop of 55 seats. Never before in the political history of the nation had the legitimacy of UMNO as the representative of the Malays been so seriously questioned. In fact, the BN appeared to have been more successful among the non-Malays, in particular the Chinese. Consequently, while UMNO was the biggest loser in the BN, the Democratic Action Party was the biggest loser in the BA. The 1999 election outcome is further discussed in Chapter 7.

Ironically, during the 1999 electoral campaign, the BA opposition parties were preaching and practising national unity while the BN ruling parties were sowing inter-racial and inter-religious distrust, discord and disunity, i.e. a throwback and regression to the communal politics of the 1980s and before. Indeed, the BN conducted a very dishonest campaign of instilling fear and spreading falsehood. Malays were told that 'the DAP plus PAS equals *Islam Hancur*' (Islam destroyed) while Chinese and non-Malays were warned that 'a vote for the DAP is a vote for PAS is a vote for an Islamic state'. There would no longer be pork, nor alcohol, nor temples, nor churches, nor karaoke lounges, nor Chinese schools, nor lipstick for women. Instead, women would have to cover their heads, beautiful women would be denied jobs, and there would be a chopping of hands.

The short nine-day campaign period, coupled with the virtual monopoly of the BN over the mass media, both printed and electronic, did not allow the BA enough time and opportunity to expose and counter the chicanery of the BN's propaganda, which was in fact contradictory in several regards. For in calling the electorate to reject the BA - the formation of which was surely an exercise in the inter-ethnic and inter-religious cooperation which the BN itself claimed as its own goal - the BN unabashedly resorted to ethnic and religious baiting. It raised the spectre of the impending destruction of Islam among potential Muslim supporters on the one hand, and the spectre of the end of non-Muslim cultural and religious rights among potential non-Muslim supporters on the other. Other items of the BN's propaganda included inculcating fear of a repeat of the 13 May 1969 racial riots and of recurring economic instability should the BA come to power. Such vicious propaganda vindicated what the prime minister, Dr Mahathir Mohamad had publicly forecast a few months before the polls - that the tenth general election would be the 'dirtiest election in history'.

Indeed, the 1999 campaign was reminiscent of UMNO's *coup de grâce* in the 1990 general election. Then, in the final lap of the campaign, all printed and electronic media were mobilized to portray the *Semangat 46* President and Dr. Mahathir Mohamad's challenger, Tengku Razaleigh Hamzah, as having sold out to the Malays and betrayed Islam. The purported 'evidence' was a photograph of Razaleigh wearing the *tengkolok*, the traditional Kadazan headgear purportedly bearing the sign of the Christian cross. In fact, the design on the *tengkolok* symbolized padi stalks. Dr Mahathir himself had donned a *tengkolok* bearing virtually the same design during his visit to Sabah a few days earlier, but the BN's propagandists chose not to highlight this. In the event, the misleading portrayal of Tengku Razaleigh resulted in massive defeats for *Semangat 46* candidates, who had until that last round of propaganda been optimistic of their chances.

Significantly in 1999, the Malay voters did not fall prey to the BN's propaganda of instilling fear and spreading falsehood. But the non-Malays did. In particular, many Chinese believed that the Democratic Action Party's cooperation with PAS would facilitate the formation of an Islamic state in Malaysia. Consequently, the BA's call to rally behind the struggle for justice, freedom, democracy and good governance, and to break the BN's political hegemony, was not heeded by many non-Malays in particular. Thus the opposition ended up 20 parliamentary seats short of depriving the BN of its two-thirds parliamentary majority.

TOWARDS ARBITRARY AND AUTHORITARIAN RULE

Yet, developments subsequent to the 1999 election indicate it is imperative that efforts be made to strengthen the multi-ethnic and multi-religious opposition front, so as to lay the basis for the creation of a two-coalition, if not two-party, political system. For the prime minister, Dr Mahathir, does not seem prepared to respond positively to UMNO's dismal performance in the general election. Neither does he seem prepared to acknowledge 'that what the people want is not just physical development but also freedom', as has been stated by his long-term nemesis, Tengku Razaleigh Hamzah. Instead, in the period following the 1999 election, Malaysia moved even more towards arbitrary and authoritarian rule. Events in this direction during that period included:

1. The utter contempt shown by Dr Mahathir Mohamad to the *Yang di Pertuan Agong*, the constitution and parliament when he unconstitutionally convened the new tenth parliament on 20 December 1999 without first forming a new cabinet. In so doing, the prime minister disregarded the constitutional provision that only the cabinet (and not the prime minister acting on his own volition) can advise the King to summon parliament. Consequently, all laws and businesses passed by the tenth parliament could be infected by illegality and even declared unconstitutional.
2. The arrest and prosecution of several opposition leaders from the BA for sedition or under the Official Secrets Act. The charge for sedition against the Democratic Action Party national deputy chairman, five-term MP and renowned counsel, Karpal Singh, was the first prosecution of its kind in the Commonwealth of Nations. Yet Karpal's allegedly seditious remarks were made in court in defence of former deputy prime minister, Anwar Ibrahim. By charging Karpal Singh, therefore, the BN government not only trampled on the traditional immunity of lawyers from state prosecution and persecution for their conduct in court (apart from being subject to court contempt proceedings). It also violated international norms and principles like the 1990 United Nations Basic Principles on the Role of Lawyers. In fact, speaking in Malaysia Hall in London at the end of January 2000, after Karpal had been arrested and charged, the prime minister not only declared that Karpal who had said 'a lot of nasty things against us ...should have been charged a long time ago' (Mahathir Mohamad, 2000a). He also went on record to say that he 'wished to hang Karpal', but that this was just his wish. For he had no

power to influence the courts, which decided on legal proceedings independently of the executive!

3. The charge for sedition against *Keadilan*'s vice president, Marina Yusoff, for stating in a speech that UMNO leaders had started the 13 May riots in 1969. This has to be seen in the context that nobody from the BN had ever been charged for sedition for claiming over the years that the opposition had started the 13 May riots.

4. The charge under the Official Secrets Act against *Keadilan*'s youth chief, Mohamed Ezam Mohd Noor, for disclosing classified information about cover-ups in anti-corruption investigations involving top UMNO leaders. This information had become an 'open secret' as it had been posted on the internet and was also the subject of police reports lodged by Anwar Ibrahim on corruption in high political circles in July and August 1999. The BN did not seem bothered that in prosecuting Mohamad Ezam it was inadvertently confirming the veracity of official documents, and that there had in fact been a cover-up of corrupt acts. Although the Official Secrets Act is a colonial anachronism, it has been amended to make it probably the most draconian piece of such legislation in the world. Conviction under the Act entails a mandatory minimum one-year jail sentence and an ensuing five-year disenfranchisement of civic and political rights even after release from jail.

5. The crackdown on press freedom taken against independent-minded publications. Actions against *Harakah, Detik, Wasilah, Tamadun* and *Eksklusif* ranged from banning their sale on news-stands through limiting the frequency of their publication to restricting their sale of publications only to members of the party, as in the case of *Harakah*, the PAS publication.

6. The massive police show of force, involving arrests and road blocks throughout the country, to forestall a planned peaceful assembly in Kuala Lumpur on 14 April 2000, to mark the first anniversary of the first jail sentences for Anwar. This action can be matched against the commendation by the Malaysian prime minister of the actions of demonstrators at the Word Trade Organization summit in Seattle and at the World Bank and International Monetary Fund meeting in Washington, D.C.

In this regard, the release of *Justice in Jeopardy: Malaysia 2000*, the joint report of four prominent international lawyers' organizations (International Bar Association 2000), merits mentioning. This report is a terrible indictment of the system of justice, rule of law and independence of the judiciary in Malaysia. It concludes that 'the extremely powerful Executive in Malaysia has not acted with due regard for the essential elements of a free and democratic society based on the rule of law'. And although in the vast majority of cases which come before the courts at whatever level there is no complaint about the independence of the judiciary, there are serious concerns that in cases of political or economic importance to the executive the judiciary is not independent. This perception is also held by members of the general public.

That these concerns are not just those of foreign observers but also of Malaysians is best attested by the recent remarks of the former chief justice (then known as the lord president), Tun Suffian, who had served under the four prime ministers Tunku Abdul Rahman, Tun Razak, Tun Hussein Onn and Dr

Mahathir. Recounting the first judicial crisis in 1988 which resulted in the removal of the lord president of that time, Tun Salleh Abas, Tun Suffian said:

> The news of the devastation that hit the judiciary resounded throughout the world and reached me in Geneva, where friends asked me what sort of country Malaysia was. I was at a loss to explain and, for the first time in my life, I felt ashamed of being a Malaysian (Mohamed Suffian 2000).

He added:

> I had predicted that our judiciary would take a whole generation to recover from the assault. Now that more than 12 years have elapsed, I doubt if the judiciary would recover in a generation from today.
>
> Judges who joined in downing their boss have been rewarded by promotion. Judges who did not, have been cowed into silence. Judges are at sixes and sevens. Some daren't speak to each other. While there are judges whose integrity and impartiality have never wavered, the public perception is that the judiciary as a whole can no longer be trusted to honour their oath of office. When I am asked what I thought, my usual reply is that I wouldn't like to be tried by today's judges, especially if I am innocent.

Tun Suffian concluded:

> It is not enough for Government to have confidence in the judiciary if the public does not. It is not enough for courts only to go through the motion of a trial. It is not enough if justice seems to be done if in fact justice has not been done.

Yet all these concerns were virtually ignored by the BN government. In fact, many concerns about the relentless deterioration of the system of justice and the marginalization of the fundamental rights of Malaysians had already been documented in an earlier report, *Malaysia: Assault on the Judiciary* published by a another team of foreign legal experts (Lawyers' Committee on Human Rights 1989). The concerns were also expressed in the book, *Freedom under Executive Power in Malaysia* by the then critic Rais Yatim (1995). The latter has since the 1999 election returned to the cabinet as minister in the Prime Minister's Department, with specific responsibility over law and justice. His views on some of the aspects treated here are canvassed in Chapter 11.

Justice in Jeopardy: Malaysia 2000 provides testimony that the fears of Rais Yatim (1995, p. 20) that 'the future of the rule of law and human rights in Malaysia is dismal', that 'the independence of the judiciary is merely illusory', and that 'the executive has come to occupy a truly supreme position that renders the other segments of government - Parliament and the judiciary - subservient to it' (p. 20) have come to pass. It is evident from the events discussed that the state of democracy and human rights in Malaysia in the year 2000 was in a worse position than in 1995. One suspects that things are going to deteriorate further before they get better. It is imperative that the multi-ethnic and multi-religious opposition front should be strengthened and consolidated, so as to be the bulwark against the further erosion of the rule of law and the denial of fundamental rights and freedoms in the country.

RE-POLARIZATION OF ETHNICITY AND RELIGION

There are two other reasons why the opposition front must be strengthened, namely, to break down the old 'divide and rule' politics dominated by race and religion, and to replace it with a new politics concerned with creating a just and democratic Malaysia.

There are clear signs that UMNO leaders are resorting to the re-polarization of ethnicity and religion in Malaysian politics, in order to win back support from Malays. They are doing so regardless of adverse consequences for inter-ethnic and inter-religious relations, as well as for Malaysia's economic future in the era of globalization and information technology.

For example, one UMNO minister urged young Malays to 'rediscover themselves' by understanding 'the Malay agenda', lamenting that many young Malay professionals did not seem aware of this agenda and of the struggles surrounding it that had been waged by UMNO on behalf of the Malay community. He said they should try and understand Article 153 of the Constitution (which elaborates on 'special rights' for the Malays), to find out what the agenda was about.

More poignantly, the themes of racial and religious re-polarization were exploited in the UMNO, UMNO Youth and UMNO Women general assemblies held in early 2000. Addressing the joint assemblies of the latter two bodies, deputy prime minister and deputy UMNO president, Abdullah Badawi, asked why UMNO faced opposition from the younger generation of Malays, who were the very group which had benefited most in material terms from UMNO's efforts. He asked: 'How could this have happened? Where did we go wrong?'

It seems beyond the comprehension of the UMNO leaders that the new generation of Malays could be committed to the aspirations and ideals of justice, freedom, democracy and good governance, all of which involve wanting more democratic space for Malaysians including a free press, an independent judiciary, public integrity and a serious war against corruption, cronyism and nepotism. Hence, Abdullah's only proposal was for Malays to unite behind UMNO again, declaring that the political programme of PAS which split the Malays and sought the defeat of UMNO was tantamount to an un-Islamic act.

In his presidential address to the UMNO general assembly, Dr Mahathir dwelt on the same need for Malays to unite. Again, PAS was criticized for collaborating with non-Muslims and sowing discord among Muslims. In one part of his address, Dr Mahathir declared:

Brotherhood in Islam is no longer practised by the Muslims. Everywhere they are at loggerheads with each other and are willing to collaborate with the enemies of Islam to defeat their fellow Muslims.

In Malaysia this has begun to happen. There are Malays who allow themselves to be influenced by the enemies of Islam, so that the efforts to develop and regain the glory of the Malays and Islamic civilisation could be prevented (Mahathir Mohamad 2000b).

Non-Muslim Malaysians who cooperated with PAS in the BA in the 1999 elections to restore justice and democracy cannot but ask themselves whether they are the 'enemies of Islam' referred to by Dr Mahathir and, if so, what are the implications of UMNO's new approach?

One effective way to check the dangers of a re-polarization of race and religion in Malaysian politics, therefore, is to strengthen the multi-ethnic and multi-religious BA. By so doing, the dangerous trends set loose by UMNO in trying to recapture support for itself, but which contradict the concept of a *Bangsa Malaysia* contained in Vision 2020,[3] might still be reined in.

LAYING TO REST THE TWO SPECTRES

However, for the BA to succeed, it must take the initiative in laying to rest the two spectres which the BN used to frighten Malaysian voters in the 1999 elections. On the one hand, this is that the Democratic Action Party is anti-Malay and anti-Islam and wants to see the destruction of Islam. On the other hand, it is that the PAS is extremist and fanatical and wants to end the religious, cultural and political rights and freedoms of non-Muslims in Malaysia. The BA must project, in particular, that the 'political Islam' represented by PAS is an Islam of tolerance and justice which is fully compatible with democracy, which upholds open and accountable government and cultural pluralism, and is compatible with a flowering of human rights and democracy in Malaysia in the new century.

However, in order to be successful in this, the component parties of the BA must acknowledge that many non-Malays feared that the Democratic Action Party's cooperation with PAS in the 1999 elections would lead to the formation of an Islamic state. That was not because they were anti-Islam, but because they feared that they would unable to exercise their full citizenship rights in such a system of governance. It was also in turn related to their belief that a theocratic state, whether Islamic, Buddhist, Christian or Hindu would be inappropriate for a plural society like Malaysia.

In the 1999 election, the Democratic Action Party in particular, and the BA in general, learned to their cost that it was not adequate for the opposition parties in the BA to reach a common accord on a wide spectrum of subjects to achieve a just and democratic society while controversial issues, such as that of an Islamic state, were avoided or deferred. Indeed, the question of an Islamic state does not lend itself easily to rational discussion and resolution in a multi-ethnic, multi-religious society like Malaysia, even less when elections approach and fears and emotions are manipulated.

Hence BA leaders made special efforts to argue and show that an Islamic state was not on the cards in Malaysia. This was because it would require a constitutional amendment, which in turn required a two-thirds majority before its passing in Parliament where PAS on its own was fielding candidates for less than one-third of the parliamentary seats. These efforts and accompanying rational arguments proved futile, however, and were blown to the winds when baseless fears of a primordial nature concerning food, religion and restrictions on women were exploited by the BN in its electoral propaganda.

The issue of an Islamic state must be addressed and settled by the BA itself, once and for all. Once resolved, greater trust and cooperation can develop among the BA component parties. The resolution of this issue can also be the basis to regain lost ground and to win new support. Towards these ends, the Democratic Action Party took the initiative of organizing inter-party, inter-religious and inter-civilizational dialogues in order to build greater inter-racial, inter-political and inter-religious understanding in Malaysia. These were only the first steps in a journey of a thousand miles.

It is hoped that through such inter-religious and inter-civilizational dialogues, which should be held in all parts of the country and at all levels of society, there will be a greater understanding among Malaysians of different races, religions and cultures of two critical issues. The first is that the political Islam represented by PAS has nothing to do with violence, extremism or fanaticism, that it is not oppressive against women and minorities, that it is compatible with religious and cultural pluralism, that it respects human rights, that it espouses political liberalization and democracy, and that in fact that it seeks to promote the development of a true civil society equipped with the institutions, values and culture which will be the foundations of a truly participatory government. The second issue is that the secular system of governance espoused by the Democratic Action Party is not atheist, anti-Islam, or anti-religion, but trans-religious.

In May 2000, another path-breaking initiative was achieved when the PAS spiritual leader, Tuan Guru Nik Aziz Nik Mat, conducted a dialogue with a group of Christians - the Conference of Churches in Malaysia. Significantly, Nik Aziz clarified to the gathering that his party fully realized that Malaysia is a multi-ethnic, multi-religious society, and that Muslims constitute only slightly more than 50 per cent of the population. Accordingly, his party's goal was not the creation of an Islamic state (*negara Islam*). Rather, it sought to create an Islamic community (*masyarakat Islam*).

His message of compassion and fair play in Islam, and his suggestion that an Islamic state is not a practical option in a society where PAS could not, on its own, get a sufficient majority to amend the constitution, could well lay the basis for the consolidation of the multi-ethnic and multi-religious opposition front. It could as well lead to the marginalization of fears and prejudices concerning Islam among non-Muslims in Malaysia.

CONCLUSION

If the BA can contribute to a new politics based on the issues of justice, freedom, democracy and good governance, and move away from the old politics dominated by race and religion, it will be making a signal contribution not only towards political development but also to nation-building.

The inter-civilizational dialogue initiated by the BA is most apt and in keeping with the times, especially since the year 2001 has, on the proposal of the Iranian President Mohammad Khatami, been designated by the General Assembly as the United Nations Year of Dialogue among Civilizations. In his proposal, Khatami expressed the hope that through dialogue among civilizations 'the realisation of universal justice and liberty may be initiated'. He declared:

> If humanity at the threshold of the new century and millennium devotes all efforts to institutionalize dialogue, replacing hostility and confrontation with discourse and understanding, it would leave an invaluable legacy for the benefit of future generations (Mohammad Khatami, 2000).

The UN Resolution establishing the Year of Dialogue emphasizes the 'importance of tolerance in international relations and the significant role of dialogue as a means to reach understanding, remove threats to peace and strengthen interaction and exchange among civilisations' (United Nations 2001).

Malaysia can indeed be the microcosm for an inter-religious and inter-civilizational dialogue. It can offer itself to the world as an example of a political system where diverse races, religions and cultures are able to build a political architecture embracing justice, freedom, democracy, and good governance in an environment of religious and cultural tolerance and pluralism. Ethnic and religious baiting, as currently practised by UMNO and its BN component parties, will then, hopefully, be rejected by Malaysians.

NOTES
1. This was for the second time in his political life, with the first occasion being after the *Operasi Lalang* mass arrests in 1987 (see note 4 of Chapter 8).
2. These were to '(1) Support the people's struggle to create a just and prosperous Malaysian nation based on a truly democratic system of government; (2) Protect and defend the rights and dignity of all the people and guarantee justice for all; (3) Enhance economic prosperity through greater productivity, efficiency, and sound economic management in order to enable the country to face global challenges; (4) Channel the country's resources not only to meet the basic needs of the people but, more importantly, to ensure that the quality of life and

social harmony are enhanced; (5) Distribute wealth and opportunities fairly among all; (6) Develop quality social infrastructure and a clean and comfortable physical environment; enhance the quality of education, health and other social services; build mosques and other places of worship; build public parks and libraries; build arts and cultural centres; and provide the widest opportunities for information technology and other methods of communication; and (7) Create a favourable atmosphere - through the provision of infrastructure, education and legislation - towards affirmation of Islam as a way of life (*ad-deen*) among Muslims, while ensuring the rights of non-Muslims to practice their respective religions or beliefs' (*Barisan Alternatif* 1999).

3. This is a visionary future scenario for Malaysia, set out by Dr Mahathir Mohamad (1991a). It looks forward to the time when Malaysia becomes a 'developed nation'.

PART IV

Conclusions

13. Conclusions

Colin Barlow and Francis Loh Kok Wah

The foregoing discussions of economics, politics and society in Malaysia explore in considerable detail the 'underlying questions' posed in the Introduction at the start of this book (p. 3). Hence successive chapters analyse issues connected with how the economy and society are organized, how the benefits from economic development are distributed, the relations of government to major national institutions, and the nature of the political process. This closing chapter addresses the views of participant authors regarding the underlying questions, doing this under the heads of 'the organization of the economy and society' and 'political and legal processes and outcomes'. It also attempts attempts to highlight issues likely to be important for the future of Malaysia, setting out possible policy approaches in each case.

As in the first volume in this series, the contributions of individual authors often contain disparate interpretations of the same policy or event, and also focus on rather different aspects of the same occurrence. This may sometimes be confusing, but is actually helpful in enriching the insights of readers into the nature of what occurred. This chapter attempts to combine the disparate views of authors into a more logical and understandable framework. The polity of Malaysia is complex and hard to appreciate in its entirety, but individual views generally contain perceptions usefully included in an assessment of the whole. The present chapter basically treats issues suggested by constituent authors, and many other crucial topics are omitted. But it is hoped these other topics can be addressed in successive books of the series.

THE ORGANIZATION OF THE ECONOMY AND SOCIETY

Thillainathan in Chapter 2, and Tan Tat Wai in Chapter 3, have much to contribute to understanding the causes of the financial crisis in Malaysia, and to appreciating adjustments desirable in improving future national economic organization.

Thillainathan in concentrating attention on Malaysian financial arrangements emphasizes the accentuation of the crisis occasioned by the high-risk and over-protected banking system, side by side with an over-regulated capital market. He perceives the continuing reliance on such a system as a dangerous feature enhancing macroeconomic vulnerabilities and systemic risk (p. 19). He sees the banking system at the commencement of the 1997 crisis as over-extended, with chronic dependence on short-term debt and other deficiencies under circumstances of moral hazard where bankers were encouraged to engage in risky lending. He argues convincingly for reduced bank protection, together with the purposive development of wider financial markets including non-bank financial institutions, freer capital trading, risk management products, risk intermediaries, and cash and futures market in bonds, all of which reduce dependence on the formal banking sector (p. 21).

Thillainathan also suggests amendments to the Employees Provident Fund (EPF), so as to allow wider choices to that majority of Malaysian employees forced to deposit savings in the Fund which are then centrally invested (p. 22). These wider choices would entail large reliance on his proposed expanded financial markets. He argues too for a strengthened legal and regulatory infrastructure of financial markets, in order to assist a progressive transition from what has been a relationship-based to a market-based investing model. Transactions in the latter are grounded on prices and contracts, and more effective adjustments are consequently made to market changes.

Tan in looking at the Malaysian economy before the 1985 and 1997 recessions makes the interesting point that the economy was much stronger in 1997 than in 1985, being marked by full employment and a good fiscal position (p. 30). Indeed, changes in the regulatory framework by the Bank Negara after 1984 - 1985 helped prevent more serious difficulties which would have otherwise occurred in 1997. Further, and in comparison with other crisis-hit countries, foreign currency loans are not viewed by Tan as the key factor in the post-1997 corporate crisis. This is in light of the high level of domestic savings and lesser need for foreign capital (p. 43). Tan observes too that, compared to Indonesia, restrictions of Malaysian bank credit following the onset of crisis were far less, and that early mistaken credit constraints were reversed when major policy changes were made in 1998. These alterations, which included the introduction of special institutions to assist restructuring together with the imposition of capital controls, appear to have been positive features assisting recovery.

Tan notes as well, however, that the slower accumulation of problems in the 1985 recession allowed an orderly and more attainable restructuring of companies not feasible after 1997, when adjustment had to be far quicker (p. 43). He indicates too that while the 'bubble' in the markets was recognized well before 1997 by the Bank Negara which suggested a credit ceiling for the broad property sector, this proposal which would have helped substantially in ameliorating the crisis was aborted under intense business and political lobbying.

Tan also looks more favourably than most outside observers at the restructuring of larger companies in the corporate sector. He submits on the basis of hard facts a picture of substantial changes to companies in difficulties, with good progress in a mix of financial and more radical restructuring, and with the latter sometimes involving assumption of control by foreign concerns. A market solution was hence being effectively applied in restructuring, and promised to enhance the future effectiveness of Malaysian industry. Such restructuring had in fact gained momentum since the departure of the previous minister of finance, Tun Daim, in 2001. Tan does not treat the further major component of Malaysian business comprising small and medium business enterprises, but there too substantial recent restructuring seems to have taken place in directions indicated by the market (Chin, 2002).

Thillainathan's and Tan's views on rather different spheres of the economy in fact complement one another, and together indicate desirable lines of reform in Malaysian economic arrangements. While both authors indicate the superiority of the Malaysian position to that of other crisis-hit countries, there are still numerous deficiencies where signal improvements can be made.

Thus in one sphere, and following the thinking of Thillainathan in what is essentially a novel policy recommendation, much requires to be done in extending and deepening Malaysian banking and financial markets, with measures along the lines of his proposals being implemented to promote better distribution of risks and more efficient reactions to economic upturns and downturns. While regulation at the level of banks and capital markets needs to be loosened, the desired changes are partly a matter of vigorous government intervention through overarching financial reform and effective legal governance to replace the previous relationship-based regime. 'Effective' is an operative word, in that much past governance does not seem to have been strictly implemented. It appears too that while official interventions to facilitate bank and corporate restructuring through *Danaharta*, *Danamodal* and the Corporate Debt Restructuring Committee have assisted alterations since 1997, these institutions have introduced difficulties of moral hazard and should be wound up in the relatively near future.

In another sphere, and within the realistic scenario of big business presented by Tan, many companies in stress owing to high and continuing losses, endemic debt, or both, still need restructuring. Sometimes financial restructuring without change of ownership will suffice, and will entail rescheduling loans, reducing existing capital, reaching agreements to debt-equity conversions, and selling non-core assets. But in other cases radical restructuring involving enlistment of local or foreign partners to the extent of losing control, may be necessary. Such restructuring following private market dictates is certainly a viable route for Malaysian industrial reorganization, deserving stress in an environment where undue emphasis has been given to government assistance in securing industrial change. It also appears far preferable to the latter less sustainable option, which Tan refers to as 'the use of state funds in attempting to salvage leading *Bumiputera* businesses' (p. 39).

It is noteworthy that both Thillainathan and Tan in scrutinizing economic organization implicitly see business and industry as best arranged through a largely private model, while still seeing a key role for government in directional policy making and establishing appropriate regulations and controls. Their suggestion of a small, albeit critical, part for government is one for further debate, with little doubt that official intervention is still needed within a system also embodying far more response to public pressures for change. This key topic will be taken up in a subsequent volume in this series.

Societal Changes

The presentation of Shamsulbahriah in Chapter 4 serves to denote the remarkable rise to prominence of the Malaysian salaried middle class, representing a dramatic shift from the earlier more traditional society comprising a huge working class and small professional and administrative elite. This change accompanied the heady economic growth and industrialization over several decades, and may be regarded as necessary in enabling human resources to propel the economy upwards. Indeed, there is also no doubt that Shamsulbahriah's further substantial group of a *petite bourgeoisie* is one of essentially middle class values, which with its independence of the corporate sector and relatively strong activity during the financial crisis also helped sustain the Malaysian economy. Even the persisting but rather smaller working class quantified by Shamsulbahriah now has a small but key component of 'skilled industrial workers' (p. 50). The switch to middle class values has been a major factor in changing political attitudes, as elaborated in the next part of the book.

Yet despite these developments, Shamsulbahriah is still able from her data to cite Malaysia as essentially a 'production-based' rather than 'knowledge-based' economy, with an extreme of a 'highly paid and highly empowered' 2 to 3 per cent of the workforce compared to many more much lesser trained persons and a large working class group of some 30 per cent unskilled labourers (p. 53). This composition actually reflects current demand for labour within an economic system where insufficient effort is made to transform the production process into one employing more sophisticated technologies and making higher value-added outputs. Such transformation is required to move Malaysia to a position where she remains ahead of her competitors in the region and elsewhere. Thus Shamsulbahriah catalogues the large presence of foreign workers in Malaysia, with her estimated average over all sectors in 1998 of one such worker to each eight Malaysian personnel (p. 56). These legal and illegal migrants are concentrated in the unskilled occupations of manufacturing, plantations and construction, and essentially do not compete with local artisans.

A desirable reform emerging from Shamsulbahriah's perception that Malaysia must become more technology-intensive is that of better provision for upgrading worker skills. Such provision should apply across the whole spectrum of the workforce, entailing training for improved routine industrial expertise at one end and for high professional ability at the other. It should comprise even more effort to enhance the quality and capacity of national vocational schools, training colleges and other tertiary institutions. While expressing this need for educational reform and a rearrangement of the workforce is not new, it is made in an industrial labour situation persisting in its inappropriateness and crying out for further change.

Distributional Issues

Ishak Shari in addressing the social implications of the financial crisis in Chapter 5 stresses the very large decline in Malaysian absolute poverty since the 1970s, additionally drawing attention to reductions in income inequality at least up to the early 1990s (p. 62). The employment situation also improved spectacularly right up to the time of the 1997 crisis and, as denoted by Shamsulbahriah, the export-oriented industrialization in the 1980s had made Malaysia a 'labour-short' economy by the early 1990s (p. 56). Ishak points as well to the increasing use of foreign workers, who in his view had reached 1.7 million persons by 1997.

But Ishak also comments significantly that 'Malaysian households still had few formal mechanisms to protect themselves from risks associated with job losses, disabilities and ageing' (p. 63), indicating that only 62 per cent of the working population contributed to the Employers' Provident Fund in 1997. There remained large numbers of persons in 'vulnerable groups' receiving minimal wages or returns, and these particularly suffered from pay reductions and higher prices after the crisis (p. 65). Yet he points out too that both these vulnerable groups and Malaysian society as a whole were crucially buffered by the presence of migrants, who could be retrenched and sent back to their original countries. Hence about 384,000 of these people had returned home by the end of 1998, and formed the group bearing the brunt of the economic downturn.

Ishak also goes out of his way to stress the major efforts of the Malaysian state over many years towards promoting welfare, boosting social services, and especially through the NEP towards rectifying inter-ethnic imbalances and improving the position of the *Bumiputera*. These official efforts are seen to have led to the remarkable social advances from the 1970s to the 1990s. It likewise seems true, however, that government policies from the late 1980s, putting even greater emphasis on private enterprise as the vehicle of economic advance, slowed improvement for less well-off social groups, as reflected in widening income disparities in the 1990s. Thus Thillainathan argues in relation to this period that 'over-reliance on privatization to achieve a distributional goal undermined efficiency and increased macroeconomic vulnerabilities' (p. 13).

Such adverse consequences from predominant state withdrawal are a general international phenomenon, and have been experienced by many countries ranging from New Zealand to the Cote d'Ivoire. As in the case of the desirable Malaysian business re-organization canvassed above, the circumstances argue for continued government leadership in determining the overall thrust of economic activity, and in establishing regulations to ensure such activity is conducted within appropriate guidelines. Ishak in fact cites the vigorous devotion of transnational corporations and advanced industrial countries to 'maximizing the freedom of financial capital around the world' (p. 73), concluding that 'states in developing countries need to assert social control and to continue to pursue redistributive policies'. This important reversion of attention to social issues and organization in Malaysia is likely to be favoured by the new emergent social movements explored in political discussions below.

All these considerations suggest the Malaysian state needs to exercise rather stronger control over local and foreign business enterprises so far as they affect employees and the populace at large, and that it should also pursue tax and other policies securing appropriate redistribution of incomes. Some of these other policies should entail stronger public social services in health and education, targeted programmes of support for particularly vulnerable groups, and enhanced safety net provisions to lessen the effects of crises on those at the bottom end of the social scale. Certain services and targeted activity can be undertaken through private and community groups, including non-government organizations. This will substantially lessen the direct burden on government itself, and increase the participation of society at large in promoting social progress.

Strategic Alterations

Russ Swinnerton in contemplating questions of defence organization in Chapter 6 scrutinizes the deployment over time of the Malaysian armed forces. He emphasizes how dramatically circumstances have altered from the heady days of the domino theory and domestic threat of the Emergency in the 1950s and early 1960s to the comparatively inert security environment of the early 2000s, at least up to September 11th, 2001 and October 12th, 2002. These changes saw a transformation in the Malaysian armed forces from an internal security vehicle to the relatively well-balanced and substantial military complex of today, seen by government as capable of repelling the mix of external threats likely to occur. Swinnerton points out that the present enhanced defence sector is significant to the economy, in terms both of contributing to gross domestic product and encouraging a wider spread of technology from state-of-the-art weapons systems.

Swinnerton indicates that Malaysia's current defence deployment is underpinned by the 1997 white paper premise that Malaysia should have the capability to act independently in 'matters concerning internal security' and in 'protecting its territorial integrity and security interests....from low to medium level external threats' (p. 86). It seems from his analysis that there tends to be a pre-occupation with 'immediate economic threats, rather than distant, hypothetical, military threats'. But this may have altered following recent developments, including especially the newly aggressive stance of the United

States against international terrorism and its willingness to intervene wherever pockets of *Al Qaeda* operatives are suspected.

It appears from Swinnerton's assessment that Malaysia may be 'too optimistic about external threats' (p. 88), and that the growing strength and possible danger from China is an aspect needing more attention beyond the country's active and desirable participation in regional security forums. It seems as well that the newly aggressive interventionist policies of the United States emphasize a need for Malaysia's military self-sufficiency, so that independence of Western anti-terrorist coalitions can be maintained. These considerations argue for even more emphasis in defence organization on building not only an effective conventional deterrent force but also more capable internal policing, giving the nation real credibility with potential aggressors and other external and internal intervenors.

POLITICAL AND LEGAL PROCESSES AND OUTCOMES

Francis Loh in Chapter 7 pinpoints a new 'fragmentation' in Malaysian politics, with 'contestations' caused by interactions between the elements of 'participatory democracy', 'developmentalism' and 'ethnicism'. He perceives the democracy element as springing from a background including the financial crisis, *reformasi*, and the arrest of Anwar Ibrahim, and as leading to more open criticism of the government's 'abuse of power' together with the formation of the *Parti Keadilan Nasional* and *Barisan Alternatif* (p. 94) and rise of non-government organizations. All these events were critically powered by 'significant numbers of the Malay middle classes', whose 'growing disenchantment' with government economic policies and shoddy treatment of Anwar is noted by Ishak in Chapter 5 (p. 72) and others.

Indeed, the revised views of many Malays may be vitally attributed to the restructuring of society through the NEP, and to what Anthony Milner in Chapter 10 (p. 135) terms the 'reform of Malay attitudes' latterly powered by Dr Mahathir's tenacious policies to encourage development of a *new Malay*. This 'rescue of the Malays' did much more than produce entrepreneurs, and perhaps inadvertently created a more egalitarian generation which did not tolerate many policies of Mahathir's own government. The rescue also in another paradoxical side effect canvassed by Milner did 'violence to the egalitarian aspirations that are so deeply embedded in Australian society' (p. 141), and may in his view be seen as a key impediment to relations with the Australian government. Indeed, it along with the differing Western interpretations of human rights cited by Rais (p. 146) were probably factors accounting for problems in relations with many Western countries.

Loh's second element of developmentalism comprises technical economic improvement and growth through a wide gamut of development policies, which together with democracy and the BN's promotion of 'cultural liberalization' (p.

98) has tended to displace his final element of ethnicism which had previously dominated Malaysian politics for so long. Interestingly, Loh's three elemental mainsprings have also been evident elsewhere in Southeast Asia, although proceeding differently. Thus in Indonesia, democracy is stronger than in Malaysia, while developmentalism has been accepted less and ethnicism is far more vicious. But ethnicism in Malaysia, and especially its mix with Islam and what Lim Kit Siang in Chapter 12 (p. 169) terms 'fears of a primordial nature concerning food, religion and restrictions on women', remains a potent political and cultural force which should not be underestimated and can emerge vehemently any time. It was indeed basic to the departure of the Democratic Action Party from the *Barisan Alternatif* in late 2001.

Yet it is important to remember as well that against these significant elements of fragmentation, Malaysia remains a peaceable and law-abiding multi-racial society, far from events like the wholesale burning-down in the late 1990s of Chinese business premises in Jakarta and other Indonesian cities, and the widespread massacre by Islamic and Christian groups in Maluku and elsewhere in the early 2000s of those with opposite religious and cultural beliefs. Ishak in fact takes note of the 'relative peace' of Malaysia (p. 71), attributing it to the long preoccupation of the Malaysian state with distributional issues, its concomitant encouragement to businesses operated by all races, and the growth of a large multi-ethnic middle class mostly interested in maintaining the status quo. This class, like its counterpart in many other industrialized societies, generally seems conservative in attitude, distinctly preferring middle-of-the-road policies and disliking abrupt changes in political direction. Shifts in the Malaysian polity are accordingly liable to be slow, with persisting influences from previous institutional arrangements. But the fragmentation and accompanying contestations are likely to impel gradual shifts to a different scenario as the new century proceeds.

Governance Changes and Voting Trends

Michael Ong in Chapter 8 looks at a different aspect of political processes, and scrutinizes the constitutional and other changes by successive Malaysian governments following Independence from Britain in 1957. These changes, including modifications to the electoral system in favour of Malay electorates (p. 110), the 'sabotaging of parliament' to become a 'zero-sum game' (p 114), and the strengthening of 'rule by law' embodied in repressive legislation (p. 115), were accompanied and indeed enabled by the continuing predominance of UMNO in the Alliance and subsequent *Barisan Nasional* coalitions. Ong indicates that the changes vastly increased the power of the executive, which since the 'watershed' 1999 election is seen by Lim in Chapter 12 (p. 164) as moving even further towards 'arbitrary and authoritarian rule'.[1] The changes far pre-dated Dr Mahathir, who continued and to some extent accentuated a long-standing trend which in the absence of remedial action could persist after his departure.

It is also evident that apart from UMNO's advantage as the party with the most seats, its Malay leaders have for most of the period since 1957 cleverly out-manoeuvred politicians of other ethnicities, enhancing their ability to push through constitutional and other policies. It was in fact only the strengthening in the late 1990s of another Malay grouping, the *Parti Islam seMalaysia*, which began to present a real challenge to UMNO in formal politics. The rise of non-government and other quasi-political civic organizations over the last few decades (p. 96) is likely as well to have weighty long-run political consequences, where these have already exercised what Ong terms 'external' pressure on the government (p. 114).

But beyond these considerations it is apparent that BN predominance has worked positively in easing the implementation of the NEP. The latter has despite problems enabled substantial progress to be made towards the goals of Dr Mahathir's Malay policy so carefully analysed by Milner (p. 135). Indeed, the behavioural and attitudinal changes contained in this policy, and foreseen by Dr Mahathir in his classic book, *The Malay Dilemma*, were then significantly pushed by him from his position of huge authority. This, as Milner relates, led to 'a substantial increase of Malays entering the modern sector of the economy' (p. 136), and in so doing contributed much to the critical long-term goal of national stability. Indeed, despite Dr Mahathir's recent 'bemoaning the fact that the Malays have made too little of the economic advantages offered them' (p. 136), the NEP represented extremely successful affirmative action for a given societal group, being unparalleled elsewhere in Southeast Asia during the post-colonial era.

Recent voting trends are addressed by several authors and notably by Loh, who sees from his scrutiny of the 1999 election results and UMNO's loss of such a dominant position a '*permanent shift....* and not merely a *temporary swing* in the pattern of voting behaviour' (p. 104). This situation where large numbers of Malays and many Chinese voted for the *Barisan Alternatif* marked a dramatic change from previous elections, in which 'most Malays readily identified with UMNO and the BN government'. Also significant were the numerous seats narrowly won by either side, following a current pattern in many democracies and suggesting that small shifts in voting behaviour could result in a future opposition victory. But Ong taking account of the BN's entrenchment of its position over many years argues that predictions of BA success at the time of the election were always too optimistic, in what were essentially only 'the beginnings of a sea change' (p. 106). In his reading, the building of an effective opposition is a long hard task, and firm policies and effective leadership are essential to ultimate success.

Analyses looking to the possible emergence of a new administration may also be questioned in light of other factors appearing to favour the BN government in the early 2000s. Hence many in the general public perceived that government as responsible for Malaysia's economic recovery, while some in the middle class both appreciated its continued pursuit of developmentalism and believed it well placed to contain Islamic fundamentalism fuelled by the late 2001 attack in New York. The opposition was also drastically undermined by the withdrawal of the Democratic Action Party from the BA, mainly in response to the pushing ahead by PAS with its plans for an Islamic state in Terengganu where it controlled the government.[2] The opposition was further weakened through dissension within *Keadilan*. The more favourable stance of the public towards the BN was indeed reflected in the results of by-elections after 1999.

Yet despite all this there seemed no doubt that important change was in the air. None of the factors positive to the BN appeared likely to permanently subdue the underlying suspicions of the electorate, while Dr Mahathir's 'resignation' announcement of mid-2002 and his plan to stand down in 2003 only further stimulated reigning uncertainty.[3] Thus, given that opposition parties can again combine effectively, there is significant long-term possibility of governmental change. Such combination could be feasible if sustained inter-religious dialogue of the nature canvassed by Lim (p. 170) successfully overcomes the persisting and deep-seated anti-atheist and related prejudices against the Democratic Action Party and other non-Islamic parts of the opposition. The latter also need to remove their own biases over fanatical Islam and a perceived widespread presence of fundamentalism within PAS. Such differences are themes which the *Barisan Nasional* has assuredly used to its own electoral advantage in what Lim most appropriately terms its 're-polarization of race and religion in Malaysian politics' (p. 168).

It is also true, however, that the age-old tradition of a tolerant and civic-minded Islam, going back to the international Muslim ascendance in the fourteenth and fifteenth centuries, is well and broadly grounded in Malaysia, especially amongst the middle class. The main players in *Parti Islam* largely hold tolerant views, and despite current difficulties springing from international Islamic militancy a meeting of minds and policies in the longer run seems eminently possible. As pointed out by Lim, however, any such meeting will require major and sustained efforts, going well beyond the 'common accord on a wide spectrum of subjects' (p. 168) illustrated by the earlier BA manifesto. It must seriously address the issue of an Islamic state and other inter-cultural matters, reaching an in-depth and robust understanding which works to remove the divisive element of ethnicism.

Justice and the Constitution

Case in his detailed treatment of the Anwar trials in Chapter 9 essentially backs up and authenticates Ong's 'rule by law' argument, presenting the legal proceedings of those trials as instancing the reining in of the judiciary and exemplifying a broader process of 'hollowing out most formal institutions while personalizing the executive' (p. 129). His vivid accounts of the trials illustrate the 'great pliancy' of the Malaysian bench under political pressures, in instances which assuredly reflected more general patterns. The instances also denote the high politicization of the police, whose behaviour denoted that they too were under direct political control. These and parallel events are disturbing signs in a society supposedly framed along democratic lines, well justifying underlying suspicions of government on the part of the Malaysian public. Case is also eminently correct in pointing to the contradiction 'in which the country modernizes its industrial base while its political institutions are demeaned' (p. 130). Although this may generate short-term economic gains, in the end 'modernization demands a sound legal structure' for the conduct of social life.

Rais Yatim in Chapter 11 argues that cultural considerations should help in formulating the rule of law and Constitution, where in Asia 'domestic governments prefer to safeguard society first followed by the individual, while in the West it is the opposite' (p. 147). He justifiably criticizes Western commentators who from a narrow cultural view condemn the absence of civil liberties in Malaysia, doing this without reference to the local context. He also comprehensively backgrounds the influences on the Malaysian law and Constitution of a mix of factors, including local social attitudes, English common law, and evolving domestic contingencies, showing how the legal system and its rules have evolved to deal with reigning circumstances while the *grundnorm* have accordingly altered. He further argues that, under the Malaysian Constitution, 'equilibrium is determined by the need to keep law and order and the uncompromising need of national security priority' (p. 153). This priority has heavily influenced public order approaches, ranging from the consequent necessity 'to contend with racial riots over political and economic issues' in 1969 (p. 149) to the 'taking of proportionate action by the authorities' following 'the emergence of violent demonstrations subsequent to the Anwar Ibrahim case' (p. 156). Rais further explains how such security situations often require appropriate subsequent adjustments to legal provisions.

These latter instances and others similar to them would undoubtedly be placed by Ong in his category of 'rule by law', in a system where all else is overtaken by executive priorities. Indeed, Rais himself appeared to condemn the accordance of such priorities in his book *Freedom under Executive Power in Malaysia*, where he classes Dr Mahathir as a person 'whose understanding or rather his misunderstanding of the concept of the separation of powers has been quite extraordinary' (Rais Yatim 1995, p. 309). Yet there is no doubt that a degree of social control is always necessary, and most circumstances quoted by Rais would appear to justify at least its limited exercise.

In practice, however, it is a question of what measures are used and how they are formulated. Where measures are sanctioned through arrangements entailing an executive fully accountable to Parliament and other institutions with proper checks and balances, their implementation can be acceptable. But it is doubtful whether such sanctioning is adequate in the supposedly democratic system of Malaysia, and for this reason numerous Malaysians from all sides of politics are critical of the ways in which laws discussed by Rais are framed and applied. It is assuredly true that much more public debate of this issue, followed by extensive debates in Parliament, are desirable. This said, there are spheres where more social control is manifestly needed, and that is true of the strengthened legal framework of financial markets suggested by Thillainathan in light of the 'growing perception of a decline in the standards to which laws have been upheld in commerce in recent years' (p. 24).[4]

CONCLUSIONS

There are manifest needs for reformed governance in Malaysia, especially in response to emerging social and political pressures at the beginning of the new century. The changes made should lead to greater openness in economic affairs, administration and the law, and to readier responses to public pressures for change. Despite the high achievements of BN governments in building a largely prosperous society with a relatively fair distribution of income and greater participation of Malays in modern society, it is time for new modifications better reflecting the requirements of the evolving nation.

The discussions of the book denote that in economic affairs there are strong advantages to relaxing many government controls, allowing the banking and financial sectors to be deepened according to mechanisms of the private market. Substantial further company restructuring following similar mechanisms is also necessary, and should be vigorously pursued. But such changes must, on the other hand, be accompanied by a key government role in directional policy making and in interventions including enhanced technological training of the workforce and social safety net measures for vulnerable groups. These interventions additionally entail the hard but vital task of giving financial markets a legal and regulatory framework, which is powerful enough to check abuses by national and international business and to eliminate the cancer of money politics. The state further has a role in maintaining a defence force capable of giving Malaysia credibility with external aggressors and suppressing internal terrorism.

In administration and the law, there are crucial needs to move towards revised governance which keeps a better balance between Parliament, the judiciary and the executive. Although such governance could well follow the unexceptional guidelines in the 1999 Manifesto of the *Barisan Alternatif* (p. 160), these intentions could almost as easily have been expressed by the *Barisan Nasional*, and what matters in practice is their actual underpinning and implementation. Indeed, Malaysia already has a basically appropriate and sophisticated framework of institutions and underlying mechanisms, which despite gross over-augmentation of the executive is capable of supporting a fully democratic society.

Hence reform to some extent involves rolling back more recent modifications, so as to balance governance more equally between the three constitutional arms and remove restrictions on vital supplementary bodies including the media. It entails as well an evolution of the framework to meet the requirements of modern society, with provisions for the new and potentially active role in social change of non-government organizations and civic groups. These are highly difficult tasks, and will not be achieved unless constructive and effective challenges are mounted by opposition and other groups, while reforms are assiduously instituted by governments in power.

As indicated in the Preface, this book builds on the first volume in the series, 'Modern Malaysia in the Global Economy', which chiefly looked back over three decades of rapid development up to the 1997 financial crisis. The present book largely considers future socio-economic adjustments, particularly addressing questions of how to overcome the serious deficiencies which the crisis and ensuing events revealed. While contributors discuss whether the 1999 elections and subsequent events were a 'watershed' in Malaysian development, there is little doubt that these occurrences demonstrated lasting shifts in the Malaysian polity with critical future implications. The planned departure of Dr Mahathir in 2003 and the upsets which this will involve give further weight to prospects of a substantially revised future. As Ishak Shari (p. 73) notes, 'the undercurrent of social discontent will not be blown away by increasingly favourable economic winds. The government's reputation....may only be restored by reconstructing institutions characteristic of a modern democratic society'. This is a vital challenge facing Malaysia in the new century, and should be scrupulously addressed.

NOTES

1. It is pertinent that similar although not such excessive trends feature many other democratic systems, and notably the British 'Westminster' arrangements on which Malaysian governance was originally modelled. It is also evident that numerous authoritarian features of Malaysian administration in the 2000s replicate aspects of the British colonial government of Malaya prior to Independence in 1957. Thus Rais Yatim (p. 149) quotes the case of Terrell, a British judge in the Straits Settlements and Federated Malay States, who was prematurely dismissed in the 1930s on the spurious grounds of ruling against colonial policies.

2. The PAS in Terengganu had appeared intent for some time on introducing punishments fixed by the *Q'uran* and *Sunnah* for both *hudud* and *qisas*. *Hudud* refers to offences like robbery, illicit sexual relations, accusing another of illicit sex but failing to prove it, drinking alcohol and apostasy. Specified and mandatory penalties for all these offences exist under *shariah* law. *Qisas* refers to retributions permitted under *shariah* law when an individual is injured or killed. In this case monetary payments may be made by offenders in lieu of being injured or killed themselves. The *Syariah* Criminal Offences (*Hudud* and *Quisas*) Bill was passed by the PAS-dominated Terengganu State Assembly in July 2002.

   In reply to the UMNO opposition leader's contention that the law discriminated against Muslims because a non-Muslim could choose whether he or she wanted to be prosecuted in the *Syariah* court, the Terengganu chief minister, Abdul Hadi Awang, stated there would be no double standards under the law: 'For now it will apply only to Muslims, but when the time comes the *hudud* and *qisas* laws will be extended to all non-Muslims...However, we will give the non-Muslims time as Islam practices flexibility' (*The Star, 2002*).

There is little doubt that the introduction of such measures entrenched the reigning suspicions of antagonists.

3.   Dr Mahathir declared on 22 June 2002 to the annual party congress of the United Malays National Organization that 'I wish to announce I am resigning from UMNO and all positions in the *Barisan Nasional*'. While he was persuaded to defer his resignation until late 2003, his pending departure raises questions of leadership and governance by the BN coalition.

4.   It is only fair to add that corporate governance is also a serious and apparently growing international problem, as illustrated by affairs elsewhere in Southeast Asia and by the gigantic Enron, WorldCom and other scandals in the United States and Europe.

References

Abdul Rahman Embong (1995), 'Malaysian Middle Classes: Some Preliminary Observations', *Jurnal Antropologi dan Sosiologi*, no. 22, pp. 31 - 54.

Abdul Rahman Embong (2000), 'The Political Dimensions of the Economic Crisis in Malaysia', in Abdul Rahman and Jurgen Rudolph (eds), *Southeast Asia into the Twenty First Century: Crisis and Beyond*, Bangi: Penerbitan Universiti Kebangsaan Malaysia.

Abdul Razak b. Abdullah Baginda (1992), 'The Malaysian Armed Forces in the 1990s', *International Defense Review*, no. 4, pp. 4-16.

Abdul Razak b. Abdullah Baginda (1995), 'The Malaysian Armed Forces and Regional Defence', in *Malaysia's Defence and Foreign Policies*, Petaling Jaya: Pelanduk Publications, pp. 11 - 24.

Abdul Razak bin Hussein (1971), Statement by the then prime minister of Malaysia, Tun Haji Abdul Razak bin Dato' Husein, Kuala Lumpur.

Abdul Razak bin Hussein (1972), Statement by the then prime minister of Malaysia, Tun Haji Abdul Razak bin Dato' Husein, Kuala Lumpur.

Acharaya, Amitav (1995), *Governance and Security in Southeast Asia*, Eastern Asia Policy Papers No. 9, Toronto: University of Toronto-York University, Joint Centre for Asia Pacific Studies.

Ackland, Richard (1999), 'Anwar's Trial: Making the Evidence Fit the Charge', *Sydney Morning Herald*, matny@usa.net, posted 17 April.

Aeria, A. (1997), 'The Politics of Development and the 1996 Sarawak State Elections', in Francis K.W. Loh (ed.), *Sabah and Sarawak: The Politics of Development and Federalism*, Special Issue of *Kajian Malaysia*, Penang: Universiti Sains Malaysia, pp. 57 - 83.

Alagappa, Muthiah (1987), 'Malaysia: From the Commonwealth Umbrella to Self-Reliance', in Chin Kin Wah (ed.), *Defence Spending in South East Asia*, Singapore: Institute of Southeast Asian Studies, pp.20-31.

Anwar Ibrahim (1999), reproduced as 'Judgement Stinks to High Heaven', *Aliran Monthly*, vol. 19, no. 4, pp. 6 - 8.

Anwar Ibrahim (2000a), reproduced as 'I Reiterate My Innocence', *Aliran Monthly*, vol. 20, no. 6, pp. 9 - 10.

Anwar Ibrahim (2000b), reproduced as 'CJ, Disqualify Yourself', *Aliran Monthly*, vol. 20, no. 8, pp. 12-17.

Arifin Jaka (2000), reproduced as 'Summary Judgment', *Aliran Monthly*, vol. 20, no. 6, p. 8.

Ariffin Omar (1983), *Bangsa Melayu. Malay Concepts of Democracy and Community 1945 - 1950*, Kuala Lumpur: Oxford University Press.

Asiaweek.com (1999), posting on 23 April.

Asiaweek.com (2000), posting on 18 August.

Athukorala Prema-chandra (2001), *Crisis and Recovery in Malaysia. The Role of Capital Controls*, Cheltenham, UK and Northampton, MA, USA: Edward Elgar.

The Australian (1990), 1-2 December, Sydney.

The Australian (1996), 22 November, Sydney.

The Australian (1999), 25 August, Sydney.

The Australian (2000a), 17 May, Sydney.

The Australian (2000b), 20 - 21 May, Sydney.

The Australian (2000c), 21 June, Sydney.

Barisan Alternatif (1999), *Towards a Just Malaysia*, Kuala Lumpur.

Barraclough, Simon (1988), *A Dictionary of Malaysian Politics,* Singapore: Heinemann.

Boyle, Kevin (1988), 'Freedom of Expression', in Paul Sieghart (ed.), *Human Rights in the United Kingdom*, London: Pinter Publishers, ch. 8, p. 85.

Burton, Sandra (1993), 'Society versus the Individual', *Time,* 14 June, p. 21.

Business Week (1998), 9 November, Singapore.

Canberra Times (1991), 28 September, Canberra.

Canberra Times (1996), 16 November, Canberra.

Case, William (1994), 'The UMNO Party Election in Malaysia: One for the Money', *Asian Survey*, vol. 34, no. 10, pp. 916 - 30.

Case, William (1999), 'Politics beyond Anwar: What's New?,' *Asian Journal of Political Science*, vol. 7, no. 1, pp. 1 - 19.

Cement and Concrete Manufacturers' Association (2000), Personal Communication, Kuala Lumpur.

Chelvarajah, R.R. (1999), 'Grave Disquiet in the Administration of Justice', *Aliran Monthly*, vol. 19, no . 4, p. 11.

Chin, Y.W. (2002), 'Globalisation and Small and Medium Industries (SMIs): Strategies for Survival', Paper presented at the Workshop on Globalization, National Governance and Local Responses: Experiences from Malaysia, Georgetown, Penang, April.

Claessens Stijn, Simeon Djankov and Daniela Klingebiel (1999), 'Financial Restructuring in East Asia: Halfway There', Financial Sector Discussion Paper 3, Washington, D.C.: World Bank.

Crouch, Harold (1996), *Government and Society in Malaysian Politics,* St Leonards: Allen and Unwin.

Crouch, Harold (1998), 'Understanding Malaysia', in Anthony Milner and Mary Quilty (eds), *Australia in Asia: Episodes,* Melbourne: Oxford University Press, pp. 37 - 60.

De Smith, S.A. (1963), 'Westminster's Export Models: The Legal Framework of Responsible Government', *Journal of Commonwealth and Political Studies*, no. 1, pp. 2 - 16.

Dicey, A.V. (1987), *An Introduction to the Study of the Law of the Constitution,* (10th edition), London: Macmillan.

Far Eastern Economic Review (1997), 18 September, Hong Kong, p. 65

Far Eastern Economic Review (1999), 24 June, Hong Kong, p. 30.

Faruqi, Shad S. (1985), 'Fundamental Liberties in Malaysia - An Overview', *INSAF Journal*, vol. XVIII, no.3, p. 7.

Fitzgerald, V. (1998), 'Global Capital Market Volatility and the Developing Countries: Lessons from the East Asian Crisis', Paper presented to the East Asian Crisis Conference at the Institute of Development Studies, Brighton: University of Sussex, July.

Foo, Lillian and Bala Ramasamy (1991), 'A Macro-Economic Analysis of the Oil Industry in Malaysia', in Sorab Sadri (ed.), *Oil and Economic Development*, Petaling Jaya: Forum Publications.

Funston, John (1980), *Malay Politics in Malaysia*, Kuala Lumpur: Heinemann.

Gomez, Edmund Terence and K.S. Jomo (1997), *Malaysia's Political Economy: Politics, Patronage and Profits*, Cambridge: Cambridge University Press.

Groves, H.E. (1964), Statement Regarding the Malaysian Constitution, Kuala Lumpur.

Haider S.M. (1978), *Islamic Concept of Human Rights,* Lahore: The Book House.

Hari Singh (2000), 'Democratization or Oligarchic Restructuring? The Politics of Reform in Malaysia', *Government and Opposition*, vol. 35, no. 4, pp. 520 - 546.

Hawkins, David (1972), *The Defence of Malaysia And Singapore. From AMDA to ANZUK*, London: The Royal United Services Institute.

Higgott, R. (1999), 'Bank from the Brink? The Theory and Practice of Globalization at Century's End', Paper presented at the Thirteenth Asia-Pacific Roundtable, Kuala Lumpur.

International Bar Association (2000), *Justice in Jeopardy: Malaysia 2000,* London: joint publication with the Centre for the Independence of Judges and Lawyers, Commonwealth Lawyers Association and the International Lawyers Union.

International Monetary Fund (1999), *Malaysia: Selected Issues,* Washington, D.C.: IMF.

Ishak Shari (1999), 'Financial Crisis in Malaysia and its Social Impact', Paper presented at The Research Workshop on Economic Crisis and Its Impacts on Social Welfare, Sun Yat-Sen Institute of Social Science and Philosophy, Academia Sinica, Taipei, June 14 - 15.

Ishak Shari (2000), 'Economic Growth and Income Inequality in Malaysia, 1971 - 1995', *Journal of the Asia Pacific Economy*, vol. 5, nos 1-2, pp. 112 - 124.

Ishak Shari and Abdul Rahman Embong (1999), 'Rapid Participatory Assessments of the Social Impact of the Financial Crisis in Malaysia', Draft final report presented for UNDP Regional Bureau for Asia and the Pacific.

Jane's Defence Weekly (1989), 'Malaysia: Planning for Change', London, 29 July, p. 32.

Jay, Antony (ed.) (1996), *The Oxford Dictionary of Political Quotations*, Oxford: Oxford University Press.

Jayasuriya, Kanishka (1999), 'Introduction: A Framework for Analysis', in Kanishka Jayasuriya (ed.), *Law, Capitalism and Power in Asia: The Rule of Law and Legal Institutions*, London: Routledge, pp. 1 - 27.

Jomo, K.S. (1998), 'Malaysia: From Miracle to Debacle', in K.S. Jomo (ed.), *Tigers in Trouble: Financial Governance, Liberalization, and Crises in East Asia*, London: Zed Books, pp. 181 - 197.

Jomo, K.S. (1999), 'A Malaysian Middle Class? Some Preliminary Analytical Considerations', in K.S. Jomo (ed.), *Rethinking Malaysia*, Kuala Lumpur: Malaysian Social Science Association, pp. 6 - 29.

Kelly, Paul (1992), *The End of Certainty*, St. Leonards: Allen and Unwin.

Kessler, Clive (1991), 'Negotiating Cultural Difference: On Seeking, Not always Successfully, to Share the World with Others - or in Defence of Embassy'. *Asian Studies Review*, vol 15 no. 2, pp. 57 - 73.

Khoo Boo Teik (1996), *Paradoxes of Mahathirism*, Kuala Lumpur: Oxford University Press.

Khoo Boo Teik (1999), 'Between Law and Politics: The Malaysian Judiciary since Independence', in Kanishka Jayasuriya (ed.), *Law, Capitalism and Power in Asia: The Rule of Law and Legal Institutions,* London: Routledge, pp. 205 - 231.

Khoo Boo Teik (2000), 'Unfinished Crises: Malaysian Politics in 1999', in *Southeast Asian Affairs 2000*, Singapore: Institute of Southeast Asian Studies, pp. 165 - 83.

Khoo Kay Jin (1992), 'The Grand Vision: Mahathir and Modernisation' in Joel S. Kahn and Francis Loh Kok Wah, *Fragmented Vision. Culture and Politics in Contemporary Malaysia*, Sydney: Allen and Unwin, pp. 444 - 476.

Khoo, Philip (1999), 'Thinking the Unthinkable', *Aliran Monthly*, June, pp. 2 - 8.

Kuala Lumpur Stock Exchange (2000), Data Supplied by the Exchange, Kuala Lumpur.

Kim Quek (2000), 'Judgment on Anwar is Thoroughly Flawed', bungaraya@listserv.net-gw.com, posted 11 August.

La Nauze, J. A. (1965), *Alfred Deakin: A Biography*, Carlton: Melbourne University Press.

Lamb, David (1999), 'Blunt Malaysian Leader Has an Answer for Everything', bungaraya@listserv.net-gw.com, posted 25 April.

Lawyers' Committee for Human Rights (1989), *Malaysia: Assault on the Judiciary*, New York.

Lim, H. and S. Fong (1991), *Foreign Direct Investment and Industrialisation in Malaysia, Singapore, Taiwan and Thailand*, Paris: OECD Development Centre.

Loh, Francis K.W. (1996), 'A New Sabah and the Spell of Development' *Southeast Asian Research*, vol. 4. no. 1, pp. 63 - 83.

Loh, Francis K.W. (2000), 'State-Societal Relations in a Rapidly Growing Economy: The Case of Malaysia, 1970 - 1997', in J. Clark and R. B. Kleinberg-Bensabat (eds), *Economic Liberalisation, Democratisation and Civil Society in the Developing World*, London: Macmillan, pp. 65 - 87.

Loh, Francis K.W. (2001a), 'Developmentalism and the Limits to Democratic Discourse', in Francis K.W. Loh and Khoo Boo Teik (eds), *Democracy in Malaysia; Discourses and Practices*, London: Curzon, for the Nordic Institute of Asian Studies.

Loh, Francis K.W. (2001b), 'Where Has (Ethnic) Politics Gone ?', in R. Hefner (ed.), *Southeast Asian Pluralisms*, Honolulu: University of Hawaii Press.

Mack, A., and D. Ball (1992), 'The Military Build-up in Asia-Pacific', *The Pacific Review*, vol. 5, no. 3, pp. 31-42.

Mahathir Mohamad (1970), *The Malay Dilemma*, Singapore: Times

Mahathir Mohamad (1988), Statement by Dr Mahathir, Kuala Lumpur.

Mahathir Mohamad (1991a), 'Malaysia: The Way Forward', Paper presented at the Inaugural Meeting of the Malaysian Business Council, Kuala Lumpur, February 28, reprinted in the *New Straits Times*, Kuala Lumpur, March 2.

Mahathir Mohamad (1991b), Statement by Dr Mahathir to the Asean Foreign Ministers on 19 July 1991, Kuala Lumpur, *New Straits Times*, Kuala Lumpur, 20 July.

Mahathir Mohamad (1995), *The Challenge*, Pataling Jaya: Pelanduk.

Mahathir Mohamad, (1999), 'Moving towards Greater Security and Prosperity into the New 21st Century', Keynote address at the LIMA 1999 Aerospace and Maritime International Conference, 2 December.

Mahathir Mohamad (2000a), Statement in Malaysia Hall, London, January.

Mahathir Mohamad (2000b), Presidential Address to the UMNO General Assembly, Kuala Lumpur.

Mahathir Mohamad and Shintaro Ishihara (1995), *The Voice of Asia: Two Leaders Discuss the Coming Century*, Tokyo: Kodansha International, Ltd.

Mahathir Mohamad and Shintaro (1995), *The Voice of Asia*, Tokyo: Kodansha.

Mak Joon Nam (1993), 'ASEAN Defence Reorientation 1975 – 1992', Canberra Papers on Strategy and Defence No. 103, Canberra: Australian National University.

Mak Joon Nam (2001), Personal Communication, Canberra.

Malaysia (1989), *Mid-Term Review of the Fifth Malaysia Plan 1986-1990*, Kuala Lumpur: Percetakan Nasional Malaysia Berhad.

Malaysia (1996), *The Seventh Malaysia Plan 1996 - 2000*, Kuala Lumpur: Percetakan Nasional Malaysia Berhad.

Malaysia (1998a), *Economic Report 1998 - 1999*, Kuala Lumpur: Ministry of Finance.

Malaysia (1998b) *Social Statistics Bulletin, Malaysia*, Kuala Lumpur: Department of Statistics.

Malaysia (1999), *Mid-Term Review of the Seventh Malaysia Plan 1996 - 2000*, Kuala Lumpur: Percetakan Nasional Malaysia Berhad.

Malaysia. Bank Negara Malaysia *(1986 - 2000), Annual Reports*, Kuala Lumpur.

Malaysia. Bank Negara Malaysia *(1986 - 2001), Monthly Statistical Bulletins*, Kuala Lumpur.

Malaysia. Department of Statistics (1999), *Monthly Statistical Bulletin, Malaysia, May*, Kuala Lumpur: Jabatan Perangkaan Malaysia.

Malaysia. Ministry of Defence (1997), *Malaysian Defence: Towards Defence Self-Reliance*, Kuala Lumpur.

Malaysia. Ministry of Finance (2000), Official Press Release of Finance Minister's Budget Speech, February 25, Kuala Lumpur.

Malaysia. Ministry of Human Resources (1997), *Labour and Human Resource Statistics 1997*, Kuala Lumpur.

Malaysia. Ministry of Human Resources (1999a), *Laporan Pasaran Buruh*, Kuala Lumpur.

Malaysia. Ministry of Human Resources (1999b), Unpublished data, Kuala Lumpur.

Malaysia. Ministry of Internal Affairs (1998), Unpublished data, Kuala Lumpur.

Malaysia. Securities Commission (1999), *Report on Corporate Governance of the High-Level Finance Committee of the Ministry of Finance*, MSC: Kuala Lumpur.

Malaysiakini.com (2000), Discussion of Media Credibility, January.

Maznah Mohamad (2000), 'Fifteen Years of Solitude for Anwar...And for Malaysia?' *Aliran Monthly*, vol. 20, no. 6, pp. 2 - 6.

Maznah Mohamad (2001), 'UMNO and the Contest for Malay Votes in 1999', in Francis K.W. Loh and J. Saravanamuttu (eds), *Reformasi and the 1999 General Election*, Penang: Universiti Sains Malaysia.

McDougall, R. (1968), Personal Communication, Kuala Lumpur.

Milner, Anthony (1982), *Kerajaan: Malay Political Culture on the Eve of Colonial Rule*, Tucson: The Association for Asian Studies.

Milner, Anthony (1991), 'Inventing Politics: The Case of Malaysia', *Past and Present*, vol 132, pp. 104 - 129.

Milner, Anthony (1995), *The Invention of Politics in Colonial Malaya*, Cambridge: Cambridge University Press.

Milner, Anthony (1996a), 'Malaysia', in Anthony Milner and Mary Quilty (eds), *Communities of Thought*, Melbourne: Oxford University Press, pp. 157 - 183.

Milner, Anthony (1996b), 'Introduction', in Anthony Milner and Mary Quilty (eds). *Communities of Thought*, Melbourne: Oxford University Press, pp. 1 - 28.

Milner, Anthony (2000), 'What Happened to Asian Values?', in Gerald Segal and David S.G. Goodman (eds), *Towards Recovery in Pacific Asia*, London: Routledge, pp. 56 - 68.

Milner, Anthony, Edward E. McKinnon and Tengku Luckman Sinar (1978), 'Aru and Kota Cina', *Indonesia*, vol. 26, pp. 1 - 42.

Mohd. Najib b. Abdul Razak (1994), Keynote address at the MIMA seminar: *CBMs at Sea in the Asia Pacific Region: Meeting the Challenges of the 21st Century*, Kuala Lumpur, 2 - 3 August.

Mohd. Noor b. Mat Arshad (1996), 'Planning the Malaysian Army for the Twenty-first Century', Paper Presented at the Conference on Land Forces in the Twenty-First Century: The Challenge for the Malaysian and Regional Armies, Putrajaya, Malaysia, 20 – 21 November.

Mohd. Salleh Abas (1986), 'Traditional Elements of the Malaysian Constitution', in Trindade F.A. and H.P. Lee (eds.), *The Constitution of Malaysia: Further Perspectives and Developments. Essays in Honour of Tun Mohamed Suffian*, Kuala Lumpur: Oxford University Press, pp. 1 - 17.

Mohammad Khatami (2000), 'Proposal by the Iranian President for a United Nations Year of Dialogue among Civilizations', Teheran.

Mohamed Suffian (2000), 'Remembering Tan Sri Wan Sulaiman', *Aliran Monthly* 20 (2), p. 24.

Moore A.M (1960), Statement by Mr Moore, an Ex-Colonial Official who had been Involved in Framing the Constitution, Kuala Lumpur.

National Operations Council (1969), Document Dealing with the 13 May Incident, Kuala Lumpur.

New Straits Times (1985), Statement by Dr Mahathir, 20 August, Kuala Lumpur.

Paul, Augustine (1999), 'Public Prosecutor v. Dato' Seri Anwar bin Ibrahim', *Malayan Law Journal*, no. 3.

Pertierra, Raul (ed.) (1999), 'Asian Ways: Asian Values Revisited', Special Issue of *Sojourn*, vol. 14, no. 2, pp 43-51.

Rais Yatim (1995), *Freedom Under Executive Power in Malaysia: A Study of Executive Supremacy*, Kuala Lumpur: Endowment Sdn. Bhd.

Rasiah, R. (1995), *Foreign Capital and Industrialisation in Malaysia*, London: Macmillan.

Rasiah, R. (1998), 'AFTA and Its Implications for Labour Mobility in ASEAN', Paper presented at a Conference on Migrant Workers and the Malaysian Economy, Quality Hotel, Kuala Lumpur, 19 - 20 May.

Rasiah, R. and Ishak Shari (1997), 'Malaysia's New Economic Policy in Retrospect', in H.M. Dahlan, J. Hamzah, A.Y. Hing and J. H. Ong (eds*)*, *ASEAN in the Global System*, Bangi: Universiti Kebangsaan Malaysia Press.

Rehman Rashid (1996), *A Malaysian Journey*, Petaling Jaya: Rehman Rashid.

Rowland, John (1992), *Two Transitions: Indochina 1952-1955, Malaysia 1969 - 1972*, Nathan: Centre for the Study of Australia-Asian Relations, Griffith University.

Sachs, Jeffrey (1999), 'Missing Pieces', *Far Eastern Economic Review*, 25 February, p. 11.

Samsudin Hitam *(1999)*, 'Pencapaian Bumiputera Dalam Bidang Ekonomi (Achievements of the *Bumiputera* in the Economic Sector)'*,* Working Paper at the Fourth *Bumiputera* Economic Congress, Kuala Lumpur, September, pp. 10 - 11.

Saravanamuttu, J. (1992), 'The State, Ethnicity and the Middle Class Factor: Democratic Change in Malaysia', in K. Rupesinghe (ed.), *Internal Conflict and Governance*, New York: St Martin's Press, pp. 44 - 64.

Scoble, Harry M. and Laurie S. Wiseberg (1997), Personal Communication, New York.

Searle, Peter (1996), 'Recalitrant or Realpolitik? The Politics of Culture in Australia's relations with Asia' in Richard Robison (ed.), *Pathways to Asia*, St Leonards: Allen and Unwin, pp. 56 - 86.

Searle, Peter (1999), *The Riddle of Malaysian Capitalism*, St Leonards: Allen and Unwin.

Sebastian, Leonard C. (1991), 'Ending an Armed Struggle Without Surrender: The Demise of the Communist Party of Malaya, 1979 - 1989, and the Aftermath', *Contemporary Southeast Asia*, vol. 13 no. 3, pp. 9-21.

Senu Abdul Rahman (ed.) (1973), *Revolusi Mental*, Kuala Lumpur: Penerbitan Utusan Melayu.

Shaharuddin Maaruf (1984), *Concept of a Hero in Malay Society*, Singapore: Eastern Universities Press.

Shaharuddin Maaruf (1988), *Malay Ideas on Development*, Petaling Jaya: Times.

Shamsul, A.B. (1999), 'From Orang Kaya Baru to Melayu Baru' in M. Pinches (ed.), *Culture and Privilege in Capitalist Asia*, London and New York: Routledge, pp. 86 - 110.

Shamsulbahriah Ku Ahmad (1996), 'Economic Development and Social Stratification: Occupational Change and Class Structure in Peninsular Malaysia under the New Economic Policy', PhD thesis, Cambridge: University of Cambridge.

Sheridan, Greg (1997), *Tigers*, St Leonards: Allen and Unwin.

Shireen Mardziah Hashim (1997), *Income Inequality and Poverty in Malaysia*, Lanham: Rowman and Littlefield.

Sieghart, Paul (ed.) (1988), *Human Rights in the United Kingdom,* London: Pinter Publishers.

Singh, B. (1993), 'ASEAN's Arms Procurements Challenge and the Security Dilemma in the Post-Cold War Era', *Comparative Strategy,* vol 12, no.2, pp. 5-23.

Spaeth, Anthony (1998), 'Whose Trial?', *Time,* 16 November, p. 21.

Star (1999), Speech of Dato' Abdullah Badawi to the 13th ASEAN-Institute for Strategic and International Studies Asia Pacific Roundtable, 20 August, Kuala Lumpur.

Star (2002), Statement in the Terengganu State Assembly by the chief minister, Abdul Hadi Awang, 8 July, Kuala Lumpur.

Stiglitz, J. (2000), 'IMF: The Cure that Kills', *New Republic,* Washington D. C., September.

Stubbs, Richard (1977), 'Peninsular Malaysia: The New Emergency', *Pacific Affairs,* vol. 50, no. 2, pp.34-43.

Sussangkarn C., F. Flatters and S. Kittiprapas (1999), *Social Impacts of the Asian Economic Crisis in Thailand, Indonesia, Malaysia and the Philippines,* Bangkok: Thailand Development Research Institute.

Thillainathan, R. (1999), 'Malaysia and the Asian Crisis - Lessons and Challenges', Paper presented at the 18th Central Bank Course of the Bank Negara Malaysia, Petaling Jaya, Malaysia, September.

Toffler, Alvin (1998), 'Malaysian Cyber Vision Clouded by Arrests', posted at http://www.apnic.net/mailing-lists/apple/9811/msg00017.html, 12 November.

Tregonning, K.G. (1964), *Malaysia,* Melbourne: F.W. Cheshire.

Trindade, F.A. and H.P. Lee (eds) (1986), *The Constitution of Malaysia: Further Perspectives and Developments. Essays in Honour of Tun Mohamed Suffian,* Kuala Lumpur: Oxford University Press.

United Nations (2001), Resolution establishing the Year of Dialogue, 21 August, New York.

Walsh, James (1993), 'Asia's Different Drum', *Time,* 14 June, p. 16.

Wazir Johan Karim (1998), *Malaysian Women in and out of the Crisis in Malaysia and Penang,* mimeo (source unknown).

Weatherbee, Donald E. (1987), 'ASEAN: Patterns of National and Regional Resilience', in Young Whan Kihl and Lawrence E. Grinter (eds), *Asian - Pacific Security: Emerging Challenges And Responses,* New Delhi: Archives Publishers.

Wilkinson, R.J. (1922), Statement by Mr Wilkinson, Kuala Lumpur.

World Bank (1993), *The East Asian Miracle,* Oxford: Oxford University Press.

World Bank (1999), *World Development Report. Knowledge for Development,* New York: Oxford University Press.

Zakaria Haji Ahmad et al. (2000), *Trends in Malaysia: Election Result,* Singapore: Institute of Southeast Asian Studies.

Index